NEGOTIATING AUTONOMY

NEGOTIATING AUTONOMY

Mapuche Territorial Demands *and* Chilean Land Policy

KELLY BAUER

University *of* Pittsburgh Press

Published by the University of Pittsburgh Press, Pittsburgh, Pa., 15260
Copyright © 2021, University of Pittsburgh Press
All rights reserved
Manufactured in the United States of America
Printed on acid-free paper
10 9 8 7 6 5 4 3 2 1

Cataloging-in-Publication data is available from the Library of Congress

ISBN 13: 978-0-8229-4666-3
ISBN 10: 0-8229-4666-1

Cover art: General plan of the colonization of Cautín by Nicanor Bologna, published in 1910.
Cover design: Melissa Dias-Mandoly

CONTENTS

ACKNOWLEDGMENTS

I acquired extensive debts and wonderful relationships on the ten-plus-year journey of researching and writing this book. The earliest portions emerged from a Theories of Ethnic Politics class with Henry Hale and a Qualitative Research Methods class with Harris Mylonas at George Washington University. The papers emerging from those classes provided the very initial embers of this project and, more importantly, started conversations about this research. I am grateful that both, joined by Manny Teitelbaum, were willing to dive into mentoring roles for research significantly outside of their areas of expertise. Cynthia McClintock provided (and provides) steady advice, leadership, and motivation to persevere through the complications and thrill of life and work in academia.

In Chile, Alejandro Herrera Aguayo graciously welcomed me to the Instituto de Estudios Indígenas at the Universidad de la Frontera, and Alvaro Bello and Hugo Zunino graciously extended that invite with thoughtful support during my time at the university and in Temuco. Sergio Toro at the Universidad Católica de Temuco provided me invaluable workspace and connections within the Political Science and Sociology Department; colleagues in the department had the joy of supporting me through my first earthquake in Chile. All at the Archivo General de Asuntos Indígenas (AGAI) helped me navigate archives and made sure the space heaters were close enough. These patchworked networks provided extensive opportunities for learning and collaboration. Among many others, I am grateful to Lientur Alcaman, Germán Bidegain, Venancio Coñuepan Mesias, Elsy Curihuinca, Hector Curiqueo Melivilu, Jael Goldsmith Weil, Gonzalo Infante Grandon, Volodia Jineo, Fernando Rosenblatt, and Victor Venegas for so thoughtfully allowing professional connections to flow into supportive friendships throughout various stages of this project. The richness of my time in Chile was facilitated by the financial support of the Inter-American Foundation's Grassroots Development Grant, and the Fulbright US Student Program. Luckily, both grants created significant opportunities for collaboration with other grantees, and I am thankful for how the grant coordinators thoughtfully created opportunities for reflection and collaboration with, among others, Carolina Arango Vargas, David Bergin, Paula Dias, Andrea Dillon, Summer Harlow, Kevin Healy, Katherine Maich, Liz Mason-Deese, Maddie Orenstein, and Manuel Prieto. Erick Langer and Todd Eisenstadt also provided thoughtful comments throughout.

This book came to life at Nebraska Wesleyan University. Navigating a heavy teaching, mentoring, and service load, I was continually supported by brilliant colleagues and friends, too many to name, who encouraged me to dive into interdisciplinarity and provided inspiring examples of how to be both a passionate teacher and scholar. The excellent students who ended up in my classrooms demanded clarity in my own thinking and writing and usefully nagged me to finish; NWU alumni Randi Knox and Carlin Daharsh provided remarkable research support during this process.

As this book became more interdisciplinary, it acquired more debts to scholars working in anthropology, geography, history, sociology, and law. I am grateful to have benefitted from the input of the interdisciplinary communities that formed around conferences, workshops, and journals. Three anonymous reviewers provided the rare sort of reviews that pulled their optimism and vision for the book through their critiques. Reviewers and editors for the *Journal of Agrarian Change* and *Latin American and Caribbean Ethnic Studies*, including Nancy Postero and Helene Risør, offered similarly useful comments on earlier stages of portions of this work that appears in those journals. Colleagues at the 2018 NEH Summer Institute, "Women's Suffrage in the Americas," at my alma mater, Carthage College, offered solidarity and energy during a particularly challenging period of writing. Kristy Johnson provided key developmental editing and encouragement through successive revisions, Josh Shanholtzer at the University of Pittsburgh Press took a chance on this book, and the UPP team provided seamless support throughout the publishing process. All remaining errors and limitations are my own.

Finally, numerous communities supported my well-being, persistence, and happiness through this journey. Jeff Roberg and Penny Seymoure at Carthage College have offered more years of mentoring and friendship than I expect they imagined. During our time at George Washington University, Dina Bishara, Kerry Crawford, Lisel Hintz, Jake Haselswerdt, Michelle Jurkovich, Fabiana Perera, and Varun Piplani became brilliant colleagues and friends. The formal and informal volleyball communities in Temuco; Santiago; Washington, DC; Lincoln; and Los Angeles put up with my inconsistencies as I jumped between research trips and long writing sessions, and offered enriching, external perspectives on my work. My US and Chilean families had the love and patience to support me through writing. Growing up, my parents taught me to see and hear the world, and my brothers taught me to fight; while they aren't always thrilled that has pulled me away from Wisconsin, their support is unwavering. The love and support of my husband, Claudio, is written into these pages, as he dives into debates about Chilean politics and research ontologies and epistemologies, supports me through the precariousness and ambiguities of academia, and attempts to perfect my Chilean Spanish. I am lucky that he knows how to strike the impossible balance of encouraging me to be fearless and knowing when to pull me out of an escalating protest, both literally and figuratively.

This work analyzes what it is to imagine what could be and fight against what is; I hope that the words that follow contribute to further individual and collective reflection.

NEGOTIATING AUTONOMY

INTRODUCTION

It was a typically frigid and rainy morning on April 12, 2013, in Temuco, the capital of the Araucanía region in southern Chile. I was awake early to attend a march, scheduled to descend from the top of Cerro Ñielol into the city to assert demands of the Mapuche Indigenous community demands with the accompaniment of *trutrukas*, long horns made of bamboo and a carved-out cow horn, and *kultrunes*, ceremonial drums.

Cerro Ñielol is a historically significant hill overlooking downtown Temuco. On November 10, 1881, Mapuche leaders supposedly ceded their land to Chilean colonists on the hill, a result of the Chilean armed forces' brutal Pacification of the Araucanía military campaign pursuing the territorial continuity of the country and space for agricultural development on previously unconquered Mapuche territory. For some, the resulting agreement, "La Patagua del Armisticio," ushered in peace and the founding of the regional capital of Temuco. For others, the agreement solidified the military conquest of the Mapuche nation and institutionalized persisting patterns of subordination, colonization, and marginalization. The presumed exact location of the agreement, la Patagua, continues to serve as a central meeting point to conduct Mapuche politics; even the dictator Augusto Pinochet was presented a *toki-kura*, a stone pendant symbolizing the authority of chief, from allied Mapuche organizations on Cerro Ñielol in 1986.

The April march was a continuation of recent events. In January 2013, assailants, alleged to be Mapuche, set fire to the house of Werner Luchsinger and Viviane Mackay, a wealthy elderly couple. The Luchsinger family owns one of the largest and historically conflictual plots of land in the region where, in 2008, the young Mapuche activist Matías Catrileo died after being shot in the back by police officer Walter Ramírez during a land occupation on a plot of land owned by the cousin of Werner Luchsinger, Jorge Luchsinger Villigier. By the time the police arrived at

Image I.1. View of Temuco, Chile, from Cerro Ñielol, April 2013. Photo by the author.

the fire, the house was destroyed and the couple was dead. However, the husband did shoot and injure one of the attackers, Celestino Córdova, who was the only detained that night. Literature from a radical Mapuche organization was reportedly found at the scene, but no individual or group claimed responsibility for the attack. The government responded quickly. By noon the following day, President Sebastián Piñera reached the region, announcing plans to improve security by declaring a security zone, allocating additional police, and creating a specialized police force. Minister of the Interior Andrés Chadwick went further, suggesting a declaration of a state of emergency. Officials called for the assailants to be charged with terrorism under a controversial, Pinochet-era law that, since the return to democracy, has nearly exclusively been applied to Mapuche activists. In the following week, there were nine additional arson attacks; prominent landowners spoke of creating armed self-defense groups; truckers blocked the Pan-American Highway, protesting the uncertain security situation; and civil society organizations criticized the application of the terrorism law.

For Mapuche activists, the government's security-focused response was insufficient and myopic; if Mapuche individuals were responsible, the violence was an expression of unheard and unmet demands about broader structural conditions. The government needed to recognize the Mapuche as Indigenous peoples with internationally recognized

Image I.2. PACMA Reunion at la Patagua, Cerro Ñielol, Temuco, April 12, 2013. Photo by the author.

Image I.3. PACMA Reunion at la Patagua, Cerro Ñielol, Temuco, April 12, 2013. Photo by the author.

rights to self-determination and autonomy, rooted in the Mapuche peoples' connection with ancestral territory. For the group of leaders that gathered in April, the events of January 2013 highlighted the need for a historically splintered movement to clearly articulate and assert the collective demands of a united Mapuche community. Diverse organizations and prominent Mapuche leaders formed the Pacto Mapuche por la Autodeterminación (PACMA, Mapuche Pact for Self-Determination). PACMA announced plans to assert their rights to self-determination and autonomy; indeed, on April 11, PACMA organized their first conference on self-determination, bringing together leaders to discuss specific demands, proposals, and processes. The march on the following day would present these decisions to the government.

We arrived to la Patagua by 8:00 a.m. on April 12, as PACMA leadership had publicized on social media. The few people who had arrived poked at a small fire and passed around steamed chestnuts, waiting for the crowds and leadership to arrive. Several prominent *lonkos* (chief, "head" in Mapuzungun) arrived by mid-morning, overseeing the ceremonies and a long discussion about whether to follow through on the march as scheduled. PACMA intended on delivering a letter declaring the group's intentions to self-govern, but everyone was concerned that a march of a hundred people would not garner enough attention. Ultimately, leaders and attendees agreed that PACMA leadership would present the letter to the government and hold a press conference, and postpone the march.

I left perplexed. PACMA was the work of some of the most prominent, experienced Mapuche leaders. There were no signs of repression beyond what could be expected at similar events. A few *carabineros* (police officers) in riot gear stood awkwardly at the exit of the hill, and an old reporter from a conservative newspaper circulated through the ceremony, taking pictures of everyone in attendance. As the march was broadly publicized, it was confusing as to why leadership ultimately seemed eager to diffuse it.

While descending the hill, a friend shared details he had pieced together in hushed conversations throughout the morning. In a last-minute scramble to cripple the planned march and any momentum for the public articulation of Mapuche self-determination demands, the government organized ceremonies throughout the region to present resources to a number of Mapuche communities. Many Mapuche leaders and community members who had planned to attend the march decided to stay in their communities to receive the visiting politicians and participate in the last-minute ceremonies. PACMA, in fact, only learned of the government's plans late the night before, leaving them scrambling to avoid appearing as if the organization and call for self-determination lacked broad support from the greater Mapuche community.

I scoured the internet, finding confirmation on the website of the Chilean government's Corporación Nacional de Desarrollo Indígena (CONADI, National Corporation for Indigenous Development). The *intendente* (appointed governor) of the neighboring Los Lagos region and the subsecretary of the Servicio Nacional de la Mujer (National Women's Service) presented subsidies and fishing equipment totaling 184 million pesos to more than five hundred Lafquenche fishermen in Castro, Chiloe. The national director of CONADI held a press conference to announce two public lotteries to fund development and productivity projects in the Araucanía region, totaling 680 million pesos. In Valdivia the subdirector of CONADI and *intendente* of the Los Ríos region announced the eighty-seven families in the region to receive a subsidy to purchase land. On the day of the planned march, prominent politicians representing various portions of the government allocated more than US$1.4 million to Mapuche individuals and communities, in addition to an undetermined amount to subsidize land purchases.[1] This government strategizing crippled the planned march, which explained the bizarre unfolding of events on April 12.

This chain of events stands in stark contrast to narratives of post–Pinochet Chilean governance as centralized, technocratic, and, above all, neoliberal. When I moved to Chile, I planned to study how Mapuche communities pursued their demands through the government, focusing specifically on communities' pursuit of territory and degrees of autonomy through land policy.[2] This policy was created with the promulgation of Indigenous Law 19.253 in 1993, which recognized a number of Indigenous demands and established CONADI to oversee implementation. Article 20B of that law created an institutional path through which Indigenous communities and individuals could apply to the government, petitioning for the government to purchase and transfer formal land titles to historically occupied land. These purchases are funded by CONADI's Fundo de Tierra y Agua Indígena (FTAI, Fund for Indigenous Land and Water), which is the budgetary focal point of CONADI's work, accounting for 50–75 percent of CONADI's yearly budget between 1994 and 2013. Even from a distance, there was significant controversy and contestation over the process.

Given the strength of Chile's neoliberal project and reputation of good governance, why are there inconsistencies over which land the government returned to which communities? How did Mapuche resistance efforts interact with state domination efforts, and what is the significance of this contestation for broader patterns of governance? I expected to find a story of Mapuche communities navigating either through or around constrained institutions that governed to extend neoliberal governance by protecting market interests in the region and by preserving transparent and technocratic policymaking. I expected that Mapuche communities' extrainstitutional mobilization stemmed from extremely constrained opportunities for institutional resolution of demands, particularly for the communities pursuing land that confronted the interests of powerful economic stakeholders. And I expected that inconsistencies in the government's implementation of Indigenous land policy occurred in rare moments when the state's efforts to extend neoliberalism through policy temporarily converged with Mapuche demands.

After living in southern Chile for sixteen months, those narratives regarding Mapuche communities navigating in or around a state operating on an insulated, hegemonic, and neoliberal logic of governance felt increasingly insufficient, if not outright inaccurate. Rather, policies and procedures were interactive and negotiated, shifting depending on the actors, place, and context. One Mapuche leader, whose story is discussed in detail in chapter 3, negotiated to exchange his community's votes in an upcoming election for a politician's help expediting their land claim. Politicians frequently took flour and oil to Mapuche communities when campaigning prior to elections. At a small We Tripantu (Mapuche New Year, celebrated in June on the summer solstice) celebration, a visiting politician acknowledged his purpose for attending at that particular moment far more transparently than I expected: "As you all know, it is an election year, so we are here to listen."[3] At the April 12 march, few were surprised that government officials strategically implemented policies and programs at that particular moment to weaken the mobilization and articulation of Indigenous demands for self-determination. I too came to expect this overt, dynamic bargaining. Yet because government officials responded to the planned march through the guise of implementing institutionalized policies, the links between these officials' work and the march were never reported, preserving the existing façade of neoliberal, insulated Chilean governance. How much of the work of government officials, and the Chilean state's governance strategies, is left off the record?

Negotiating Autonomy interrogates the Chilean government's land policy response to Mapuche Indigenous communities' territorial demands, focusing specifically on when and how the work of government officials shifts in response to actors operating both inside and outside the state. I argue that the dominant narrative about the ideological and insulated neoliberalization of Chilean governance inadequately characterizes how the Chilean government responds to Mapuche communities' demands for territory. Rather, the state dynamically interacts with and responds to actors working inside and outside institutionalized procedures—public policy is not exclusively the outcome or expression of state domination but rather a middle space where Mapuche demands and Chilean governance are consequentially contested. State officials rely on a combination of formal and informal governance strategies, working to assert a vision of the nation-state that preserves and extends both neoliberalism and the hegemony of political and economic elites in the region. Simultaneously, Mapuche communities and individuals present institutional and extrainstitutional demands that challenge and work within these governing efforts. Negotiations between these efforts produce contradictory, uneven outcomes, highlighting the importance of studying public policy as a consequential arena of contestation structuring both Mapuche resistance and Chilean domination.

This contextualized contestation and negotiation is significant in revealing internal contradictions in the neoliberal project. I analyze neoliberalism as the economic, political, and social restructuring of state and society according to a market-driven logic. The anthropologist Aihwa Ong describes neoliberalism to task the state with "governing through freedom" (2007, 4), working to center politics and citizenship around the individual's responsibility to resolve demands through market mechanisms, and the state should work to funnel demands toward the market. Foucault (2008, 116) describes this as the neoliberal anti-state, with the objective for "the state [to be] under the supervision of the market rather than a market supervised by the state." Accordingly, neoliberalization is far more than economic reform. As Read (2009, 26) describes of these broader ideological premises, neoliberalism is:

> Generally understood as not just a new ideology, but a transformation of ideology in terms of its conditions and effects. In terms of its conditions, it is an ideology that is generated not from the state, or from a dominant class, but from the quotidian experience of buying and selling commodities from the market, which is then extended across other social spaces, "the marketplace of ideas," to become an image of society. Secondly, it is an ideology that refers not only to the political realm, to an ideal of the state, but to the entirety of human existence. It claims to present not an ideal, but a reality; human nature.

If neoliberalism works to govern according to the market by presenting a particular vision of human nature, ethnic relations and identity politics also need to be restructured to that end. This presents a challenge to the state; as James (2013, 31) asserts, "Multiculturalism has been a particularly important target of neoliberal change." Frequently, the resulting policies work to translate ethnic relations into competitive and valuable market assets and commodities, often evidenced by the promotion of ethnotourism, multilingualism, and intercultural communications. Neoliberalism seeks not to create "a tolerant national citizen who is concerned for the disadvantaged in her own society but a cosmopolitan market actor who can compete effectively across state boundaries . . . [and] govern themselves in accordance with the logic of globalized capitalism" (McNeish 2008, 34). The implications of project for Indigenous communities is discussed later in this introduction.

Crucial for the argument presented in *Negotiating Autonomy* is that this "transformation of ideology" mandates that the work of neoliberalism takes on several forms. It is, as David Harvey (2007, 19) conceptualizes, both a "utopian project" and "political project," furthered by particular techniques of governance. I focus particularly on this second form, the techniques of government used to implement a project of neoliberalization; in this book, the presentation of neoliberalism as a utopian project justifies and legitimizes the underlying political project. Considering the vastness of this project, neoliberalization is nuanced, inconsistent, and contradictory. Understanding neoliberalization as an "articulated, processual, hybridized, protean, variegated, promiscuous, and travelling phenomenon" (Springer 2011, 2567), scholars have documented the uneven diffusion and execution of neoliberal projects across time and space (see Peck and Tickell 2002; Brenner, Peck, and Theodore 2010; Ferguson 2010; Peck, Theodore, and Brenner 2010; Springer 2011). This unevenness in the processes of neoliberalization is understood to result from the negotiated convergence of international and local neoliberalism as well as how the interests of local stakeholders map onto these debates (Ong 2006). Effectively, it is not surprising that other governing priorities bend to neoliberalism, or that there is backlash as people demand protections from reforms.

Yet, the Chilean case reveals an additional puzzle. How, why, and under what conditions do these contradictions and inconsistencies in the implementation of the techniques of neoliberal governance undermine the neoliberal project itself? Further surprising, how, why, and to what effect are bureaucrats and government officials carrying out this work? Bureaucrats, responsible for processing Indigenous demands that fit uncomfortably with neoliberal policies, are interestingly positioned in the processes of subject formation. Subject formation, according to Foucault (1982, 777), is "the different modes by which, in our culture, human beings are made subjects," modes that serve to bring individuals and groups into a specified governing logic. Neoliberalism structures the production of subjectivity around the extension of a market logic focused on the individual, disciplined to be empowered in all aspects of society as an individual and, more precisely, a consumer that is self-directing and autonomous, isolated from structural or collective organizations. As Wendy Brown (2003, 43) describes, "The model neoliberal citizen is one who strategizes for her or himself among various social, political, and economic options, not one who strives with others to alter or organize these options." The collective demands of Indigenous communities for degrees of self-governance and autonomy, then, pose a challenge to this individualistic, market-motivated understanding of subjectivity and threaten to undermine efforts to extend this governing logic. Yet there is potential for actors working both inside and outside of the state to subvert governing intentions and intended forms of subject formation. Actors are simultaneously making and being made within the state's governing logic, creating the conceptual space for actors to subvert this logic. Bureaucrats are positioned in the middle space, representing discipline and resistance, and policy outcomes are the visible outcome of the how bureaucrats work to strategically negotiate and maneuver between the ideals of the state's governing logic and discourse, and the local application of that governing logic. For Mapuche communities pursuing degrees of autonomy through territorial rights claims through Chile's Indigenous land policy, these outcomes of bureaucrats' work are consequential, particularly when considering the uneven extension of neoliberalism over space and time.

The chain of events that developed the morning of the April 2013 march highlighted this puzzle about the role of bureaucrats in the work of both extending and contradicting the neoliberal project. The resources distributed that day were processed through institutionalized programs, each of which required communities or individuals to apply through policies that worked to funnel Indigenous demands into market mechanisms. Yet the timing and process of the distribution of those resources undermined a neoliberal logic that self-empowered, competitive, and autonomous individuals access resources pursuant to their relative human capital. Effectively, the logic that governed the policy-implementation process was in tension with the logic that governed the policy regulations. The former sought to demobilize a march the government perceived to threaten the hegemony of the Chilean state by subverting institutionalized policy procedures that followed a neoliberal logic; the latter sought to extend a market policy logic by preserving the same policy procedures to pursue the same neoliberal logic. In the specific policy analyzed in this book, Chile's Indigenous land policy works to govern land in the region with market mechanisms, purchasing land from willing buyers; often, this allows large landholders and corporations to sell off less valuable land above market value. Simultaneously, the policy works to translate

Mapuche demands, and the organization of Mapuche communities and citizenship itself, into a neoliberal logic by requiring communities to document their demands according to that particular governing logic. From the perspective of the government, these policy mechanisms would ideally extend the neoliberal project in both ways, extending the strength of the market to those already operating within these market mechanisms, while bringing more actors and commodities into that market and those market mechanisms. But what if these interests contradict each other? Would the state protect the market interests of those who are already in this logic of governance? Or work to extend the reach of the market? What does the state do when policies that work to extend the scope of the market contradict with the same policies that work to preserve and extend the strength of the market? These contradicting articulations of neoliberalism, in the context of how the Chilean government processes Mapuche territorial demands through land policy, produce surprising variation in which communities receive land through government policy. Calling attention to these different articulations of neoliberalism takes up the call to study "actually existing neoliberalism" (Ferguson and Gupta 2002) and, in doing so, reveals the moments in which communities can take advantage of the contradictions of neoliberalism.

In Chile the façade of neoliberalism, as both a governing logic and ongoing political project, is extensively upheld, but masks underlying contestation over and contradictions of neoliberal governance. While it is often assumed that this project preserves and extends the strength and scope of the market, post-Pinochet governments in Chile have favored the preservation of the strength of the market that has already been created when governing Mapuche territorial demands. In doing so, Mapuche demands have the potential to split apart the state's interests both to extend the scope of neoliberalism as a governing logic and to preserve the strength of market interests of political and economic elites in the region. This represents moments when the state is forced to choose between efforts to make Indigenous demands into something legible to the governing logic of the state, and its work to extend the benefits of the model to those already made legible within this state logic. Effectively, the state is caught between its work to discipline subjects into a legible form of neoliberal citizens by preserving institutional procedures that work to make citizens into consumers, and its work to privilege those who are already legible neoliberal citizens by preserving market investments in the region.

For Mapuche communities, these moments are costly and fleeting, and reveal unexpected variation in which communities the government processes land transfers for. I argue that these inconsistencies result from how actors operating both inside and outside the state (Indigenous communities, bureaucrats, politicians, administrators) take advantage of the inconsistent, contradictory nature of neoliberal governance through the work of government officials. The most dramatic stories in this book emerge when Mapuche communities pit the pursuit of the expansion of neoliberalism against the interests of economic and political elite, challenging the state to choose between two usually complementary governing neoliberal logics; as Harvey (2007, 19) predicts of this tension, "When neoliberal principles clash with the need to restore or sustain elite power, then the principles are either abandoned or so twisted as to be unrecognizable." Indeed, Mapuche mobilization around broad territorial demands, perceived to be a threat to the integrity of the Chilean state itself, prompts dramatic interventions from national-level politicians whose work bends neoliberalism to the state's efforts to extend its hegemony and, by extension, the power of elites and their market interests. This is not to say that the Chilean state does not pursue the extension of neoliberalism through its response to Mapuche demands. Indeed, the majority of the state's governance of Mapuche demands fits into a neoliberal logic, characterized by an effort to translate Mapuche demands for territory and degrees of autonomy into specific demands for enough property to ensure the socioeconomic viability of the community, to be processed through market mechanisms overseen by the government. Yet the contradictions revealed throughout this book highlight the potential conditions under which public policy can provide a way for communities to creatively navigate through neoliberalism.

This introduction underscores the importance of studying these contradictions in neoliberal governance through the lens of Mapuche territorial demands and state land policy responses, situating the conversation within evolving patterns of Indigenous mobilization, neoliberal multicultural reforms, and territoriality in Latin America. This research provides insight into the persisting *brecha de implementación* (implementation gap) between the recognition and exercise of Indigenous rights in Latin America, exacerbated by the uneven extension of state governance over space and time; this book documents and analyzes the governing logics motivating and served by this implementation gap, emphasizing how rights demands for degrees of autonomy are undone and remade through policy.

INDIGENOUS DEMANDS AND NEOLIBERAL REFORMS IN LATIN AMERICA

PACMA's demands, and the Chilean government's response, needs to be contextualized within decades of Indigenous mobilization throughout the country and region.[4] In the 1980s and 1990s, Indigenous communities throughout Latin America organized around a collective identity in pursuit of rights recognitions that would facilitate the acquisition and restructuring of political power. While there is broad variation in the nature and demands of this mobilization, this represented a splintering of previous class-based mobilization organized by national-level peasant or labor organizations into combinations of women's, Indigenous, landless, environmental, Afro-American, and religious interests. Indigenous activists and organizations challenged the notion of a unitary, homogenous nation, demanding a different relationship with the state based on individuals constituting themselves as political subjects with collective social identities. This frequently took the shape of calling for the recognition as "peoples" to set a legal precedent for such communities to articulate rights to self-determination and degrees of autonomy within a plurinational state. This recognition could translate into rights to degrees of autonomy in the use of land and resources, and judicial, and administrative space at the local or regional level (Sieder 2002, 7). These demands for self-determination also implied the creation of space for Indigenous conceptualizations of democracy that reject the separation of public and private spheres of association in favor of consensual, direct, collective, and accountable decision-making embedded within kinship relations and cultural identity (Van Cott 2008, 22). This stage of Indigenous mobilization did not necessarily seek to restructure the government according to this governing vision rather pursued rights recognitions that allowed for the exercise of this form of governance. While class-based labor or peasant mobilization traditionally sought to acquire and redefine political power, these new movements operated "over and above—and in spite of—institutions" (Calderón, Piscitelli, and Reyna 1992, 20), pursuing participation in, yet autonomy from, the political arena (Burdick, Oxhorn, and Roberts 2009; Levitsky and Roberts 2011; Eisenstadt 2013). For example, in 1990 Indigenous communities from the Bolivian eastern lowlands and Andean highlands participated in the seventy-day march to La Paz, demanding *territorio y dignidad* (territory and dignity), successfully pushing the government to officially recognize some Indigenous territories. As Rice (2012, 56) noted, the 1990 *levantamiento* in Ecuador "marked the first time in Ecuadorian history that an indigenous movement forced the government to enter into serious dialogue about national politics."

Much of this mobilization represented a backlash to the neoliberal reforms implemented throughout the region from the 1970s through the 1990s. Economically, Latin American governments worked to shrink the size of the state, employing structural adjustment and austerity programs that privatized state-owned industry, reduced government spending, and liberalized trade, on the recommendations of the World Bank, the International Monetary Fund, and the Inter-American Development Bank, commonly known as the Washington Consensus. These reforms disproportionately affected situations of economic vulnerability of Indigenous peoples and communities in several ways. Neoliberal reforms brought land reform back to the policy agenda, calling for the regularization of individual property rights to strengthen land markets and provide investment security (discussed in detail in chapter 1; Thiesenhusen 1995; Kay 1998; Deininger and Binswanger 1999; Deininger 2003; Veltmeyer 2005). This focus on individual property rights removed restrictions on the sale of Indigenous land, dismantled formal recognitions of Indigenous communities' collective rights, and titled land that Indigenous communities had informally owned, controlled, or accessed. Furthermore, Latin American countries promoted national development strategies that infringed on Indigenous communities' land. Often referred to as the Commodities Consensus, governments prioritized the export of primary products, encouraging the development of extractive industries in ways that disproportionately affected Indigenous communities (Haarstad 2012; Hindery 2013; McNeish 2013; Svampa 2013; Yates and Bakker 2013; Burchardt and Dietz 2014; López and Vértiz 2014; Veltmeyer and Petras 2014; Acuña 2015). Indigenous communities' territorial rights recognitions, then, quickly came into conflict with these national development strategies.

The neoliberal project also restructured state-society relations through a series of political and social reforms. While democratic political transitions in the 1980s and 1990s increased political participation, the negotiated, pacted nature of many of the transitions often cemented elite privileges and failed to reshape citizenship, representation, and participation (Hagopian 1992; Weyland 2004). Combined with efforts to decrease the size of the state, policymaking became increasingly separated from political pressures and popular demands (Garretón 2003; Kurtz 2004; Silva 2009). As the Chilean economist and politician Alejandro Foxley (1982, 149) argued, "The final objective of neoliberalism in Latin America is nothing less than radically transforming the way the economy operates and, in its most extreme version, the way society and political institutions are organized." The potential for collective action was further undercut as Latin American governments employed the "politics of antipolitics" (Loveman and Davies Jr. 1997), dismantling and demobilizing labor unions and leftist parties to prevent politics from undermining restructuring efforts, shifting mobilization to local levels (Roberts 2002; Eckstein 2006). This decreased leaders' accountability and reduced the state's role as the distributor of social goods. As Francis Fukuyama (2004) documented how neoliberal reforms inadvertently reduced both the size and scope of the state, Latin Americanists warned of the emergence of delegative democracy throughout the region, in which presidents were held limitedly accountable by weakened intermediary organizations (O'Donnell 1994); Weyland (2004, 143) summarized, "Thus, by putting economic and political elites at greater ease, neoliberalism has substantially lowered internal challenges to democracy in Latin America."

Paradoxically, restructuring citizenship in line with broader neoliberal reforms resulted in some Indigenous rights recognitions through neoliberal multicultural reforms (Sieder 2002; Van Cott 2002; Postero and Zamosc 2004). Sponsored by the state, these reforms recognized ethnic differences and promoted cultural inclusion through language, education, and healthcare programs. Donna Lee Van Cott (2007, 132) defines neoliberal multicultural reforms to include: "(1) Rhetorical recognition of the existence of Indigenous peoples as collective entities preceding the establishment of national states; (2) recognition of customary Indigenous law as binding public law, typically limited by international human rights or higher-order constitutional rights, such as the right to life; (3) protection of collective property rights from sale, dismemberment, or confiscation; (4) official status for Indigenous languages; and (5) access to bilingual education."

Notably, these reforms were an extension of a neoliberal logic. As neoliberal reforms shrunk the size of the state to facilitate the functioning of the market, neoliberal multicultural reforms shifted responsibility for guaranteeing individual rights from the state to citizens—citizens, not the state, would solve societal problems (Yashar 1999, 2005). By the end of the 1990s, eight countries in Latin America amended or rewrote constitutions to recognize the country as multiethnic and pluricultural (Sieder 2002, 4).[5]

PERSISTING INDIGENOUS-STATE TENSION

While Indigenous rights recognitions and ensuing reforms prompted some optimism, these initiatives have fallen short of movement demands (Van Cott 2000; Hale 2006; Postero 2007, 2017). There is a tension inherent in multicultural reforms motivated by a neoliberal logic. Recognizing, incorporating, and encouraging Indigenous participation, if not accompanied by shifts in the distribution of economic and political power, turn the project to recognize the "politics of difference" into "empty rituals of recognition" (Gordon and Hale 2003, 379; see also Gustafson 2002; Hale 2002; Laurie, Andolina, and Radcliffe 2003;

Postero and Zamosc 2004; Hale 2006; Postero 2007). Charles Hale's analysis of neoliberal multicultural reforms in Guatemala found that *ladinos* (elites) endorsed "modernizing" multicultural reforms to the extent that the reforms did not challenge productivity or state power. Privileging nonthreatening expressions of Indigeneity in the form of the *indio permitido* (authorized Indian) over more radical expressions of indigeneity, neoliberal multicultural reforms reinforced existing power relations (Hale 2006; Lucero 2008). Neither changing structural inequalities nor opening spaces for democratic participation, "Neoliberal multiculturalism holds out the promise of both equality and cultural recognition, but grants only the latter, and then promotes intercultural exchange anyway. Under these conditions, multiculturalism produces mutual incomprehension and strife" (Hale 2006, 38). For the state, neoliberal multicultural reforms provide a means of diffusing opposition to economic reforms, in line with what Gramsci refers to as *aggiornamento*, an "updating" of the governing façade to preserve and support the hegemonic style of governance. In Bolivia, where academics and activists were perhaps most optimistic about the potential construction of a decolonized, Indigenous state after the election of Evo Morales, Nancy Postero (2017, 4–5) argues that "the country has not only continued but expanded its reliance on market capitalism. . . . indigeneity has been transformed in Bolivia from a site of emancipation to one of liberal nation-state building." Rather than remaking the state in these negotiations, these reforms most often worked to pull Indigenous demands into existing models of citizenship.

Because of the limited impact of the reforms, prominent international observers of Indigenous rights have called attention to, as indicated previously, a persisting *brecha de implementación* (implementation gap) between these formal recognitions and the meaningful exercise of internationally recognized Indigenous rights (UN Commission on Human Rights 2006). Rodolfo Stavenhagan (in Sieder 2002, 36) warned: "Some . . . fear that the new legislation is not really meant to be implemented and represents more of a cosmetic tinkering with the constitutional system than a real thorough change of power relations . . . the open question is how the new legislation will be implemented and how Indian communities will benefit. The answer is not at all clear. Complaints are constantly heard that the new laws are not being implemented as they should be, or that secondary legislation has not been adopted after general principles were laid down in the new constitutions." These concerns are echoed throughout the region. Deborah Yashar (2005, 219–20) reviews that "the institutional success of the 'indigenous reforms' has depended on the political will of Bolivian presidents to promote them and the institutional capacity of the state to implement them." Rachel Sieder (2002, 8) similarly observes that the "the discourse of 'participation' has not yet translated into effective oversight mechanisms in practice."

This book enters the conversation, exploring how, why, and to what effect the *brecha de implementación* left by neoliberal multicultural reforms in Latin America exists, and how it is contested. More than thirty years after a wave of Indigenous mobilization and rights recognitions in Latin America, many governments have translated Indigenous demands into recognitions and policy, directing a significant amount of Indigenous participation and engagement toward institutionalized policy frameworks that frequently operate at local levels. Relegating policy implementation to local government offices often empowers local bureaucrats, occasionally to challenge national directives, and often exposes substantial subnational variation in state capacity often referred to as "brown zones" (O'Donnell 1993; see also Eaton 2017; Giraudy and Luna 2017). Holes in state capacity create the potential for actors to utilize specific policy implementation in ways that can undercut policy, potentially strengthening clientelistic networks, increasing social conflict, and reinforcing patterns of unequal access to power (Laserna 2009; Selee and Peruzzotti 2009). As Lucero (2008, 135) demonstrates of these processes in the Bolivian case, "By breathing new life and channeling more money in the previously weak government, incentives now exist to work on local levels . . . The targets of indigenous political activism became local and not national." This variation is particularly consequential for the neoliberal project, as inconsistency characterizes the extension of the project across space and subjects (Ferguson and Gupta 2002); as Ong (2007, 4) describes of this state logic: "But in emerging non-Western contexts, the strategy of governing and self-governing is not uniformly applied to all groups and domains within a nation. Indeed, neoliberal policies are all about the recalibration of the capacity of groups in relation to the dynamism of global markets. Not all populations or areas can or should be subjected to techniques of self-governing and the free play of market forces." The outcome of these local, ongoing negotiations over degrees of autonomy are equally, if not more, consequential for the exercise of Indigenous rights.

As should be evident thus far, *Negotiating Autonomy* interrogates the middle space between resistance and domination structured within public policy. More specifically, this book is a study of negotiations over the state's governance of Indigenous demands carried out by politicians and bureaucrats, understanding governance as a broad "catch-all to refer to any strategy, tactic, process, procedure or programme for controlling, regulating, shaping, mastering or exercising authority over others" (Rose

1999, 15). I do not assume that the state structures all power relations; that the state is a homogenous, unitary actor with specific intent (Pringle and Watson 1992); or that the state is the only actor that governs. Rather, I see the state, and policy, as "not just functional bureaucratic apparatuses, but powerful sites of symbolic and cultural production" (Gupta 2012, 43), and the site where "movements wage their principal struggles, and where the Indian Question will be played out" (qtd. in Postero and Zamosc 2004, 3). I adopt a Foucauldian and poststructuralist view of the state as both a site and instrument of contestation (Lemke 2007) and a fragmented "coagulation of power" (Ferguson 1990, 274), where "governing people is . . . always a versatile equilibrium, with complementarity and conflicts between techniques which assure coercion and processes through which the self is constructed or modified by himself" (Foucault and Blasius 1993, 203–4).

This conceptualization of the state and governance opens conceptual space for actors to have unexpected influence, particularly when considering the contradictions of neoliberalism introduced here. Indeed, there are key moments when Mapuche communities obtain policy outcomes contradictory to key state interests. Nancy Postero similarly documents how "subjects of neoliberalism find in it a number of resources and tools. This is because neoliberalism is not an all-encompassing or hegemonic paradigm that dominates society but rather a philosophy that is expressed in various policies, practices, and institutions that are constantly being conserved and/or contested" (Postero 2007, 18). *Negotiating Autonomy* documents the moments in which and conditions under which creators and subjects of neoliberalism create these inconsistencies.

TERRITORIALITY AND THE STATE

Territorial rights are one of the most salient demands of the Mapuche community, underpinning broader demands for autonomy and self-determination. The Mapuche[6] identify themselves as people of the land (*mapu*, "land"; *che*, "people"); the strength of Mapuche identity is dependent on the health of the land and the peoples' relationship to it, as is discussed in chapter 1. A Mapuche university student most profoundly articulated this to me. After describing his community on the outskirts of Temuco early in our friendship, he asked where I was from and, accustomed to the question of how I ended up in Temuco, I described the short version. My Minnesota birthplace; Wisconsin childhood home; Carthage College dorm room; Buenos Aires host family; and Washington, DC, studio jointly, but not separately, defined where I was from. His puzzled response has become increasingly significant to this project:

"What does all that mean? Where are you actually from?" The litany of experiences that I understood to shape my own identity stood in stark contrast to his conceptualization of his identity by *tuwün* (place of origin) and *kupalme* (ancestry). My first few weeks of Mapuzungun ("the talk of the land," with land understood to include all natural beings, including humans, mountains, animals, and wind) language classes further reinforced this difference; introductions focused on identifying and situating a person within a territorial space by the person's *tuwün* and *kupalme*.

This conceptualization of territory as the basis of identity conflicts with the Chilean government's use of land as a primarily economic resource and commodity. How does the state govern this tension between understandings of Mapuche territory and Chilean land? At its core, this question asks how states attempt to extend or reconfigure governance through processes of territorialization. Territory has been traditionally theorized as "the bounded space of national territorial sovereignty," recognizing the role of the nation-state in defining and controlling space (Sassen 2013). As states have gradually weakened or lost their control over sovereign territory, scholars have described sovereignty as "fragmented" or "graduated" (Ong 2000), and territory as "blocks of space" (Agnew 2005, 441; see also Agnew 1994; O'Donnell 1999; Agnew and Oslender 2010). Decoupling territory, conceptually and empirically, from the nation-state is not necessarily an abdication of state sovereignty, but a recognition of "the use of territory for political, social, and economic end" by diverse actors (Agnew 2005, 437), and "a displacement from formal to informal techniques of government" (Lemke 2002, 84).

These shifts in territoriality accompany and mirror the neoliberal reforms introduced earlier, with the state strategically governing, formally or informally, particular spaces in particular ways so as to facilitate market efficiency and prioritize individual responsibility (see, for example, Rose and Miller 1992; Agnew and Oslender 2010; Bryan 2012; Gregory and Vaccaro 2015). As Bryan (2012, 218) summarizes: "State control over territory thus becomes less important than the ability to preserve a spatial order necessary to economic growth, security, and the task of governing itself . . . Neoliberalism has altered that perspective by recasting the role of the state as coordinating the interests of the private sector and civil society in order to maintain the socio-spatial order necessary for the functioning of markets." Land policy scholars similarly call attention to the local exercise of power, arguing that "land tenure regulation is contested at the level of policy *implementation*, that is, how regulation at different levels in society undoes or reworks state efforts to regulate land tenure in accordance with policy objectives" (van der Haar 2000,

285, emphasis added). The significance of Indigenous rights recognitions, then, comes to depend on these local, bureaucratic, and political calculations.

These transitions in territorial politics provide a window into a state's shifting approach to governance, in which the preservation or extension of an existing socioeconomic order in particular areas is paramount. Hale (2011, 204) more broadly observes, "The fate of black and indigenous land claims has come to vary widely, depending on location in relation to the empty spaces or brown areas that neoliberal development has left behind." Considering the strength and scope of neoliberal reforms in Chile, Mapuche demands for degrees of autonomy are subject to local and national economic interests at play in the same region. The Chilean government's response to Mapuche territorial demands provides a window into ongoing, contested state formation and restructuring occurring within policy.

NEOLIBERALISM AND INDIGENOUS POLITICS IN CHILE

The Chilean case is often excluded from literature on Indigenous politics in Latin America, which usually explores more dramatic or successful instances of Indigenous mobilization and rights recognitions. This limits our understanding of the broader range of Indigenous demands and the governance of Indigenous demands in the region, highlighting some experiences over others. For example, Postero and Zamosc (2006, 18) observe a split between countries in which Indigenous communities comprise the majority and those in which Indigenous communities comprise the minority, summarizing that "in the case of small minorities, it is a matter of survival, expressed primarily through demands for territory, autonomy, and special rights which would allow them to maintain their ways of life as indigenous peoples." Observing that lowland Indigenous communities in Ecuador prioritized negotiation over institutional rights, Lucero (2008, 107) similarly calls for analysis of Indigenous politics in countries where Indigenous groups comprise a minority of the population in order to fully understand the range of experiences in the region. Extending our understanding of the scope of Indigenous politics in the region, the Chilean case offers key insight into how Latin American states have responded to Indigenous demands through policy. Chile is regionally known for its centralized, technocratic, neoliberal governance and the strength through which the early implementation of neoliberal economic and political project permeated society and disarticulated civil society's links with the government. Chile reluctantly implemented neoliberal multicultural reforms, lagging behind its regional counterparts,

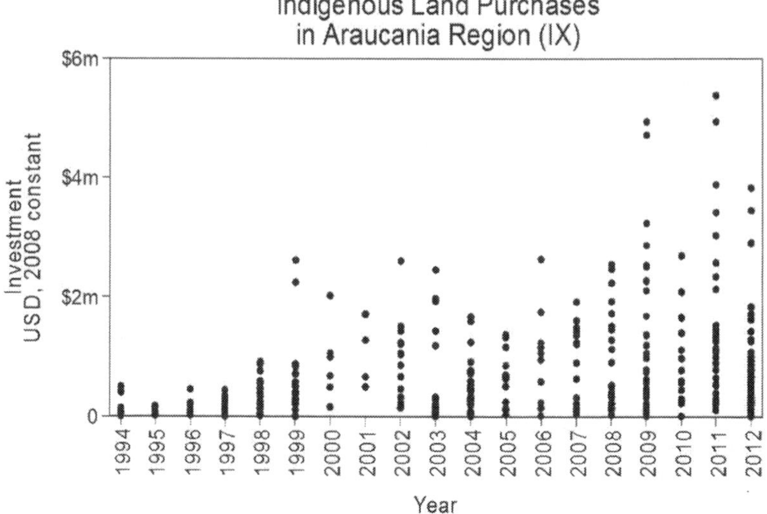

Figure I.1. CONADI land purchases, 1994–2013.

which constitutionally recognized Indigenous communities. Because of these established patterns of governance, distance between state and society, and tentative implementation of neoliberal multiculturalism, the Chilean case is a most likely case for capable policy implementation that follows a neoliberal logic, and a least likely case in which groups would be expected to influence policy implementation. These dynamics are analytically useful for isolating when and how policy outcomes deviate from these expectations.

This analysis focuses on Chile's piecemeal policy response to Mapuche territorial demands, which allows for nuanced analysis of specific implementation decisions. This policy response is outlined in Article 20B of the Indigenous Law 19.253. The 1993 law tasked CONADI with implementing Indigenous public policy.[7] With the expressed objective of responding to historic land disputes by purchasing ancestral land from a private landowner for a community if and when that particular Indigenous community submits the application, Article 20B is one of the cornerstones of this law. *Negotiating Autonomy* analyzes the implementation of Article 20B from 1994 (when it was first implemented) to 2013 (the end of the first Piñera administration). Based on public CONADI records, 266 Mapuche communities acquired land through Article 20B during this time period, with an additional 500 placed on a waiting list. While there are more than 3,000 state-recognized Mapuche communities, there is no publicly available data on communities still working through the process, those which qualify but have not applied, or those which have been rejected. These 266 communities received a total of 435 land purchases, covering 137,953 hectares. Purchases range in total cost from US$3,313 to $4,751,502 (2008 constant). In total, from 1994 to 2013, four presidential administrations spent US$303 million to purchase over 100,000 hectares for 11,000 families through Article 20B, amounting to 3 percent of all land in the region.[8] Implementation has been less than smooth, as evident in figure I.1, with inconsistencies in which communities access land through the policy, when, and at what total cost to the Chilean government.

After the central government hesitantly recognized some rights in Article 20B, responsibility for the recognition of these rights shifted to the local level. As such, policy implementation is situated between national priorities on development and Indigenous rights recognitions, and local narratives attempting to balance those priorities while considering local power dynamics. What accounts for the inconsistencies in when, where, and how much the government invests in responding to the territorial demands of particular communities?

RESEARCH DESIGN

Empirically, *Negotiating Autonomy* deconstructs variation in Chile's policy response to Mapuche territorial demands, exposing how government officials navigate through tensions in the extension of neoliberal governance in the region. This book adopts the intellectual stance of analytical eclecticism, which works to understand the "complexity and messiness of particular real-world situations" by "forgo[ing] parsimony in order to capture the interactions among different types of causal mechanisms normally analyzed in isolation from each other within separate research traditions" (Sil and Katzenstein 2010, 412). In doing so, this book draws on multiple methodologies and disciplines to unpack the conditions under which we see variation in policy implementation, an indication of how state officials and bureaucrats govern the middle space between citizen demands and state governing logic. Each subsequent chapter traces out one type of contestation over the implementation of Article 20B, relying on different data and different methods to analyze inconsistencies in Chilean governance, with the intention that each chapter separately and jointly further the argument introduced in this chapter.

Chapter 1, "Bureaucratizing Territory into Land Policy," documents the evolution of the formal procedures governing the implementation of Article 20B, situated within a broader discussion of the challenges governments faced to translate Indigenous demands for territory into rights recognitions and specific implementation procedures. Based on analysis of regulatory documents, chapter 1 details the ways in which Mapuche demands for territory become bureaucratically entangled with the Chilean state's efforts to recognize Indigenous communities' territorial rights and establish policy regulations governing implementation. In policy regulations, the Chilean government has increasingly interpreted Mapuche territorial claims as if they were for socioeconomic development, responding through land policy. This transition provides evidence of efforts to extend a neoliberal logic of governance through formal policy procedures.

Chapter 2, "Negotiating Land for Peace," considers the bureaucratic dynamics that condition if, how, and why government officials act on the motivation to extrainstitutionally bend bureaucratic procedures to respond to Mapuche mobilization. Drawing on interviews with politicians, activists, and bureaucrats, chapter 2 reveals that, across four presidential administrations spanning the political spectrum, the Chilean government strove to use land policy, in addition to well-documented militarization and criminalization of Mapuche protest, to demobilize (*apagar incedios*, "put out fires") Mapuche mobilization. While this motivation persists over twenty years, the government's ability to use policy becomes constrained over time, confronting increasingly institutionalized procedures and requiring the intervention of higher-level policymakers and/ or politicians. This institutionalization is the result of CONADI officials and bureaucrats working to shield themselves from blame for persisting Mapuche mobilization.

Chapter 3, "Navigating Land Policy," develops the mechanisms through which mobilization drives policy implementation from the perspective of Mapuche community leaders, based on case studies of eight Mapuche communities in the Padre Las Casas district outside the regional capital, Temuco. Their stories highlight that the Chilean government strategically employs a range of formal and informal governance strategies to demobilize certain Mapuche communities; while the preservation and extension of neoliberal governance motivates many policy decisions, these interviews highlight that demobilizing the threat posed by Mapuche mobilization is a superseding motivation. These stories reiterate that CONADI does see and respond to very local power dynamics, and works to preserve existing market interests in the region. Mobilization and political connections can shape policy implementation, but CONADI will only respond in a way that undermines the interests of powerful stakeholders if high-ranking officials call for it. Policy implementation decisions are not, however, a proportional response to perceived threats as expected but rather shaped by a combination of bureaucratic and local power dynamics. Chapter 3 expands the scope of the study by incorporating Mapuche communities who have sought, but have yet to receive, land through the government.

Chapter 4, "Quantifying Mobilization and Land Purchases," explores the extent to which broad patterns of policy enactment follows formal procedures through a quantitative analysis of the impact of Mapuche mobilization, perceptions of Mapuche communities, and the presence of forestry companies on the likelihood of land purchases. Drawing on an original data set of mobilization by the 266 Mapuche communities that received land through Article 20B over twenty years, chapter 4 quantitatively highlights the inconsistencies in the Chilean government's response to Mapuche communities. The government is more likely to purchase land for communities that mobilize, or are in a region with more forestry companies, in what appears to be a calculation about how to most efficiently appease communities that could pose a threat to economic investments and regional stability.

As discussed throughout this introduction, *Negotiating Autonomy* puts theoretical conversations about the role of government officials in extending neoliberal governance in conversations with empirical conversations about Chilean governance. The concluding chapter brings these conversations together. Those interested in how actors navigate neoliberalism will be most interested in the empirics presented in chapters 1–4. The epilogue considers the relevance of these patterns of the governance of identity politics for the October 2019 protests in Chile.

CONDUCTING RESEARCH IN TEMUCO

Chile first caught my eye in 2007. I was living in Buenos Aires at the time, but became captivated by very visible, simmering societal transformations after spending a week in Chile. Despite the comparative success and stability of post-dictatorship Chile, I saw visible contestation over the entrenched neoliberal transformation of politics, economics, and society. More puzzling was the unexpected visibility of the state, particularly in its coercive and disciplinary elements, in these negotiations over Chile's future. Where neoliberalism perhaps most dramatically deconstructed and reconfigured the state, how did the state navigate contestation over neoliberalization while further extending neoliberal governance? And why were the state's efforts so visible?

These questions first took me to Temuco in 2011, for sixteen months in 2012 and 2013, and several trips since in attempts to understand patterns of Chilean governance. Very quickly, I met Chilean and Mapuche scholars more qualified to document, analyze, and contextualize the construction and articulation of Mapuche demands than I, much of which has been recently published (see, among many others, Marimán et al. 2006; Cayuqueo 2012; Llaitul and Arrate 2012; Marimán 2012; Tricot 2013, 2014; Pairican Padilla 2014, 2017; Cayuqueo 2014; Rodríguez 2015; Cayuqueo 2017). In conversation with those I met in Temuco and Santiago, this focus narrowed over time in response to what seemed to be a remaining link in the narrative on the recognition of Indigenous rights in Chile: the very bureaucratic ways the state negotiates conversations over the politics of recognition through the work of bureaucrats and politicians. As one Mapuche friend often encouraged, "We know ourselves and our demands. What we don't know is what the state is doing and how to change it."

Choosing this focus raises valid concerns about assuming and legitimizing the hegemony of the Chilean state. The wonderful linguists, lawyers, anthropologists, historians, sociologists, and teachers at the Instituto de Estudios Indígenas at the Universidad de la Frontera, which I was affiliated with, constructively questioned and critiqued if this focus on governance of Indigenous rights legitimized the Chilean government as the arbiter of the these rights, undermining the autonomy (and legitimacy of demands for that autonomy) of the Mapuche and other Indigenous communities in Chile. Many were simultaneously curious about what government bureaucrats and officials would tell me. Certainly, engaging with the state is only one of the ways Mapuche communities and individuals pursue territory and territorial rights. At its core, this is the tension inherent in neoliberal multiculturalism and the pursuit of territorial rights through land policy; as Hale (2011, 202) summarizes: "The predicament, in sum, rests on the premise that these two modes of struggle—one immediate and pragmatic—the other expansive with sights set on the horizon are incompatible." Their questions and critiques honed my research to focus on naming the exercise of power through Chile's Indigenous land policy, in hopes of better informing and empowering those who do engage with these state procedures; as Boaventura de Sousa Santos (2010, 63) describes, this debate about the potential for state reforms to be a counterhegemonic force plays out throughout Latin America. Throughout this book I note resistance to and the limits of engaging with these state procedures, and return to these more normative questions about resistance and domination within neoliberal hegemony in the conclusion.

My time in Temuco was spent understanding Chilean governance of CONADI's land policy from a range of perspectives, including bureaucrats, politicians, activists, academics, lawyers, and Mapuche community leaders. Because of this focus, I did not seek out the Mapuche activists, leaders, communities, or regions that most frequently appear in the media or prominent court cases, although I crossed paths with many whose stories appear in this book in reference to particular requests presented to the government. I only occasionally heard the often-repeated assumptions that international researchers are either supporting radical mobilization or conducting surveillance. While I have my suspicions that my cell phone was tapped at one point because of degrees of connections to specific Mapuche activists of interest, my presence did not raise the suspicions that others have noted while in the region. While I did not sufficiently realize the implications of these decisions as I was planning and adapting the research design of this work, I resisted pressures to engage in intimate, solitary, and dangerous fieldwork presumed to produce a particular type of disembodied data. Hanson and Richards (2017, 603) appropriately call for reflection on how "all bodies are instruments of research, and all research projects are shaped by the gender, sexuality, and embodiment of the ethnographer," and, indeed, these dynamics strongly shaped much of my research, particularly in relationships with government bureaucrats, nearly exclusively men, who were flattered by my interest in mid-level bureaucracy, unthreatened by my presence and accent, and quick to agree to a conversation (Milkman 1997). Many of these conversations turned into two-hour conversations and ended with a scribbled list of phone numbers of their friends and colleagues who had more nuanced details about a different bureaucratic position or time period. But that access also brought limits to what could have been useful follow-up conversations, which often implied meeting in less public and/or professional settings. All this to say, my identities were not set aside as I conducted this research.

When interviewing bureaucrats and politicians who were working or formerly worked on the policy, I explained that my work sought to understand how the Chilean government responds to Mapuche territorial demands through policy, which they frequently took as an opportunity to share what they perceived to be lost in the narrative that usually focused on more on activism and violence than on their bureaucratic work. These people were selected based on their familiarity with Chile's Indigenous land policy, largely based on their time working on the development or implementation of Indigenous land policy from 1994 to 2013. Many of these individuals no longer worked in the government at the time of our interview. These interviews centered on situating that person's experience into a continuum of the Chilean government's approach, in hopes that I could understand how the Chilean state created and updated policy implementation and rhetoric over time. Many of these conversations started with a discussion of how that person understood the government's response to Indigenous demands before starting their position, and evolved to discuss how they kept or worked to shift that response, and how they interpreted the direction of the policy since leaving in efforts to detail which individuals, offices, and organizations were involved in which decisions at which points in time, and to understand key moments that changed or entrenched the Chilean government's response. Interviewees usually discussed CONADI as a well-intentioned institution staffed by well-intentioned bureaucrats motivated to mediate between Mapuche communities and the interests of the national government. Fifteen minutes into the conversation, the narrative was usually about how CONADI was on the side of the communities, wanting to return land, but continued to be undercut by the national government, who persistently intervened into their carefully designed policies and regulations to appease concerns about Mapuche terrorism. News reports triangulated this information to provide additional background and context around these events.

A friend came to act as a research assistant to contact and guide me to the homes of local Mapuche community leaders who could speak of their community's process. Born and raised in the Makewe district right outside Temuco, he was distantly related to many in the region and frequently crossed paths with these leaders at community meetings and local events (details of these interviews are discussed in chapter 3). The interviews addressed how the community learned about the policy, the steps they took to present their demand, whether the communities have connections to civil servants/politicians/academics/lawyers/political parties, if they participated in any type of protest or mobilization while presenting their demand, how they would characterize the government's responsiveness, their general challenges and successes navigating the policy, and their perceptions of why some communities were more successful than others. The experiences of these eight communities are interwoven with local news reports on Mapuche communities in pursuing territorial rights in the same district.

All of the interviews were semi-structured and, when given permission, most were recorded. These interviews lasted between thirty minutes and two and a half hours, with the average interview lasting sixty minutes. I conducted all the interviews in Spanish; when personal interviews are cited in this text, they are my own translations from Spanish. In total, I conducted interviews with about seventy politicians and bureaucrats, twenty Mapuche leaders and activists, and twenty professionals, including academics, lawyers, and community leaders. Those categories are not mutually exclusive but categorized by how the person was most directly involved in the policy process: creating or implementing policy, utilizing or opposing the policy, or observing.

Image I.4. Community meeting announcement in Padre Las Casas, reading, "Se sita a reunion todo socios asunto de la tierra. Hora 15.30." May 2013. Photo by the author.

Image I.5. Local bus stop. Graffiti on the left reads, "La tierra no se vende se recupera. Marrichiweu Lof Muco." November 2013. Photo by the author.

Most interviews were conducted in or near Temuco, Chile, an eight-hour drive south of Santiago, and the location varied dramatically as most convenient for the interviewee. A former political appointee and current politician asked his assistant to schedule our conversation at the upscale Café de la P, a café on the west side of town between the newer shopping mall and upscale casino. Others were at exclusive law firms in Santiago. Many interviews with current bureaucrats were held in the national and subnational CONADI offices in Temuco. Most often, I traveled to the homes of Mapuche leaders, navigating buses and long walks on muddy roads, collecting a broader understanding of territory and mobilization around territory in the process; thankfully, my friend and research assistant stopped scheduling interviews during the rainy season.

Interviewees are not referred to by name, in accordance with university human subjects research requirements and in recognition of shifting conditions in the region. I do include the names of individuals when using secondary sources, meaning that some individuals are mentioned both anonymously and by name. I regret that specific individuals and communities are not able to publicize their demands and stories through this medium; I can only hope that the collection of stories jointly presented here uncovers previously shielded patterns of governance and contributes to the future interrogation of the Chilean state and its governance through Indigenous policies.

CHAPTER 1

BUREAUCRATIZING TERRITORY INTO LAND POLICY

While it is possible that land problems will continue to be important for the rural indigenous population in the next decade, economic and social change will undoubtedly demand that indigenous communities broaden their economic base beyond agriculture. This has occurred with non-indigenous peoples in all countries. With this perspective, it is likely that education, development of indigenous human resources, and commodification of economic activities will be some of the strategic work for the next millennium.

It is not possible to reconstitute ancestral territory through land purchases at market prices because there is not sufficient public funding to buy them and because often the current owner does not want to sell them.

—1999 Land Policy, CONADI, Ministerio de Planificación y Cooperación

The Chilean case offers key insight into variation in the neoliberal governance of identity politics, analyzed here through the lens of Indigenous territorial demands and land policy. Chile is regionally known for the strength and continuity of such governance, and post–Pinochet Chilean governance is characterized by its ongoing efforts to reshape politics, economics, society, and citizenship according to a neoliberal governing logic; as Silva (2004, 65) concludes, "Probably nowhere else in Latin America has the objective of political deactivation been pursued so consciously and tenaciously by authoritarian as well as by democratic governments as in the case of Chile." In southern Chile, successive administrations extend this logic by expanding extractive industries, translating collective demands into bureaucratic requests processed by market mechanisms, making communities responsible for pursuing their demands, and disarticulating mobilization that opposes these governing efforts. This work attempts to strengthen the economic market in the region, and make Mapuche demands legible to neoliberal state logic; this chapter explores how the Chilean government pursues these governing motivations through evolving Indigenous land policies.

When responding to the territorial rights demands of Mapuche communities, the Chilean government works to extend both the strength and scope of neoliberalism in southern Chile. This happens through the work of bureaucrats and politicians, who reshape formal policies by shifting when, how, why, and if the government can respond to the demand. This chapter details the ways in which CONADI officials evaluate and regulate this policy, understanding the regulatory documents governing Chile's policy response to be "constitutive of bureaucratic rules, ideologies, knowledge, practices, subjectivities, objects, outcomes, and even the organizations themselves" (Hull 2012, 253). As officials work to shield themselves from pressure by updating policy regulations and procedures, they gradually converted a policy with the potential to respond to Mapuche territorial demands into a policy infused with a neoliberal logic, promoting socioeconomic development in those communities through land transfers. In doing so, they exacerbated the gap between Mapuche demands and Chile's corresponding Indigenous land policy. Certainly, we should not assume that implementation always follows these formal procedures; indeed, it is precisely the argument of the book that both policy regulations and implementation are contested and fluctuating in Chile. Yet the evolution of the formal procedures and regulations defines which Mapuche communities can pursue which territorial demands through land policy and, accordingly, reveals governing priorities.

This chapter situates Article 20B of Indigenous Law 19.253 (1993) within a broader history of (1) recent regional trends in the recognition of Indigenous territory throughout Latin America, and (2) formal and informal Chilean governance of Indigenous territorial demands. Historically, Chile followed regional trends in policy governing land as property with economic utility. However, beginning in the 1990s, many Latin American countries started to formally recognize Indigenous communities' territorial rights. Frequently referred to as the *territorial turn*, these recognitions reconceptualized territory as economically, socially, politically, and historically constructed spaces. Optimism about these recognitions was short-lived, as implementation frequently extended neoliberal governance by reinforcing existing socioeconomic and political hierarchies. Chile adds nuance to this narrative of the territorial turn, revealing the processes of neoliberalization in a context where Indigenous territorial rights protections were only weakly established, and where land continues to be conceptualized primarily as property with economic utility.

LAND AND TERRITORY IN POLICY IN LATIN AMERICA

Latin American governments historically conceptualize land as an economic resource capable of facilitating development. Dating back to the Mexican land reform and persisting across authoritarian, liberal reformist, and revolutionary regimes, land reform seeks to shift the productive use of land to promote long-term development, reduce rural unrest, and encourage agricultural efficiency (Zoomers and van der Haar 2000a; Veltmeyer 2005). While there have certainly been swings in perceptions of how to best accomplish these objectives, economic interests are paramount in these instances of government efforts to reshape patterns of land tenure. For example, land reform was particularly prominent on Latin American political agendas in the 1960s. Hoping to avoid a repeat of the 1959 Cuban Revolution and supported by the 1961 Alliance for Progress, nineteen Latin American countries passed land reform legislation, and twelve countries enacted reforms between 1960 and 1964 (Dorner 1992, 33). During import substitution industrialization programs, land tenure was blamed for lags in agricultural output; land reform offered to supply inexpensive, domestically produced food to growing urban populations, reducing a country's reliance on imports (Zoomers and van der Haar 2000b, 60). Furthermore, reform would prompt agricultural efficiency by transferring unproductive land to new owners, often in the form of cooperatives or collectives. Effectively, land reform was a tool to benefit the nonreformed sector; by selling less productive land, landowners would keep their most productive agricultural lands and acquire capital to reinvest in new technology (De Janvry 1981).

As the region shifted away from import substitution industrialization policies and state-directed economic policies, most Latin American countries adopted a neoliberal developmental model. Beginning with the Pinochet dictatorship in Chile and accelerating with the worldwide economic recession following the 1982 petroleum crisis, concerns about the distribution of land and agrarian reform were subsumed into macroeconomic concerns about debt, tariffs, and inflation (Thiesenhusen 1995, 13). The Chilean government reduced its role in the agricultural sector and halted or reversed land redistribution efforts, often referred to as the "reform of the reform." Land titles were returned to previous owners and communal or state-owned land was separated into constituent parts under Washington Consensus structural-adjustment programs.

While removing restrictions limiting land markets was understood to be the most appropriate way of facilitating rural development in the first stages of neoliberal reforms, limitations of this approach brought the "land question" back to the policy agenda in the 1980s and 1990s

(Thiesenhusen 1995; Kay 1998; Deininger and Binswanger 1999; Deininger 2003; Veltmeyer 2005). The focus remained on the promotion of land markets within a neoliberal framework, but called for the government to adopt a more active role to strengthen land markets and provide investment security by regularizing individual property rights (Deininger 1999), referred to as negotiated or market-led agrarian reform. This neoliberalization of agrarian reform shifted understandings of how the state should be involved in land politics. Rather than selecting, acquiring, and redistributing land, the government would work to facilitate the function of land markets, providing access to credit and abolishing communal lands to increase the quantity of available land and ensure land access for the most efficient producers. Land reform, then, would be accomplished through buyer-willing, seller-willing transactions. The promotion of free markets and private enterprise, accomplished through land titling and registration, would encourage profit-maximizing behavior, efficiency, and rural development. This policy shift is most prominently seen in the focus on land titling programs, which were understood to facilitate land transfers, provide a source of credit, encourage investment in the land, and ensure security for the landholder (Deininger 2003). Governments also set up land taxation programs, encouraging the productive use of land, generating government revenue, and improving public records. By the early 1990s, every Latin American country had shifted its approach to land reform in accordance with this neoliberal policy agenda, enacting constitutional reforms to eliminate communal lands and entitlements for small landowners and freeing up land for the land market (Veltmeyer 2005, 300). While there has been recognition of nuances in these recommendations, there is notable continuity in the promotion of land markets as a development tool. The 2003 World Bank report "Land Policy for Growth and Development" recognizes the utility of communal tenure arrangements in particular situations, and the potential for meaningful community-based reform based on buyer-willing, seller-willing transactions. By doing so, it acknowledges that land sales were previously overemphasized, considering the systematic exclusion of many living in situations of poverty (Deininger and Binswanger 1999, 248–49). As Courville and Patel (2006, 3) summarize of the significance of this evolution, "Policy discussions now highlight considerations of efficiency, making issues of equality and distributive justice secondary, if they are considered at all. Many of the most prominent and recent arguments for and against agrarian land reform since the Cold War have come to pivot on economic questions." While addressing these exclusions, the objective continues to be the integration of historically excluded groups into land markets, facilitating the exchange and distribution of land and improving land allocation and utilization.

Somewhat unexpectedly, these trends in land reform and policy converged with and facilitated the articulation of emerging Indigenous demands for territorial rights. As most prominently articulated on international stages, these demands challenge the dominant perception of land as property with economic utility, calling instead for recognizing territory as economically, socially, politically, and historically constructed spaces representative of deeper, mutually constitutive relationship between Indigenous peoples and spaces (Davis and Wali 1994; Assies 2000; Bryan 2012). While Indigenous territorial demands were largely subsumed into class demands for property rights through agrarian reform in the 1960s and 1970s, ethnicity reemerged as a prominent nexus of political organization in the 1980s and 1990s, partly in response to the implementation of neoliberal reforms (Sieder 2002; Postero and Zamosc 2004; Yashar 2005). Politically, neoliberal reforms entailed a liberalization of relations between state and society toward individual, rather than group or corporate, rights. Neoliberal economic policies had a particularly significant impact on Indigenous land holdings, encouraging the development of industries that drew on natural resource extraction and restructuring of land markets around individual rather than collective land titles. In response to these shifts, Indigenous territorial demands were first discussed at the 1984 meeting of the Coordinating Body of the Indigenous Peoples of the Amazon, where Amazonian communities discussed territory as "an integral part of an indigenous political project" (Lucero 2008, 105). These demands called for the recognition of territory not for its productive value but rather for its political, cultural, and social significance (Healy 2001, 81; Lucero 2008, 92). This decolonizing project later spread to the highlands, throughout the region (Healy 2001, 393), and to international forums.[1] At the 1985 meeting of the United Nations Working Group on Indigenous Populations, the president of the Central Organization of Indigenous Peoples and Communities of Eastern Bolivia expressed:

> Our defense of the land and natural resources is for the cultural and human survival of our children, and is the foundation of a moral security for peoples who have different languages and customs . . . We indigenous peoples think and plan in terms of the territory, not only the individual plot; in this way, we assure the access of the community to the diverse resources of the forest (wood, soil appropriate for agriculture and cattle, and wild fauna) . . . We indigenous peoples know that without land there can be no education, there can be no health and there can be no life. (qtd. in Ortega 2004, ix–x)

UN Special Rapporteur José R. Martínez Cobo similarly emphasized, "It is essential to know and understand the deeply spiritual special relationship between indigenous peoples and their land as basic to their existence as such and to all their beliefs, customs, traditions and culture . . . land is not merely a possession and a means of production . . . Their land is not a commodity which can be acquired, but a material element to be enjoyed freely" (qtd. in International Labor Organization 2009, 91). This conceptualization of land stands in stark contrast to understanding land as an economic commodity.

Indigenous communities' territorial demands are about much more than land, requiring more policy tools for full recognition and exercise of these rights. As the Inter-American Court of Human Rights (IACHR, 2010, ¶ 55) described, this "special relationship" means that "the use and enjoyment of the land and its resources are integral components of the physical and cultural survival of the indigenous communities and the effective realization of their human rights more broadly." As most commonly expressed, Indigenous communities pursue territory by claiming rights to historically occupied land, land sufficient to fulfill economic and social functions, protection of claimed land from the state or private actor, environmental protection, rights to adjacent or subsoil resources, degrees of autonomy or self-government within the claimed land, and protection from violent conflict if the state does not enforce land rights. While a land claim pursues redistribution within the existing institutional framework, territorial claims demands "an alteration of the rules" (Offen 2003, 47) and are at the root of Indigenous communities' demands for power, autonomy, and self-determination. Territorial rights necessitate both the recognition of territory as a jurisdictional space as well as the recognition of a community's jurisdiction over this territory (Zuñiga Navarro 1998).

Coalescing international standards on territorial rights called on governments to recognize and act on the legitimacy of these demands. The 1989 Indigenous and Tribal Peoples Convention (ILO 169) of the International Labor Organization (ILO), the most significant and only binding international law on Indigenous rights, recognizes that "governments shall respect the special importance for the cultures and spiritual values of the peoples concerned of their relationship with the lands *or territories*, or both as applicable, which they occupy or otherwise use, and in particular the collective aspects of this relationship" (emphasis added).[2] The recognition of territory as the "the total environment of the area" represents a significant conceptual shift from the first international convention on Indigenous rights (ILO 107, 1957), which called for Indigenous communities to have a "land reserve adequate for the needs of shifting cultivation," deploying language that understands land as a commodity for subsistence. ILO 169 recognizes Indigenous rights to land beyond that necessary for subsistence, stating that "measures shall be taken in appropriate cases to safeguard the right of the peoples concerned to use lands *not exclusively occupied* by them, but to which they have traditionally had access for their subsistence and traditional activities" (Article 14, emphasis added). Importantly, this right is recognized regardless if these lands were ever formally recognized or documented by the state and calls on signatory states to establish legal procedures to claim territory (Articles 14, 2, and 3). The ILO supervisory bodies have repeatedly emphasized that this clause should not be interpreted as requiring "regular and permanent presence" on specific land as governments sometimes interpret, ruling in favor of Indigenous communities' rights to land based on traditional land tenure, and recent rather than historical occupation.[3]

Latin American governments recognized more than two hundred million hectares of the communal property rights of Indigenous and Afro-descendent communities' territorial rights during the 1980s and 1990s, resulting in the "the most ambitious and radical territorial reorderings ever attempted in Latin America" (Offen 2003, 44). In some countries, these recognitions are substantial (Ortega 2004). By 2014, 28 percent of Nicaraguan national territory was recognized in collective land titles (Larson et al. 2016). Demands for territorial recognitions appear more common in countries in which Indigenous communities comprise the minority of the national population, or for lowland Indigenous groups, often smaller in number (Postero and Zamosc 2004, 16). The extent of the reforms also depends on patterns of land tenure of the region under analysis, with reforms more likely instituted where land is not held by powerful economic stakeholders with clear property rights regimes.

As expected, there is broad variation in the recognition, implementation, and exercise of these rights. Most authors note the chronological evolution of how countries recognized Indigenous territorial rights, from recognition of limited forms of autonomy (Guatemala 1985, Nicaragua 1987, Brazil 1988), to acknowledgement of Indigenous communities as collective actors with collective rights (Colombia 1991; México 1992, 2001; Perú 1993; Bolivia 1994; Ecuador 1998), to the identification of Indigenous communities' status as nations with rights to degrees of legal plurality and territorial autonomy (Ecuador 2008, Bolivia 2009) (Aylwin Oyarzún 2003; Yrigoyen Fajardo 2010; Galvis Patiño and Ramírez Rincón 2013). Ortega (2004) catalogues the extent to which Latin American countries constitutionally protected Indigenous territorial rights, classifying Bolivia, Brazil, Colombia, Costa Rica, Panama, Paraguay, and Peru as having advanced protections (including the legal framework and a sufficient commitment to implementation); Mexico, Guatemala, Honduras, Nicaragua, Venezuela, and Argentina began making commitments, but had not sufficiently regulated or implemented these commitments; and El Salvador, Guyana, Suriname, and Uruguay made no commitments. Notably, the Chilean case drops out of these conversations, with very weak protections of Indigenous rights in law, but not in the current 1980 Constitution.

Implementation of this range of rights recognitions was most often folded into broader reforms focused on the regularization of property rights regimes and strengthening of market reforms. Effectively, the territorial turn frequently served to extend neoliberal governance, with the World Bank serving as an unexpected but key supporter and financial backer of these recognitions (Offen 2003; Ortega 2004; Anthias and Radcliffe 2015). These reforms removed restrictions on the sale of Indigenous land, dismantled formal recognitions of Indigenous communities' collective rights, and titled land informally held by Indigenous communities. While neoliberal economic reforms partly facilitated Indigenous rights recognitions to advance the expansion of property rights, they also encouraged the growth of the extractive industries that relied on natural resources and prioritized exports of primary products. This development strategy was often sold politically as a means to fund domestic social welfare programs, but the costs and benefits are disproportionately distributed, requiring what has been referred to as "large-scale foreign investment in the acquisition of land," "land-grabbing," and "accumulation by dispossession" (Haarstad 2012; Hindery 2013; Svampa 2013; Veltmeyer and Petras 2014; López and Vértiz 2014; Burchardt and Dietz 2014; Acuña 2015; Veltmeyer 2016). As Veltmeyer (2016, 779) describes: "Perhaps the most serious 'contradiction' of nature resource development is that a large part of the benefits of economic activity are externalised, i.e. appropriated by groups outside of the country and region, while virtually all of the costs—economic, social, and environmental—are internalized and disproportionately borne by the indigenous and farming communities." While some Indigenous communities acquired some territorial rights, the state most often maintained subsoil rights, effectively limiting Indigenous communities' legal recourse to prevent the expansion of the extractive industries on or surrounding Indigenous land (Anthias and Radcliffe 2015; Erazo 2013; Hindery 2013; McNeish 2013; López and Vértiz 2014; Veltmeyer and Petras 2014; Acuña 2015). This increased reliance on extractive industries "extends a particularly neoliberal approach to governance, one that compels property owners to simultaneously make use of land and resources in economically productive ways and maintain a broader social order equated with the security of property rights" (Bryan 2012, 218).

In addition to being folded into economic restructuring, territorial rights recognitions also required Indigenous communities to work through the state to recognize, administer, and manage the exercise of these rights. By turning to the state, Indigenous peoples risk reinforcing their position as objects of the state, confirming the government's legitimacy and authority. This bureaucratic entanglement with the state threatens to reinforce rather than reconstruct territoriality, ultimately preserving or advancing existing political economic structures (Wainwright and Bryan 2009; Hale 2011; Bryan 2012; Erazo 2013; Bauer 2016; Finley-Brook 2016; Sylvander 2018; Correia 2019). Effectively, the territorial turn opened unexpected "hybrid, double-edged and not-quite-neoliberal" spaces' for Indigenous communities (Anthias and Radcliffe 2015, 257), offering only limited potential to purse the radical reconfiguration of territoriality itself. As Fabricant and Gustafson (2011, 64) concluded of the Bolivian experience: "The risk is that the proposal of territorial ordering—the remapping of Bolivia—and of indigenous autonomies becomes simply . . . 'state matter.' That is to say, the remapping is transformed into a state reform that deepens the mechanisms of indigenous participation in the state but does so through their subordination, without changing the structures of the state itself." Erazo (2013, 1–2) similarly summarizes, "Thus, collective indigenous land titling, whose apparent purpose is to allow native peoples the freedoms to escape from the everyday workings of bureaucracy and the state, paradoxically initiates new governmental structures within the territory and new dynamics of rule and discipline." This bureaucratic entanglement with the state undermines communities' broader mobilization potential. For example, in Nicaragua, "Multiple layers of authority have led to infighting, tensions and conflict, opportunities and opportunism. Policies and processes of demarcation, the construction of territorial governments and mestizo colonisation—or the failure to address it—have led to a weakening of the foundations upon which the indigenous movement was historically constructed" (Larson et al. 2016). Similarly, in Mexico, "The national neoliberal land certification program has nevertheless served to further fragment indigenous lands, which may threaten their well-being and survival as culturally distinct peoples over the long term" (Kelly et al. 2010, 163).

As evidenced, the potential significance of the territorial turn was undone as states extended neoliberal governance through the policy reforms. While Indigenous communities call for the recognition of territory as economically, socially, politically, and historically constructed space, the pursuit of territory risks bureaucratic entanglement within state's efforts to extend governance. Indeed, governments often responds with land policy, preserving or advancing existing political economic neoliberal structures of governance and too often failing to fundamentally reshape Indigenous-state political, economic, or social relations.

MAPUCHE TERRITORIAL DEMANDS

How do these regional and international trends relate to and interact with Mapuche demands for territory in Chile? Territorial demands are one of the Mapuche community's most salient demands, calling for the Chilean government to recognize land not for its productive value but for the deeper, mutually constitutive relationship between Indigenous peoples and territory. The strength of the Mapuche identity and community is dependent upon the health of the territory and the peoples' relationship to it (*mapu*, "land"; *che*, "people"). Mapuche identity stems from this constitutive relationship (Chihuailaf 1999; Marimán et al. 2006; Quilaqueo and Quintriqueo 2010; CEPAL and Alianza Territorial Mapuche 2012), which Di Giminiani (2018, 11) characterizes as defining both land and people as sentient subjects. Mapuche individuals situate their individual and collective identity within this *tuwun* (used as a noun, place of origin, and verb—"to come from") and *kupal* (family descent). Demands for territory, then, are based on this historical connection rather than on a formal land title establishing a right to a particular plot of land; as the Mapuche poet Elicura Chihuailaf (1999, 19) describes, "La tierra no pertenece a la gente" (the earth does not belong to people).

The Mapuche have a long history of mobilization and resistance in defense of lost territory (Bengoa 2000; Aylwin 2001; Boccara 2002; Pinto Rodríguez 2003; Correa, Molina, and Yáñez 2005; Marimán et al. 2006; Rodriguez and Carruthers 2008; Correa and Mella Seguel 2010; Pairican Padilla 2014; Tricot 2017). It is important to avoid assuming that the Mapuche movement or Mapuche demands are unified, due to both the importance of an individual's autonomy, independence, and responsibility in Mapuche society (Foerster 2004; Course 2011; Gonzalez Galvez 2012), and the protracted history of state policies that reshaped the organization of Mapuche society (Bengoa 2000; Aylwin 2001; Morales Urra 2002; Pinto Rodríguez 2003; Marimán et al. 2006; Correa and Mella Seguel 2010; Webb 2014). Rather, demands and mobilization take on several forms over time and space (Bidegain 2017). For example, the Coordinadora Arauco Malleco (CAM, Arauco Malleco Coordinating Committee), a more radical Mapuche organization sought to change the strategy of political engagement from one of "symbolic land recoveries" to "body-to-body" conflict with police (Pairicán and Álvarez 2011, 75). One of the founders of CAM summarized that the anti-systemic organization's vision was to arrive to a plot of land, tear down the existing infrastructure of the landowner, and plant crops; this initial self-defense of Mapuche territory would allow for the reconstruction of sociopolitical spaces, facilitating cultural revitalization, autonomy, and eventually Mapuche national liberation through the self-defense of Mapuche territory (Pairicán and Álvarez 2011, 73–74). The group's land occupations, acts of arson on state and corporate properties, and violent encounters with state police draw a significant amount of media attention, used to publicize their demands for autonomy. This escalation in direct action has been accompanied by a convergence of collective rights demands, based in Mapuche demands as a nation (Marimán 2012). Many, however, however, do not see CAM's tactics as the most appropriate way to present demands to the state. For example, Aukiñ Wallmapu Ngulam or Consejo de Todas las Tierras (CTT, Council of All the Lands) largely pursues self-government through international law by pursuing sanctions against the Chilean state for violating international standards on Indigenous rights (Kowalczyk 2013). This portion of the Mapuche movement is frequently contrasted with a portion of the movement that mobilizes within institutionalized domestic paths to degrees of autonomy through, for example, municipal and congressional elections, domestic recognitions of international agreements on Indigenous rights, and constitutional reforms. One of the most notable expressions of this strategy is the formation of the Wallmapuwen Political Party, pursuing decentralization of the regional government in the short-term to the end of creating an autonomous region. In 2006 they declared "the necessity of taking a leap forward in the organized struggle of our peoples through the formation of a Mapuche Political Party, of nationalistic and autonomist character," arguing that the institutional path is most effective, as "it makes no sense for the Mapuche movement to escalate violence when our people have to pay for the costs of a conflict that can only have political solutions" (Wallmapuwen 2009). These few examples evidence the variation in strategies of Mapuche mobilization.

HISTORY OF INDIGENOUS LAND POLICY IN CHILE

Historically, Mapuche territorial demands have been met with strong resistance from governing officials and elites, who argue that Indigenous peoples comprise part of one Chilean nation. A few examples highlight the continuity of this response, and are further contextualized shortly.

During the nineteenth and twentieth centuries, Chile promoted *chilenidad* (Chilean identity, Bengoa 2004); during the political and economic swings from the 1950s to 1970s in Chile, Indigenous demands were largely subsumed into class-based demands (Correa, Molina, and Yáñez 2005). When in 1974 the Pinochet dictatorship issued Decree 701 and in 1979 Decrees 2.568 and 2.750 to privatize Indigenous communal land and to facilitate the rapid expansion of the monoculture plantation industry (specifically pine and eucalyptus) in southern Chile, officials established "indigenous lands and indigenous landowners do not exist, because there are only Chileans" (Government of Chile 1979, see chapter 4 for details on these policies). The 1980 Constitution declares that "the Chilean State is unitary" (Article 3), and during discussions over Indigenous Law 19.253 (1993), the opposition argued that the concept of "peoples" was reserved for the Chilean people; the resulting law recognizes "Chile indigenous races . . . [as] an essential part of Chilean Nation roots" (Article 1) and subsequently refers to "ethnic group of indigenous communities" or "indigenous populations." Throughout Chilean history, the government has repeatedly rejected efforts to recognize Indigenous communities and rights.

Simultaneously, much of the history of relations between the Mapuche community and the Chilean state is characterized by the Chilean state's efforts to access the economic potential of land historically occupied by the Mapuche community, understanding land policy as a developmental tool to best utilize the commodity of land. The Mapuche were the only Indigenous group to resist incorporation into the Inca Empire, and were the only Indigenous community granted autonomy from the Spanish crown between 1641 and 1803 in numerous formal treaties after a series of uprisings, beginning in 1592, culminating with the destruction of all Spanish forces, forts, and settlements south of the Bíobío River in 1598. After Chile declared independence from Spain in 1818, the government became increasingly concerned about the country's dependence on imports; colonizing the "Indigenous zone" was necessary to ensure the country's development and national security (Bengoa 2014). The resulting military campaign was known as the Pacification of the Araucanía; as the Chilean historian Diego Barros Arana later justified, the Mapuche were "lazy and improvident," necessitating that Chile conquer these lands (qtd. in Richards 2013, 37).

This narrative of needing to turn unproductive Mapuche territory into productive Chilean land continued to drive policy. After Chilean forces militarily defeated the Mapuche in 1883, the government surveyed the land and allocated plots of land to Mapuche communities. Yet they only granted communities rights to the land they currently resided on, splitting the Mapuche community and territory into approximately three thousand reservations by 1927, 6.39 percent of the land originally claimed by the Mapuche (Bengoa 2000; Aylwin 2001; Boccara 2002; Pinto Rodríguez 2003; Correa, Molina, and Yáñez 2005). Marimán et al. (2006, 121) cite that only 5.5 percent of land in regions occupied by Mapuche communities before 1884 was Indigenous territory in 1930. The boundaries of these reservations, as drawn out in a *título de merced* (land title) issued between 1883 and 1929, form the basis for most present-day land demands and policy under analysis. During the nineteenth and twentieth centuries, Chile promoted *chilenidad*, calling for racial mixture and assimilation (Bengoa 2000; Pinto Rodríguez 2003), and Indigenous communities were viewed as "non-nationals" who did not fit into the homogenizing nation-building project. The state promoted colonization to the region, offering *colono* (settler) families sixty-two hectares of land, thirty additional hectares for each son over the age of ten, free passage to Chile, board, nails, two oxen, cow and calf, plow, cart, trunk-removing machine, monthly pension for a year, and medical care for two years (Richards 2013). Fraudulent purchases and "spontaneous colonization" by *colonos* informally encroached on Mapuche land through *corridas de cerco* (fence-running) and trades in bars, utilizing their connections in government to legitimize the transactions (Bengoa 2000; Pinto Rodríguez 2003; Richards 2013). Land that Mapuche communities historically occupied but lost rights to were auctioned off. In the 1940s, the southern regions of Chile where most Mapuche communities resided were known as "suicide belt" on the country, serving as the "barrier against greater progress in the regional economy" (Richards 2013, 57). As one elite argued, "How is it possible that it is permitted that the most fertile lands in these provinces, which are Chile's granary, remain in the hands of Indians and that they produce absolutely nothing?" (57).

Indigenous demands in Chile were largely subsumed into class-based demands during the political and economic swings from the 1950s to 1970s (Correa, Molina, and Yáñez 2005). Until the 1960s, rural politics were separated from the national political arena; power was internally organized through the *latifundia* (large landed estate) system, "Sealed off from the direct influence of the state and was considered outside the bounds of legitimate party competition" (Kaufman 1972, 26). This structure, however, was increasingly pressured by external forces as the emerging urban upper class acquired rural land, raising the number of absentee landowners (22–23). This system began to fall apart with an economic crisis in the 1960s, blamed in part on the inequitable distribution of land. The agricultural sector of the economy was considered to be, according to reports from the United Nations and the Chilean government, characterized by "extreme irrationality" due to inefficient land use and low output (22–23).

This concern became a key policy platform of Eduardo Frei Montalva, a Christian Democrat who served as president of Chile from 1964 to 1970. Land reform would allow new property holders to access land, expected to bring about the "transformation of male inquilino farmers into yeoman farmers who produced adequate surpluses for domestic markets" (Tinsman 2002, 85). Mapuche communities recovered over 152,000 hectares during agrarian reforms from 1962 to 1973, largely mobilized through alliances with Chilean political parties. It is important to note that while Mapuche communities accessed land through these policies, these acquisitions served broader efforts to promote socioeconomic development in the region by breaking up large plots, rather than to respond to Indigenous demands. Particularly revealing of these trends was Indigenous Law 17.729 (1972). While working to facilitate the consolidation and expansion of Mapuche–held communal lands, it also established the Directorate of Indian Affairs to pursue "the promotion of the social, economic, educational and cultural development of the communities, while seeking their gradual and harmonious integration into the national society, respecting their distinctive ethnic characteristics" (Del Anaquod and Taylor 1984).

The Pinochet regime dramatically transformed land policy in the region, but preserved the focus on economic production. While much of this transformation resulted from changes in land policy, there was also an immediate backlash against the prior agrarian reform in the region. As a 1978 report by the Working Group on Indigenous Populations of the United Nations documents: "On the day of the coup, the big landowners, the land barons, the military and the carabineros started a great manhunt against the Mapuches who had struggled and gained their land back . . . The counterrevolution of 1973 hit the Mapuche populations harder than most other sectors" (qtd. in Del Anaquod and Taylor 1984). Broadly, the Chilean government incentivized development in the region by supporting the growth of industries relying on natural resources. Previous administrations had also promoted pine plantations as a solution to ecological challenges in the region and means of expanding the territorial reach of the state (Klubock 2014), but the Pinochet regime sold off recently privatized land well below market value and deregulated the industry. Decree 701 (1974) actively encouraged the expansion of forestry companies in eighth through twelfth regions of Chile. Subsidies covered more than 75 percent of the costs of establishing plantations on unused land, and more than 90 percent of costs during the economic crisis in the

1980s. Because of economic restructuring, many landowners were willing to sell to logging companies that were tightly affiliated with national and international capital (Haughney 2006, 57); ties with international capital strengthened during the 1980s debt crisis as Chilean investors turned abroad. These favorable policies resulted in the rapid expansion of the industry. In 1965 an estimated 418,000 hectares of land (1.4 percent of sown land in Chile) was tree plantations; by 1997 the industry accounted for more than 1,098,500 hectares (4.1 percent of sown land), which replaced between 400,000 and 900,000 hectares of native forests between 1985 and 1994 (Haughney 2006). Most of this expansion was in pine and eucalyptus, which grew from 300,000 hectares in 1974 to 2,700,000 in 2013 (Andersson et al. 2016); Monterey pine alone accounts for an estimated 85 percent of all tree plantations in Chile (Klubock 2014, 2). Most of this production is for export; forestry companies grew from US\$42 million in the 1970s to US\$5.4 billion in 2008 (Reyes and Nelson 2014, 3), and timber is the second largest export after minerals.

Pinochet-era reforms also worked to undo protections of Indigenous communities' access to ancestral territory by privatizing collectively held land and encouraging the development of industries relying on natural resources (Aylwin 2001; Correa, Molina, and Yáñez 2005). Understanding private property to be the key to the productive use of land and the economic development of the country, the Pinochet government declared in Decree 2.568 (1979), "Indigenous lands and indigenous landowners do not exist, because there are only Chileans" in an effort to eliminate the need for communal property on the basis of ethnicity (Government of Chile 1979; Aylwin 2001; Correa, Molina, and Yáñez 2005). Decree 2.568 preserved recognitions of Indigenous peoples after significant opposition, but eliminated restrictions on the sale of Indigenous land in hopes of improving productivity, addressing Indigenous poverty, and opening up communal property to the land market.[4] A request from one occupant of a plot of land, who did not need to be the owner or Mapuche, was sufficient to divide a plot of Indigenous land into individual holdings. The title of the decree, "For the Indians, Indian lands, the Division of the Reserves and the Liquidation of the Indian Communities," is particularly revealing of ongoing framing of Mapuche communities as a hindrance to national development. As the special rapporteur to Chile reported in 1979, Decree 2.568 "is intended to promote the forced integration of indigenous communities in the socioeconomic structures established by the Government without any regard for the traditional forms of organization and work or the special cultural characteristics of such communities" (qtd. in American Anthropological Association 1980). As a result, around two thousand Mapuche communities were divided into plots of, on average, 6.4 hectares of land per family (Aylwin 2001; Marimán et al. 2006; Silva and Rodrigo 2010); Haughney (2006) estimates that by 1990, Mapuche communities held titles to 300,000 hectares of land, 40 percent less than established in *títulos de merced*.

Similar to previous governments, the Pinochet regime justified shifts in land policy as necessary to bring economic development to the region. For example, the Instituto de Desarrollo Agropecuario (Agricultural Development Institute, INDAP, part of the Ministry of Agriculture) noted that "zones of extreme cultural and economic stagnation, like the Ninth Region [Araucanía], 'justified an action prevailing from the State and the Private Sector in the search to alleviate their [rural inhabitants'] condition'" (Crago 2015, 46). In 1979 regional political authorities declared that the state "must manage to grant equal opportunity to all citizens in a way in which they can participate in the benefits generated by economic growth" (46). In addition, the Ministry of Agriculture declared, "Any land, of any size, and located in any part of the country is a factory. And, as such, must produce not only products but also profit. What the campesino is lacking, therefore, is his conversion into a businessman" (48). And in the development of mechanisms for Mapuche men to privately own land and produce for the market: "The Ministry of Agriculture relied on existing portrayals of irrational Mapuche agricultural practices, which had first gained prominence in the nineteenth century, to justify programs to eradicate Mapuche cultural traits that officials argued limited scientific and modern agricultural development. Furthermore, Plan Perquenco continued the goals of earlier agrarian reform efforts, which the military regime ridiculed as ineffective, to argue that the formation of male-headed nuclear families would solve rural economic and cultural stagnation" (vii-viii). As the Mapuche political scientist José Marimán (2012, 2) summarized, "Until recently, Chilean interest in the Mapuche focused exclusively on regulating contact; in other words, the most important question was always, 'What to do with the Mapuche?'"

Mapuche protest reemerged in 1978 in response to these reforms and the military regime, and, as a result, effectively positioned Indigenous demands on the agenda of the center-left opposition to the Pinochet dictatorship. These efforts culminated in the 1989 Acuerdo de Nueva Imperial (Nueva Imperial Agreement) between Mapuche leaders and future president Patricio Aylwin (Christian Democrat, PDC), who agreed to address territorial land disputes, the constitutional recognition of Indigenous peoples, and the adoption of ILO 169 if elected. Aylwin also agreed to create a state agency and special commissions to voice Indigenous demands within the government (Carruthers and Rodriguez

2009, 4). Many observers note that despite this agreement, the administration's commitment to Indigenous demands was, at best, tenuous, and the agreement was the result of several key connections between indigenous leadership and the Comision Chilena de Derechos Humanos de Temuco (Vergara, Foerster, and Gundermann 2004, 8).

Discussions over proposed constitutional reforms reveal ongoing resistance to recognition. Proposals in 1991, 1999, and 2000 called for state recognition of Indigenous communities as part of the Chilean nation. A 2006 proposal, originating from right-wing senators, states that the Chilean nation, one and indivisible, recognizes and values Indigenous communities. A 2007 proposal called for recognition of the Chilean nation as multicultural. Even with the limited scope of these reforms, none advanced out of Congress; most opposition to these proposed amendments centers around the term *pueblos*, which politicians fear would challenge the unity of the Chilean nation and legitimize a range of Indigenous demands (Sanhueza et al. 2013). Jose Aylwin, a prominent observer of Indigenous rights in Chile, concluded that these debates over the politics of recognition are indicative of "the incapacity of the Chilean society to accept the existence of sociopolitical groups that pre-date the Chilean state and are distinct from the rest of society" (Instituto de Estudios Indígenas 2003, 16).

As its regional counterparts implemented neoliberal multicultural reforms recognizing the rights of Indigenous communities within a neoliberal framework during the 1980s and 1990s, Chile has only recently, and with strong trepidation, recognized minimal international standards on Indigenous rights. Chile's recent patterns of governing difference are an anomaly in the region, as one of the first to adopt the broader set of neoliberal reforms, yet one of the last to adopt neoliberal multicultural reforms (Hale 2006; Postero 2007; Richards and Gardner 2013). As of writing in 2020, Chile is one of the few Latin American countries that has yet to constitutionally recognize Indigenous peoples and only became a signatory to ILO 169 in 2008.[5]

INDIGENOUS LAW 19.253

Given that Chile's current constitution dates to 1980, Chile's primary response to Mapuche territorial demands, and the response under analysis, is in Article 20B of Indigenous Law 19.253 (1993).[6] Due to the difficulty of amending the 1980 Constitution, the demands in the Acuerdo de Nueva Imperial agreement were enumerated in Indigenous Law 19.253. The bill was modified seven times between its introduction in 1991 and promulgation in 1993, severely weakening the law's recognition of Mapuche rights. Land and territory were principle topics of debate. Mobilization and the resulting law project sought to end the land divisions initiated by Pinochet and defend Indigenous lands, as documented by *títulos de merced*. As a result, land acquisitions for Indigenous communities would be based on well-documented, historic documents rather than historically occupied land or territory more broadly; while defensive, the strategy was the minimum by which negotiations could be advanced. In negotiations, the category of "Indigenous peoples" was changed to "ethnic group of Indigenous communities" (*pueblos indígenas* to *etnias de comunidades indígenas*) and "territories of Indigenous development" to "areas of Indigenous development" (*territorios de desarrollo indígena* to *áreas de desarrollo indígenas*) (Aylwin Oyarzún 2003); stronger recognition of Indigenous land would have given the community preferential rights to natural resources on the land (Aylwin Oyarzún 2000, 2003; Vergara, Foerster, and Gundermann 2004). Most of these modifications were made due to the fears of conservative sectors in Congress that recognizing the territorial rights of Indigenous communities would result in fragmentation (Aylwin Oyarzún 2000, 2003; Vergara, Foerster, and Gundermann 2004). The law project articulated Indigenous territorial rights recognitions, yet the changes to the law project undid these recognitions, highlighting how the Aylwin government and politicians in Congress understood these demands to be an agricultural or economic issue.

It is important to reiterate that Article 20B is a very narrow, insufficient response to the majority of the territorial demands of Mapuche communities. While this law represented a significant step forward for Indigenous rights in Chile, activists maintain that the law does not meet the terms of the Acuerdo de Nueva Imperial, and, specifically, the agreement that the incoming Aylwin administration would recognize territorial rights. While the law grants Indigenous peoples the right to pursue traditionally held land, this land can only be pursued if it was formally titled as Indigenous land in accordance with laws enacted from 1823 through 1979 and acknowledged in Indigenous Law 19.253. The map of Ercilla (image 1.1) shows these tensions; *títulos de merced* are labeled by number. Indigenous communities do not have the right to pursue land without proof the land was previously, formally defined as such. Many Mapuche organizations, communities, and individuals rejected the whole legislative project, seeking a broader definition of territorial rights premised on access to ancestral territory, resources, and spaces that were never recognized by the state, rather than state-documented Indigenous land (Núñez 2013, 45). These broader territorial claims were legally supported by treaties signed with the Spanish crown in the eighteenth century as well as by UN special rapporteur Miguel Alfonso Martínez's study (Martínez, Daes, and Hatano 1999), which concluded the colonizers "aimed at di-

Image 1.1. Map of *títulos de merced* and Mapuche communities in Ercilla. Photo by the author, taken at the Archivo General de Asuntos Indígenas in Temuco, Chile, in July 2013.

vesting those [Indigenous] nations of the very same sovereign attributes and rights, particularly their land rights." Many Mapuche organizations rejected Indigenous Law 19.253, for the fact that it *"recognized* the division of the land, accomplishing the main objective of DL 2.568 (1979) that Mapuche organizations have rejected for more than a decade, calling not only for its repeal, but demanding the annulment but also its negative effects" (qtd. in Pairicán and Álvarez 2011, 113, emphasis added).

Title 2 of Indigenous Law 19.253 specifies state policy on the recognition, protection, and development of Indigenous land. It recognizes that an Indigenous community can collectively hold the land title, but does not recognize that the relationship between an Indigenous person and their land is in any way distinct from that of a non-Indigenous person. Land considered to be Indigenous land is protected as imprescriptible and inembargable (unmortgagable), but is not inalienable or indivisible, except within individuals or communities of the same ethnicity (Article 13). Article 20B gives CONADI the authority to establish "mechanisms allowing to overcome land issues, specially, by reason of compliance with judicial or out of court resolutions or transactions concerning indigenous lands in which there are solutions on indigenous lands or these are assigned to indigenous people, coming from land grants, or acknowledged by commissioner's titles, or other assignments or transfers made by the

State in favor of indigenous people" (Government of Chile 1993b). Notably, there are two other paths established in Indigenous Law 19.253 through which communities can request land. Article 20A establishes a lottery through which individuals and communities can apply for a subsidy to purchase land; this path more directly responds to situations of poverty and conceptualizes land as a commodity, an economic resource to promote development. Article 21E allows for public lands to be passed to Indigenous communities, through an agreement with the Ministerio de Bienes Públicos.[7] Article 20B, however, is Chile's most direct response to territorial, historic demands, and is applicable to a much broader group of communities.

However, because the implementation and regulation over the fund were left largely undefined in the Indigenous law regulatory policy, the potential for Indigenous Law 19.253 to address territorial demands remained open. The only requirement, as suggested by the final wording of the law, was historical documentation of the Indigenous community's relationship with the plot of land. Because of this ambiguity, politicians and bureaucrats have worked to specify policy regulations to further narrow the scope of demands that can be processed through CONADI.

DECREE 395

Decree 395, passed in November 1993, established implementation procedures to regulate the Indigenous Land and Water Fund (FTAI). It defines the scope of the fund to be one of financing mechanisms for the solution of land problems (Article 1). Article 6 of Decree 395 regulates this objective, further emphasizing the importance of historic documentation of the community's connection to the land; the policy only extends to land claims supported by *títulos de merced* and other state-issued recognitions of Indigenous land. The national director of CONADI is to resolve each request based on the number of people, severity of the social situation, and the antiquity of the land conflict (Government of Chile 1993a). While in hindsight these regulations appear to be insufficiently broad, they suggest that the high demand and resulting controversy over implementation were unforeseen. One CONADI public official described to me that officials only expected forty cases to be resolved through Article 20B; as a result, the policy did not necessitate significant administrative oversight or more specific regulation (Interview, October 2012). Yet the requests of eighty-nine communities were processed in the first five years, involving 2,025 families and 22,747 hectares.

This gap between expected and actual demand grew over time, frequently appearing in conversations about policy implementation. The historian Florencia Mallon documents these debates through interviews and evaluations, which highlight the Chilean government's ongoing efforts to use these funds for socioeconomic development. As she describes: "So deep were the problems encountered by the land subsidy program [Article 20A] that in November 1997 CONADI's National Council concluded, as a part of their institutional plan for 1998, that investing money in the program to purchase lands in dispute [Article 20B] was a great deal more efficient than a similar investment in land subsidies . . . It recommended, therefore, an increase in the budget for the form and a decrease in budget for the latter" (Mallon 2005, 211). Interviews with officials further revealed that "the goal of the program is to recuperate between 180,000 and 200,000 hectares of Indigenous Lands that were lost during the military government's agrarian counterreform. In this sense, the goal would be the restitution to indigenous peoples of the lands lost during the dictatorship" (qtd. in Mallon 2005, 226).

1999 LAND POLICY

The first formal clarification of these implementation procedures came in 1999, when CONADI released "Land Policy," acknowledging that Article 20B had "low efficiency in its implementation due to errors and omissions" and sought to clarify implementation procedures "to prevent the price speculation and external interferences in the organization" (Ministerio de Planificación y Cooperación 1999). CONADI officials were aware that they were increasingly caught in the center of controversy emerging surrounding Indigenous-state relations. CONADI was simultaneously responsible for responding to Indigenous demands and, specifically, territorial demands, but insufficiently equipped with resources or institutional capacity. The 1999 document was the first effort to clarify processes to avoid controversy, justified by one administrator that "it is very unlikely that current land problems in southern Chile can be solved if it is not possible to work in an environment free of pressure and if there is not a program for land solutions within a span of a few years" (Interview, October 2013).

The tension between land and territory appeared to motivate much of the controversy the 1999 policy attempted to address. The policy cites confusion between the concept of *land* (an economic concept) and *territory* (a political concept), suggesting that "the populism of the period" wrongly disseminated the idea that the land eligible for restitution was defined by the collective memory of the community elders (Ministerio de Planificación y Cooperación 1999). Responding directly, the policy states that "it is not possible to reconstitute ancestral territory through land purchases at market prices because there is not sufficient public funding to buy them and because often the current owner does not want to sell them" (Ministerio de Planificación y Cooperación 1999). It concludes with an assertion that "the irresponsible dispersion of these ideas motivated significant pressure towards CONADI and a great frustration from communities and individuals who cannot have their expectations met" (Ministerio de Planificación y Cooperación 1999). A director of FTAI suggests similar tension, asserting that "many indigenous people or indigenous leaders who had constructed small corrupt practices with the land owners rejected the changes. They provoked conflict [to pressure a response from CONADI]" (Interview, September 2013).

To these ends, the reform established that social, productive, legal, and anthropological studies would be completed for each community's request, prompting the hiring of a number of new CONADI employees with these technical capacities. The policies developed in this document mark a significant shift in the goals Article 20B is working to serve. As one CONADI employee expressed to me, the document develops the "grounds for decision-making" by establishing specific procedures to clarify the quantity and cost of land (Interview, November 2012).

This 1999 document also includes the first written expression of CONADI's objective to use Article 20B to promote socioeconomic development. As the document justifies: "While it is possible that land problems will continue to be important for the rural indigenous population in the next decade, economic and social change will undoubtedly demand that indigenous communities broaden their economic base beyond agriculture. This has occurred with non-indigenous peoples in all countries. With this perspective, it is likely that education, development of indigenous human resources, and commodification of economic activities will be some of the strategic work for the next millennium" (Ministerio de Planificación y Cooperación 1999). To this end, CONADI prioritized communities with higher incidences of poverty and sought to return a quantity of land based on the productive capability of the plot of land. Certainly, socioeconomic concerns are prominent, important demands of the Mapuche community and worthy of being a focus of CONADI's work. Yet the emphasis attributed to this socioeconomic perspective marks an important policy development, representing an early shift away from a policy with the potential to respond to historic land conflicts and broader territorial demands.

This shift toward a socioeconomic development perspective was accompanied by active efforts to deemphasize any focus on territory. For example, the 1999 document confirms the policy applies to land, not territory, asserting that CONADI interprets the scope of the law to be finite. The study cites that the lack of initial studies objectively quantifying the number of expected claims resulted in a high, unbudgeted, and unexpected demand. It estimates that principal land conflicts will be resolved by 2010, as "the mechanism was designed from the perspective that there are solutions to land problems . . . that is, land problems are not eternal" (Ministerio de Planificación y Cooperación 1999). Indicative of criticisms, CONADI asserts it will not respond to illegitimate sources of pressure, such as land grabs, and will only pay up to 10 percent more than the estimated value of the land. Finally, and perhaps most importantly, a bureaucrat shared that CONADI also began to buy alternate land if the land the community lost was too expensive and/or if the landowner was not willing to negotiate with the government (Interview, November 2012). Each of these transitions limited CONADI's capacity to respond to historic territorial claims.

RESOLUTION 878

Resolution 878, "Manual for the Application of Procedures for Land Purchases through Article 20 Letter B of the Land and Water Fund of CONADI," was introduced in 2003 to further clarify the regulatory procedures governing the implementation of Article 20B. Focusing on establishing technical procedures, it represents a significant point of departure from previous procedures in that it establishes four stages of the land purchase process: (1) applicability, (2) feasibility, (3) viability, and (4) completion. More than any previous description of the decision-making process, Resolution 878 establishes specific procedures to be carried out by specific offices. For example, the process is initiated when a community's leadership submits a written request to their respective regional CONADI office; the office will "create a numbered folder to contain all the presented records duly foliated and ordered consecutively in agreement with the logical development of the process. The first document of the folder should be the community's request, foliated and stamped with the date received by the reception office" (Government of Chile 2003, 2). This level of specificity continues for each step of the process outlined in the document and, notably, is the first instance in the history of the policy in which this level of specificity is outlined for the implementation of Article 20B. CONADI would also conduct social, occupational, and judicial/administrative reports for each community. Notably, there is no discussion of which cases are to be prioritized over others in terms of CONADI's limited time and resources.

While not directly appearing in Resolution 878, interviews with current and former CONADI employees revealed that the clarification of these procedures also brought the size of the land transfer into question. While previous land transfers processed through Article 20B were determined by the quantity of land documented in the community's *título de merced*, Resolution 878 clarified that CONADI officials needed complete social, occupational, and judicial/administrative reports specific to each community; the social report would include levels of poverty in the community and the number of children and young adults that would soon be requesting land from their parents. With these studies, CONADI began to, ideally, allocate ten productive hectares of land per family. While Article 20B was regulated by Decree 395, the number of people and quantity of land did not affect the land transfer; only ancestral land lost before 1993, based on the *título de merced*, was bought.

CENTRO EULA SURVEY

While not a policy or regulatory document, one of the most significant documents affecting the implementation of Article 20B was a survey of Indigenous lands carried out by the Centro EULA, the Center for Environmental Sciences at the University of Concepción, in 2004. The final evaluation, "Model of Supply-Demand for Indigenous Waters, Land, and Irrigation," had the explicit objective of "improving efficiency and equality in the functioning of the Land and Water Fund" (Centro EULA 2004, 5). The study determines that Chile has an excess supply of land, based on calculations of the current and future land needs of the Indigenous population in Chile. It cites that Indigenous communities in Chile have historic claim to 1,239,289 hectares of land, 42.8 percent of which were already registered to Indigenous individuals or communities in CONADI's Registry of Indigenous Lands (121). The Mapuche community in the Araucanía region would require 510,664 hectares of workable land (131). In a revealing shift, the study proposes that if land was substituted for pensions to heads of households older than 60, the demand for land would fall to 193,844 hectares. The study estimates the supply of land in the region to be 1,503,857 hectares, leading to the conclusion that there is an excess of supply (135).

While the introduction and conclusion of the study recognize the importance of the relationship between Indigenous culture and territory (172), the report focuses on calculating land demands, as necessary to promote development in Indigenous communities. This perspective is evident in the inclusion of ways to lower land demand through more cost-effective policies, such as providing pensions rather than land to elderly community members. This shift also brings the price of land into question; if the relationship between the community and a particular section of territory was not prioritized, the government could purchase other land at standardized prices.

CONADI's interpretation of these results had a significant impact on the management of Article 20B and the Land and Water Fund. One official described the survey as creating evaluative goals and an end to the policy which made calculations based on the remaining land demand and price per hectare the government would pay (Interview, November 2012). After the government resolved a certain number of requests corresponding to a certain investment and quantity of hectares, the land demand would be met and the program would no longer be necessary. This perspective was prevalent in my interviews; CONADI gradually established guidelines for the prices it will pay for certain sections of land, not to exceed US$5 million per hectare. Usually, the government spends approximately US$3 million per hectare—this makes it nearly impossible, regardless of a community's historic claim to the land—to acquire land of higher quality or from large landowners or companies demanding a higher price.

RE-CONOCER

The incoming Bachelet administration took explicit steps to reach the policy goals established from the land survey. Her full Indigenous policy is outlined in the 2008 document "Re-Conocer: Social Pact for Multiculturalism," discussed in detail in chapter 2. While reformulating Indigenous land policy was not the primary focus of this policy document, it worked toward "improving and optimizing the public response to land demands" by specifying the order in which communities' claims should be processed. The cases of 115 communities were prioritized, on the basis that the case had already been documented, studied, and approved through the established requirements. An additional 308 communities were placed on a waiting list, comprised of communities that had submitted their documents, but CONADI had not yet evaluated if the case qualified.

UFRO EVALUATION

In 2010 CONADI commissioned the first external evaluation of the Land and Water Fund, conducted by the Universidad de la Frontera in Temuco, Chile. The study, "Social-Productive Evaluation Study of Lands Acquired by the Land and Water Fund of CONADI," is justified by the assertion that despite the policy being responsible for transferring more than one hundred thousand hectares of land over more than ten years at a high cost to the government, there had not been a thorough study of the benefits of the program (Instituto del Medio Ambiente 2011). Nearly 70 percent of the communities that benefitted from the program between 1994 and 2009 were interviewed about the social, cultural, productive, and economic effects of the program. One of the strongest findings of the report was that only 40 percent of the acquired land was occupied, and families moved to the acquired land, on average, 21.7 months after the transfer (Instituto del Medio Ambiente 2011). A CONADI official emphasized that this statistic highlighted the program requirements needed reconsidered due to a lack of substantial results. Throughout this conversation, *results* were defined as increases in economic production and improvements in standards of living. As he explained, land transfers could be replaced by much more cost-effective, targeted socioeconomic development programs (Interview, November 2012). By quantifying Indigenous demands, CONADI gradually transitioned away from processing requests based on the history of the community and the territory.

CONCLUSION

In contrast to regional trends, Chile presents an extreme version of the neoliberalization of Indigenous land policy where the lack of territorial rights recognitions at the national level undercut the potential for local government offices to reshape territoriality. In other Latin American countries, these degrees of rights recognitions and protections went through a process of neoliberalization as they were translated into policy, creating contradictions between the conceptualization and implementation of Indigenous territorial demands. In contrast, Chile's Indigenous land policy response more directly merged conceptualization with implementation, with a neoliberal logic motivating both.

Working within this context of weakly defined Indigenous rights recognitions and high demand, CONADI officials attempted to assert their decision-making capabilities by clarifying implementation procedures according to a neoliberal logic. One professional in the FTAI in the national CONADI office described, "Ministers have told us that no one cares about CONADI's policies. Other ministries do not respect CONADI. Processes of evaluation and changes only come from within CONADI" (Interview, November 2012). One CONADI employee spoke of the need to *resguardarnos* (to shield or protect ourselves) from this external pressure (Interview, November 2012). To do so, CONADI officials made the implementation process more detailed and technical; the policy documents analyzed in this chapter reveal when and how this context meant that an economic and technical, and more specifically neoliberal, logic crept into the documents governing Chile's policy response to Indigenous communities' territorial demands. Over time, this work converted a potential response to Mapuche demands for territory into a socioeconomic development policy, tasking Mapuche communities with making their demands legible to technical procedures structured to expand economic productivity.

CHAPTER 2

NEGOTIATING LAND FOR PEACE

When there was sufficient conflict and sufficient legal motivations, we designed and used a policy that allowed us lower the levels of conflict. Why? The Fund was conceived of as a valve to decompress conflict. If the valve functioned poorly, it generated pressure, pressure, pressure. We diffused, through purchases, the principle focal points of land conflict.

—Former CONADI official, referring to 1999 work (Interview, September 2013)

It is not surprising, as was documented in chapter 1, that a logic of neoliberal governance is infused into how CONADI officials and bureaucrats shape policy to process Mapuche territorial demands through land policy. Yet the implementation of these policies are far from the centralized, technocratic, neoliberal, efficient governance we expect in Chile. The narrative that policy implementation bends toward neoliberal governing priorities insufficiently explains variation in which communities successfully finish the policy process and acquire land through Article 20B of Indigenous Law 19.253. And, bureaucrats responsible for implementing Indigenous land policy are at the center of these inconsistencies, working to demobilize and disarticulate Indigenous demands by bending the same bureaucratic procedures that they helped establish. Over four distinct presidential administrations spanning twenty years, these motivations and resulting patterns of inconsistent policy implementation are remarkably stable. Politicians, administrators, and bureaucrats turn to similar rhetoric to justify using Article 20B to negotiate "land for peace" with mobilized Mapuche communities. Examples from my interviews with CONADI administrators highlight this continuity:

"We diffused, through purchases, the principal focal points of land conflict," CONADI official working in the Frei administration (1994–2000). (Interview, September 2013).

"The Government's indigenous policy is to reward the most radical groups," CONADI official working in the Lagos administration (2000–2006). (Interview, October 2013).

"The strategy was to calm the issue," CONADI official working in the Bachelet administration (2006–2010). (Interview, September 2013).

"[The Piñera administration] put out fires," CONADI official reflecting on the Piñera administration (2010–2014). (Interview, July 2013).

This chapter contextualizes each of these quotes, revealing the pressures, relationships, and negotiations between levels of government that explain when, how, why, and to what effect the government engages in these land-for-peace agreements. While this motivation to use land policy to demobilize Mapuche communities persists over the twenty years under analysis, the Chilean government's ability to do so becomes constrained over time. As politicians confront increasingly the institutionalized regulations and procedures documented in chapter 1, they take fewer, but more dramatic deviations to implement land-for-peace agreements. These stories of policy implementation dramatically contradict expectations of post–Pinochet Chilean governance.

This chapter is novel in its demonstration that the Chilean state pursues the demobilization and disarticulation of Mapuche demands through land policy. Scholars have extensively documented how the state works to demobilize and isolate Mapuche demands and mobilization through criminalization and militarization (Namuncura 1999; Pinto Rodríguez 2003; Mallon 2005; Marimán et al. 2006; Di Giminiani 2012; Llaitul and Arrate 2012; Marimán 2012; Crow 2013; Richards 2013; Tricot 2013; Klubock 2014; Pairican Padilla 2014). While this chapter draws on this secondary literature highlighting these trends in criminalization and militarization of Mapuche mobilization, the intention is not to definitively document or review these historical trends. Rather, this history of the criminalization and militarization of Mapuche mobilization is discussed as it influences and intersects with the Chilean government's land policy work. Interviews with administrators and bureaucrats highlight the ongoing motivation to pursue the demobilization and disarticulation of Mapuche demands through criminalization, militarization, *and* land-for-peace policy implementation. The patterns documented in this chapter highlight how the Chilean government responds when efforts to extend the scope of neoliberalism to Mapuche territorial demands conflicts with efforts to extend the strength of the existing articulation of neoliberalism, ultimately prioritizing the preservation of elite market interests.

BUREAUCRATS IN CHILEAN HISTORY

As in the previous chapter, which discussed patterns of neoliberal governance of land policy, the work and positioning of Chilean bureaucrats needs to be historically situated. As is well documented, one of the hallmarks of the Chilean model of governance is its removed, technocratic,[1] elitist style of governance, which has persisted through democratic and authoritarian regimes; this section briefly summarizes those trends. Through these moments of change and continuity is an underlying tension; bureaucrats both hinder and support elite governing interests.

The early history of the Chilean state is characterized by the persisting strength of a closed, strategic, and self-aware elite, referenced as *cupulismo* (politics taking place at the *cúpula*, or apex) (Carruthers and Rodriguez 2009). Elites were those who acquired large haciendas through land grants and encomiendas during colonization; until the middle of the twentieth century, these elites preserved strong connections with the state. With the growth of the urban middle class, traditional elites preserved their influence by allowing the promotion of industrial development in exchange for the preservation of landed estates. As Petras (1969, 84, 93) described of the success of these efforts in 1969: "The Chilean elite was singularly adept at shaping historical circumstances and institutions to further its own particular interests- chief of which are economic and social stability. . . . To a considerable degree, representative political institutions became agencies for the transaction of business by the elite; the political structure was forged into a mechanism for maintaining the elite's power and wealth." Carrière (1975, 19) summarized how this was accomplished:

> Ownership of land has always been the ultimate status symbol in Chile and the most prestigious families since colonial days have been associated with the large estates of the Central Valley. These 150 to 200 families were the unchallenged masters of Chile . . . Not only did they control their own personal fiefs in the Central Valley but they also supplied the leadership of the Conservative and Liberal parties, ran the banks and a good deal of real estate, and were strongly represented in almost all of the Cabinets until the Christian Democrats came to power in 1964. It is quite clear that this 'traditional oligarchy,' as it has been called, has been forced to share power with other groups . . . Instead of trying to eliminate them as an archaic social force, middle class leaders have tended to play by the rules drawn up by the oligarchy in the hope of gaining admission to the inner sanctum.

The result for Chilean politics was the "dominance of a single, unified, self-conscious elite" (Carrière 1975, 17).

Chilean bureaucracy developed in this context of elite control. Elites strategically deployed vertical links between national and local government and politicians (Garretón Merino 1989; Carruthers and Rodriguez 2009). Local politics were broker politics, dominated by national-level competition between political parties over centralized resources (Valenzuela 1977; Rehren 1996). As Valenzuela (1977, 80) documents, the "lack of resources in the society as a whole contributed to the trend of the more powerful political forces in the center taking over an increasingly large share of the nation's resources for central dispensation." Local leaders were responsible for implementing national projects, yet spent most of their time channeling local demands up through national networks to ensure the local electoral success of national political parties. Local state officials were "individual political entrepreneurs," utilizing petty cash, state jobs, and social benefits to satisfy the *vicio de los chilenos* (Chilean vices) (Valenzuela 1977, 73, 89; Gil 1966; Ferraro 2008). A 1969 study found that half of petitions to municipalities originated from the bureaucracy itself, and half sought particular, individual benefits (Rehren 1996). Groups that petitioned the government pursued specific benefits rather than broader change; as one local politician from the Socialist Party argued, "All [the people] think of is the political favor" (Valenzuela 1977, 78). Chilean bureaucracy developed within this context of a governing style dominated by centralized, elite interests.

This pattern of bureaucracy being subsumed within broader governing objectives largely continued during the dictatorship and the consolidation of the neoliberal development model. The Pinochet regime implemented a series of market-oriented economic restructuring policies that privatized and deregulated the market and the provision of social services through the 1970s and 1980s, drawing on the technical support of a group of technocrats trained by free market economists at the Chicago School of Economics. While traditional elites first opposed these reforms, they came to see the reforms as a tool to reestablish their historic control over the state (Madrid 2012). This was perceived to be threatened by the emerging middle class of the early twentieth century, who had come to see the state "as a formidable institution from which a series of radical changes could be introduced in Chilean society" (Silva 2008, 220). In response, the dictatorship incorporated technocrats into prominent positions, constructing an emerging technocratic elite that tightly aligned with the neoliberal project despite lacking the political background of the traditional elites (Silva 1991). As Silva (2008, 221) summarizes, "Although most of the Chicago Boys also had middle-class roots, the openly pro-business polices they deployed rapidly eliminated any trace of self-identification of this social sector with the state technocracy." The Pinochet regime reworked vertical brokerage networks into a form of bureaucratic brokerage. Local government managed the distribution of resources and services after decentralizing reforms tasked municipalities with the intermediating local interests, as was previously done by political parties. Local politicians no longer needed to extract resources from the center but rather acted as "bureaucratic activists within the administrative apparatus of the state" (Rehren 1991, 245). This shift distanced citizens from national policy debates, in a shift referred to as the *alcaldización de la política* (mayor-ization of politics) (Valdivia, Álvarez, and Donoso 2012). Effectively, neoliberalism provided an organizing mechanism through which traditional elites could preserve their power, through the work of bureaucrats.

The Concertación did not challenge this model in their pragmatic approach to the transition. Not only was the incoming Aylwin administration severely constrained by the 1980 Constitution left by the authoritarian government, which preserved the influence of the armed forces and limited space for democratization at the regional and local levels, but political elites from the Left and Right converged to protect the uncertain transition by preserving and consolidating the neoliberal model. The Concertación struck a number of deals after the transition with right-wing veto players, agreeing to consider the economic and political interests of the right and to govern a *democracia de los acuerdos* (democracy by agreement) rather than by popular consensus or through congress (Silva 1991; Siavelis 2009). Alejandro Foxley, minister of finance from 1990 to 1994, described of this strategy: "The *main thing* we had to do was to make sure that there was an equilibrium between change and continuity. Mature countries are countries that don't always start from scratch. We had to recognize that in the previous government the foundations had been established for a more modern market economy and we would start from there, restoring a balance between economic development and social development" (qtd. in Fernandez and Vera 2012, 8). Elevating the status of bureaucrats and tasking them with implementing national policy objectives served this governing priority. As the Concertación sought to centralize power in Santiago, local elections were restored but with limited consequence (Eaton 2004). The combination of centralization and privatization left local politicians with fewer resources to distribute; between 1987 and 2007, local government expenditures account for, on average, 12.5 percent of total governmental expenditures (Horst 2009, 215). These patterns left local organizations in primarily advisory roles, with little incentive to encourage participation (Posner 2004).

Technocratic rule, then, remained on the policy agenda, offering stability to the negotiated and uncertain return to democracy in 1990.

Gradually, technocrats' roles were strengthened and further distanced from the public. After first-generation neoliberal reforms shrunk the size of the state with privatization and deregulation, "second-stage reforms" worked to strengthen state capacity through administrative reform (Ross-Schneider and Heredia 2003, 5; Domínguez 2010). Administrative modernization projects worked to promote oversight, evaluation, and bureaucratic professionalization in hopes of further distancing bureaucrats from politics (Ross-Schneider and Heredia 2003; Rehren 2008). The creation of the general secretariat of the presidency further distanced policymakers from popular demands (Weyland 1999). Garretón (2003) went as far as arguing that the modernization of the state during the Frei administration was more consequential than democratization.

Despite these shifts toward centralized, technical governance, there are indications that brokerage politics, albeit reconfigured, persisted. After privatization, the state no longer exercised control over contracting and financing investments, opening space for business interests to develop tight relationships with politicians, particularly at the local level. Rehren (1996, 327) observed the "penetration of the locality by the market and the introduction of private enterprises as a new component of local political machines and clientelistic networks." Johnston (1997) reached similar conclusions that privatization reconfigured Chilean politics, merging previous forms of "clientelism and patronage" politics with more recent forms of "interest group bidding" politics in the form of market corruption. Silva (2004, 73) concludes that Chileans take a "*cosista* approach in defining which candidate can deliver the goods." As might be expected, these trends also increased allegations of corruption at these local levels. Rehren found that 66 percent of corruption allegations were directed at mayors and 24 percent at municipal councilors, offering, "It is plausible that the accusations of corruption are nothing less than a manifestation of well-entrenched clientelistic networks operating within the local political process" (Rehren 1996, 327). As early as 1996, the limited power of local leaders and government prompted observers to conclude that many "local political practices have been partially restored," returning to be an arena for competition between centralized political parties (324).

What is the significance of these trends for Indigenous land policy governance? Throughout most of Chilean history, the role of bureaucrats fluctuates in response to elite interests. Most of the time, policies further elite interests, meaning that bureaucrats' work seamlessly extends both elite interests and institutionalized priorities. Yet tensions become overly evident when examining CONADI bureaucrats and their work processing Mapuche territorial demands vis-à-vis elite interests. The institutionalization of neoliberal interests in the policy regulations of Article 20B of Indigenous Law 19.253 occasionally come into conflict with elite interests to make Mapuche demands legible to the neoliberal state and to demobilize more radical Mapuche demands. As is documented below, while the Chilean government's motivation to use Indigenous land policy to demobilize perceived threats to elite interests posed by Mapuche mobilization persists over the twenty years under analysis, its ability to do so becomes constrained over time as politicians and bureaucrats confront increasingly institutionalized procedures.

1990–1994: PATRICIO AYLWIN

Article 20B of Indigenous Law 19.253 was not implemented during the Aylwin administration (Partido Demócrata Cristiano), yet the drafting and formulating of Article 20B and its broader bureaucratic structure established key precedence for the governance of Indigenous-state relations and policy. Problematically, this precedent came in the form of institutional ambiguity and contradictions that would characterize the future implementation of Article 20B. Was CONADI a way for Indigenous communities to present their demands to or within the state? Or for the Chilean government to implement its policy to Indigenous communities? And how would these contradicting understandings of CONADI's work be resolved?

The participatory process of drafting the law project created hope for future Indigenous-state relations. Once elected, President Aylwin created the Special Commission for Indigenous Peoples (Comisión Especial de los Pueblos Indígenas, CEPI) to develop a law project as agreed with Mapuche leadership in the 1989 Acuerdo de Nueva Imperial. The commission was comprised of ten Indigenous representatives, ten government representatives, and a three-person directorate. Approximately 100,000 Indigenous peoples indirectly participated in the project led by CEPI; 2,800 community assemblies elected 3,000 representatives to attend one of fifteen provincial congresses held throughout 1990. Each of the provincial congresses elected ten delegates to attend the culminating National Congress of Indigenous Peoples in 1990. While these processes were more participatory than future efforts, tensions over working to address Mapuche demands through the state were evident. Some prominent Mapuche leaders refused to participate in the Acuerdo de Nueva Imperial and resulting CEPI project, noting their perceptions that the state was maliciously requiring that "Indigenous peoples, specifically the Mapuche people, had to commit to channel their demands through institutional paths, forgoing using land recoveries as an instrument of political pressure" (Pairican Padilla 2014, 64).

Despite aspirations about the potentially participatory nature of Indigenous-state relations, engaging with the state ultimately limited the recognition of Mapuche territorial rights. The resulting CEPI law project focused on specific, discrete land demands based on well-documented, historic documents, rather than a much broader understanding of Mapuche territory. Participants considered this defensive strategy to be necessary, calculating that the political climate during the return to democracy would not allow broader conceptualizations of territorial rights. As one member of the CEPI project described to me of the strategy to focus on recovering rather than expanding Indigenous lands, "At the time, no one expected to recover lands. That would be absurd" (Interview, October 2012). As many expected, and/or feared, CEPI's law project was modified seven times between being introduced in December 1990 and passed in 1993, largely due to the influence of the Right in Congress. Chapter 1 further describes how these debates structured formal policy formulations.

The resulting promulgation of Indigenous Law 19.253 created CONADI, representing the first time in Chilean history that one office was tasked with responding to Indigenous demands through coordinated policy programs. Yet the law did not clearly specify the relationship between demands and policy response. CONADI was formally tasked with "promoting, coordinating, and executing, as the case may be, State actions in favor of integral development of indigenous persons and communities, specially, in relation to economic, social, and cultural aspects, and to encourage their involvement in national life," suggesting that CONADI represented the state to Indigenous communities (Title VI, Article 38, Indigenous Law 19.253, Government of Chile 1993b). Yet CONADI also created structures to represent Indigenous demands to the state. Another key first in Chilean history was Indigenous peoples electing elect representatives to a state institution (Carruthers and Rodriguez 2009, 746). CONADI's national advisory board fully encapsulates CONADI's internal contradiction, which is to be comprised of eight elected Indigenous representatives, eight government-appointed representatives, and an appointed national director to serve as a tie-breaker. As is evident throughout CONADI's history, the national director is positioned to resolve conflicts between Indigenous demands and state policy; yet the central government holds, and frequently uses, the ability to replace the national director.

This fundamental tension left communities and activists with the challenge of deciding on what terms to engage with or distance from the work of CONADI. Some activists saw CONADI as an effort by the Chilean government to make Mapuche demands legible to the state, inevitably undermining the demands themselves. Indigenous councilor José Santos Millao articulated this opposition, arguing, "I will be 100 per cent behind our communities, and I will not give in so easily when the intention [of political participation] is for us to make concessions to the government" (qtd. in Rodriguez and Carruthers 2008, 6). Yet many Indigenous communities, activists, and organizations saw this participation and representation within the state as a significant victory, understanding CONADI to be a representation of Indigenous interests to the state. For example, Mauricio Huenchulaf, the first national director of CONADI, situated that "CONADI must support an initial process of development, but in the future indigenous groups must decide themselves on their own development. CONADI will also embrace the missions of dignifying the original peoples, stimulating their participation, and contributing to tolerance and respect for ethnic differences" (6). Rodriguez and Carruthers summarized, "Indeed, leaders and citizens alike adopted a proprietary sense, thinking of CONADI as an institution of their own" (6).

This optimism was short-lived as the central government quickly worked to exert control over the new office. Mapuche activists wanted CONADI to be based in Temuco, while national politicians called for Santiago, preventing CONADI from working on its inauguration date (Rodriguez and Carruthers 2008). Today, CONADI is the only agency of the Chilean government whose national office is not in Santiago; the national office of CONADI is in Temuco, with subnational offices in each region. CONADI was created as part of the powerful Ministry of Planning and Cooperation (Ministerio de Planificación, MIDEPLAN), "Raising additional concerns about its independence and capacity for implementation, particularly for policies that would require cooperation with other ministries" (Rodriguez and Carruthers 2008, 7). The initial functioning of CONADI was also constrained by its limited budget and technical capabilities. In 1994 the director estimated that CONADI would need 14 billion pesos, but was only allocated 3.5 billion, most of which was dedicated to administration, infrastructure, services, technical support, soil productivity, and education (7).

In addition to establishing these institutional frameworks, the Aylwin administration also set a strong precedent for how future administrations would respond to Mapuche mobilization. The Mapuche organization Consejo de Todas las Tierras (CTT) most prominently organized and participated in a number of highly publicized takeovers of ancestral territory during the 1990s, frustrated with the Aylwin government's limited response to Mapuche territorial demands and CONADI's limited scope. As early as 1991, CTT carried out land takeovers in efforts to publicize demands for territory, self-determination, and autonomy (Correa and Mella Seguel 2010, 136). In 1991 CTT organized a thirteen-day series of land takeovers, culminating with leaders traveling to Santiago to inform President Aylwin that the takeovers "were a means of recovering the territory that 'historically belongs to us'" (Pairican Padilla 2014, 77). Future administrations frequently copied the Aylwin administration's strategy of responding with criminalization and militarization of Mapuche mobilization. Under the Pinochet regime's antiterrorism law, 144 protestors were charged and imprisoned for their participation in land takeovers and "conspiracy" (Haughney 2006, 72; Rodriguez and Carruthers 2008). The leader of CTT, Aucan Huilcaman, was jailed for presenting a "threat to society" (Pairican Padilla 2014, 77). The Chilean government openly discredited the legitimacy of the demands, particularly at the regional level. For example, the *intendente* Fernando Chuecas objected that the Mapuche people could not be considered "peoples," as they were not "native" to Chile, and were "ethnic minorities" organized into family groups (Haughney 2006, 72). Minister of the Interior Enrique Krauss concluded that the "Mapuche activists were nothing more than a group of common delinquents" (qtd. in Pairican Padilla 2014, 77). These land takeovers did not result in land acquisitions (80).

The Aylwin administration set a clear precedent for how the Chilean state would respond to the Mapuche community's territorial demands. Pursuing the dismantling of Mapuche mobilization, the government established ambiguous institutional structures and procedures to, in constrained ways, hear and respond to the demands of Indigenous communities in Chile, while simultaneously responding to Mapuche mobilization for territory with criminalization and militarization. Future administrations would navigate how to accomplish this work through the implementation of Article 20B.

1994–2000: EDUARDO FREI RUIZ-TAGLE

The year 1997 represents a point of departure in Mapuche-state relations, referenced by many Indigenous activists and communities as the point when the central government made clear it would not allow institutional paths to sufficiently respond to Mapuche demands. Rather, from 1997 onward, the national government worked to use CONADI to implement its own policy priorities (Namuncura 1999; Carruthers and Rodriguez 2009; Pairicán and Álvarez 2011; Tricot 2013).

The construction of the Ralco hydroelectric dam in 1997 fully revealed the extent to which the central government would intervene in

CONADI. Construction required CONADI approval, as it would require evicting Pehuenche (Indigenous community in the Andes) communities from recognized ancestral land. To obtain CONADI approval, the Frei administration, of the Partido Demócrata Cristiano, removed two national directors of CONADI who would not cast the deciding vote to approve construction. As Mauricio Huenchulaf Cayuqueo, the first director of CONADI, summarized of the circumstances surrounding his resignation in 1997: "I became an obstacle to the implementation of a political-economic path that does not take into consideration the damage it can signify to the indigenous population . . . Those in government who believe that this institution is simply another instrument for the state to accommodate a diversity of interests are wrong . . . [the president's intervention] will only provoke an end to the pact between the state and indigenous peoples" (qtd. in Rodriguez and Carruthers 2008, 8). As Huenchulaf came to understand, the position of national director, and CONADI more generally, should not be understood as a representation of Indigenous interests to the central government. Rather, the central government was increasingly exposing its willingness to intervene in CONADI to pursue, as Huenchulaf understood, "The implementation of a political-economic path" (8).

In 1998 two government appointees in CONADI switched their votes, aligning with the elected Indigenous representatives in opposition to the construction of the dam. President Frei immediately replaced them with two representatives who swore to support the construction of the Ralco dam (Rodriguez and Carruthers 2008). With the vote once again split between elected Indigenous representatives and political appointees, the deciding vote fell to the new national director, Domingo Namuncura, a Mapuche politician from Santiago known for his involvement in human rights campaigns during the end of the dictatorship. Frei asked for Namuncura's resignation when learning he would not support the construction, replacing him with Rodrigo Gonzalez, the first non-Mapuche national director of CONADI. Namuncura reflected on the irony of being the only director of CONADI whose appointment and resignation was protested by the same group of people for, first, not representing Mapuche demands, and, at the end, for representing Mapuche demands.

These interventions by the executive branch had a significant impact on Indigenous-state relations; one observer summarized that "Ralco generated bitter disillusionment. Revealing vestiges of an enduring, autocratic style of politics, the executive had 'usurped' and 'de-indianized' 'our CONADI,' and reconfigured it as a development agency rather than an entity for indigenous voice" (Rodriguez and Carruthers 2008, 9). Another summarized that it had become clear that CONADI "is the most perverse result of the Mapuche struggle" (Rice 2012, 111). Marimán argues that these actions displayed, "For the first time since the end of dictatorship, Mapuche desperation erupted in violence; for the second time in one year, the Concertación government . . . took the side of Chilean business interests. . . . That year triggered a spiral of violence and protests against the state, logging companies and the economic model" (qtd. in Mella Seguel 2007, 87).

As the Ralco controversy made clear that CONADI would not meaningfully represent or resolve Mapuche demands, communities increasingly looked to extra-institutional strategies and direct action to advance their demands. One activist summarizes that "from that point forward, the idea of 'conflict' spread; people from indigenous communities were no longer considered ignorant and backward people, but rather active" (Llaitul and Arrate 2012, 130). The most visible expression of this turn occurred in October 1997, when the Mapuche communities Pichiloncoyan and PilinMapu in Lumaco occupied ancestrally claimed land held by the Bosques Arauco Forestry Company (Marimán et al. 2006, 244). Both communities had submitted paperwork to CONADI, but the lack of government response pushed communities to look for solutions outside of institutional procedures. These initial strategies spread; by September 1998, 473 Indigenous families and several forestry companies disputed 15,000 hectares (Rodriguez and Carruthers 2008, 10).

In the late 1990s, this shift in strategies is more broadly associated with two organizations: the established Consejo de Todas las Tierras and the emerging Coordinadora Arauco Malleco. CTT, arguably the most prominent organization during the 1990s, organized and participated in several highly publicized takeovers of ancestral land. These takeovers were targeted and extremely instrumental; CTT knew which communities qualified for Article 20B, helped prepare their paperwork, coordinated mobilization, and informed CONADI of the mobilization. Yet the year 1997 shifted the strategy of political engagement, legitimizing more direct, radical actions among many Mapuche communities and individuals. As the historian Fernando Pairican (2014, 126) summarized, "This megaproject [Ralco] represented a major political defeat for the Mapuche people, which in turn supported the most radical arguments of a section of the movement. The autonomist, utopian portion was strengthened, discursively replacing the 'institutional political strategy' in the government." Most importantly, this mobilization did not pursue a resolution in the form of a land purchase on behalf of the community through Article 20B.

This shift in the patterns of Mapuche mobilization was troublesome to the central government, prompting a multifaceted response. More violent instances of mobilization, including land takeovers and road blocks, were largely met with repression, with the primary objective to contain Mapuche protest (Mella Seguel 2007, 173). As one author describes of the government's militarization strategy: "The presence of additional squadrons of police in zones of conflict, police escorts of caravans of logging trucks, police roadblocks to check identity papers, and searches of public transport led both indigenous community members and visitors to complain of a de facto state of siege. . . . To end land occupations or to conduct searches in Mapuche communities, the police resorted to intimidating and violent search-and seizure operations, using helicopters, busloads of police, *guanacos* (armored vehicles), and tear gas" (Haughney 2006, 199). Crucially, these police strategies meant that the police directly confronted Mapuche community members (Mella Seguel 2007, 173). Activists strongly criticized the Chilean government's security-focused response to Mapuche mobilization, accusing the government of militarizing the region. Some activists went into hiding to avoid repression and criminal charges. Militarization was accompanied by the criminalization of Mapuche protest. In 1999 the *intendente* of the Araucanía region, Oscar Eltit, presented a request for the Ley de Seguridad Interior del Estado to be applied to the Mapuche communities provoking territorial conflicts with forestry companies (Mella Seguel 2007, 89; Pairican Padilla 2014, 93). The shift was supported by private corporate interests; in 1997 Corporación Chilena de la Madera (Chilean Wood Corporation, CORMA), one of the most powerful organizations in the region, argued that the actions of Mapuche activists were "clearly criminal, with characteristics of terrorism," which "could have disastrous consequences for the national development and foreign investment" (qtd. in Pairican Padilla 2014, 106).

During the Frei administration, CONADI started using policy, in conjunction with militarization and criminalization, to purse the demobilization of Mapuche communities. Specifically, the central government worked to channel Mapuche territorial demands and associated mobilization through institutional channels, rhetorically emphasizing that CONADI had the capacity to respond to land demands. For example, "MIDEPLAN Minister Germán Quintana made regular press announcements to address the crisis, calling for a national consensus on indigenous issues, and assuring the public that CONADI would have sufficient money to satisfy Mapuche land demands" (Rodriguez and Carruthers 2008, 11). As Pairican Padilla (2014, 155) describes, the final years of the Frei administration were characterized by work to "reposition CONADI as a legal instrument of indigenous communities after its loss of legitimacy after Ralco." Importantly, however, the central government formally and informally tasked CONADI with making land purchases through Article 20B, but preferred other solutions to Mapuche land demands, previewing the ways in which the Chilean government undercut CONADI's capacity to respond to territorial demands.

Facing this convergence of responsibilities and limited resources, CONADI responded to the communities participating in direct action, negotiating with activists and leaders to funnel their demands through institutional procedures. These negotiations incentivized mobilized Mapuche communities and organizations to work through established, institutionalized CONADI procedures, and were conditioned on the community or organization's willingness to stop using extrainstitutional strategies. An administrator of FTAI (the fund within CONADI tasked with implementing the land policy) during this period, describes that:

> During the Frei government [1994–2000], the central government intervened in CONADI. It was very worried about the emergence of the indigenous movement. . . . The Minister of the Interior called us every Monday morning for news of Aucan's [Huilcaman, leader of CTT] land takeovers with the people of Malleco. On the other side, on the set list of communities [those formally approved by the policy], nothing happened. . . . We negotiated a lot with communities that were associated with the *Consejo Todas las Tierras* and bought 7 pieces of land. Generally, we used that strategy; when there was sufficient conflict and sufficient legal motivations, we designed, we used a policy that allowed us lower the levels of conflict. Why? The Fund was conceived of as a valve to decompress conflict. If the valve functioned poorly, it generated pressure, pressure, pressure. This indicates that we diffused, through purchases, the principle focal points of land conflict. (Interview, September 2013)

A different administrator repeated: "With communities that opted for direct action, we had a working relationship with them to incentivize their application to the institutional route. . . . The CTT wanted to pressure, to bend back the hand of CONADI and the ministry. We went to the community itself [rather than the organization] and ask if they wanted to submit papers. Usually, they applied. They used nonviolent actions to generate publicity. We could call the leaders. Everyone ended up negotiating with the government" (Interview, October 2013). CONADI bureaucrats understood these land takeovers as communities' instrumental effort to acquire land. One administrator described that many of these protests were "land grabs via fax . . . CTT sent a fax to the media and said 'We have taken over this land!' Sometimes I took CON-

ADI's truck to the plot and no one was there. They had just been there in the morning with a reporter" (Interview, October 2013). Yet CONADI responded by funneling particular demands into policy in attempts to legitimize the office.

These negotiations resulted in public agreements that delicately and often only momentarily negotiated land for peace. In 1999 CONADI transferred fifty-nine hectares to the communities of Juan Loncoyán and Traiguén after Mapuche organizations threatened further land invasions on Forestal Mininco's land (Carruthers and Rodriguez 2009). These negotiations were strongly criticized for prioritizing private interests by working to deescalate mobilization that threatened security and productivity in the region (Rodriguez and Carruthers 2008), when the Chilean government was not willing to concede to broader Mapuche demands for autonomy and self-determination (Pairican Padilla 2014, 164). One activist strongly challenged these early land for peace negotiations, accusing the government of negotiating with the wrong people: "What dialogue are we talking about? With whom does the government suppose it is dealing, if the principal grassroots leaders, who have initiated the mobilization, are in jail?" (Haughney 2006, 205–6).

These early agreements were challenged and critiqued from all directions. CTT mobilized two months later after the government did not follow through on the agreements (Pairican Padilla 2014, 164). Allegations of bureaucratic mismanagement first emerged in 1998 (Rodriguez and Carruthers 2008), prompting conversations about CONADI's purpose. As these tensions expressed themselves, Representative Eugenio Tuma said in July 1999, "CONADI should become an exclusively statist technical organization that could function in unison with another indigenous entity that would resemble an indigenous parliament. That is the only form of legitimate representation of the demands of these peoples, since its hybrid character today enables the opinions of the government always to take precedence over those of indigenous community representatives" (qtd. in Rodriguez and Carruthers 2008, 14).

The Frei administration proposed several broader policy reforms toward the end of his administration, which also worked to isolate radical Mapuche mobilization and redirect Mapuche demands toward institutional responses. The "Pact for Citizen Respect" proposed a series of programs that would distribute resources to Mapuche communities over three years. As Pairican Padilla (2014, 173) describes, the pact "called for discarding violence as an instrument to resolve demands and for creating a 'fraternal space that we call Chile.'" Like the implementation of Article 20B, the Chilean government used policy to shift the dynamics of contention and demobilize Mapuche mobilization. Discursively, Frei framed Mapuche demands and the government's response as a "violation of public order and social peace by small, violent groups that did not represent the majority of the rural Mapuche communities, rather than as a grassroots mobilization by a variety of organizations expressing a widely held sentiment of having suffered wrongs" (Haughney 2006, 208). The Frei administration also proposed constitutional reform to recognize Indigenous communities, calling for recognition of ethnic diversity within a singular Chilean nation rather than the stronger recognition of Chile as a multinational society (208), and prioritized economic development projects. Through their control of the budget, MIDEPLAN prioritized these economic development projects over more short-term and controversial policies, most prominently land acquisitions. As the minister of the interior at the time concluded, the Frei administration worked to "deactivate future conflicts and avoid the political exploitation of the Mapuche's own demands" (qtd. in Pairican Padilla 2014, 155). Indigenous leaders concluded that these government efforts were "nothing more than a distortion of the underlying themes" and a "show put on by the government" (173).

The Frei administration clearly established the range of ways in which the Chilean government would respond to both Indigenous mobilization and Indigenous territorial demands. Working to disarticulate Mapuche mobilization, the government repressed such mobilization by framing their demands as militant or criminal actions, simultaneously restructuring Mapuche territorial demands to work through public policy and, specifically, through Article 20B. Politicians and bureaucrats hoped that negotiating land for peace, processed through the institutional procedures of Article 20B, would rebuild CONADI after the Ralco controversy.

2000–2006: RICARDO LAGOS

In contrast to the Frei administration's strategy of publicly merging policy responses with repression and negotiations, the Lagos administration, of the Left/center Left Partido Socialista, continued but hid land for peace negotiations. While the Chilean government continued to negotiate land for peace, it could not ensure that the Mapuche communities who engaged in these negotiations would disavow contentious action. A number of public cases highlighted the irony and contradictions of this state logic; many Mapuche communities continued to mobilize after a land-for-peace agreement was reached, prompting the Lagos administration to work to obscure if, when, and how the land policy responded to ongoing mobilization. The result was ongoing tension between the spoken and unspoken policy agendas, resolved through the work of bureaucrats.

The 1999 presidential campaign previewed these tensions in the Lagos administration's Indigenous politics agenda. Ricardo Lagos's election was uncertain, as the center-Left coalition of parties faced internal divisions, a strengthened political opposition, an economic crisis, and concerns about a Socialist president (Salvador Allende was the last Socialist president, in office 1970–73). To appease concerns, Lagos presented himself as a "new Socialist," who would pursue "growth with equity," similar to other moderate Socialists calling for a "Third Way," which simultaneously embraced neoliberal and redistributive economic policy. Lagos's Indigenous policy platform represented a similar tense balance of policies. While campaigning in the south, Lagos tried to appease security fears about Mapuche mobilization in the region by promising to "respect the rule of law against any threat to property, like the land takeovers carried out by violent groups" (Pairican Padilla 2014, 185). He also called for eliminating restrictions on the sale of Indigenous properties to open a significant amount of land to the market, raising the number of Indigenous representatives in CONADI, constitutionally recognizing Indigenous peoples, and transferring 150,000 hectares of land to Indigenous communities. For Lagos, economic demands were at the root of Indigenous demands and mobilization, which could be addressed through incentives and effective "development with identity" policies (Richards 2010). During Lagos's 1999 presidential campaign, the Concertación presented a "gesture of openness to the demands of rural Mapuche communities while they repressed organizations that challenged capital interests and raised territorial political demands . . . The Concertación government continued to conceive of the solution to the conflict in terms functional to the major economic interests" (Haughney 2006, 205, 210).

These tensions continued after Lagos's election. A cornerstone of his administration's Indigenous policy agenda was the Comisión de Verdad Histórica y Nuevo Trato (Commission of Historical Truth and New Deal). Led by former president Patricio Aylwin, the appointed commission was tasked with reviewing Chile's treatment of Indigenous peoples and offering "a new relationship between Indigenous Peoples, Chilean society, and the State" (Aylwin Oyarzún 2003, 442). The final 2003 report, as José Aylwin (2003, 440) summarizes, recognizes that "both processes-the denial of the existence and identity of indigenous peoples in favor of the formation of a single national identity, and of appropriation of their territory for the consolidation of national territory-although successful in their objective of serving to form the Chilean nation state, had consequences, in some cases disastrous, for indigenous peoples."

The Comisión de Verdad Histórica y Nuevo Trato called for the Chilean government to constitutionally recognize Indigenous peoples and establish procedures for self-determination. Without underscoring the importance of rhetorical recognition, the Comisión de Verdad Histórica y Nuevo Trato had limited impact. As the Mapuche activist Jose Llancapan expressed after the report was published, "I'm worried it will have no practical implication. The last word is with the Executive" (qtd. in Ray 2007, 141). Indeed, Lagos did not take the Comisión de Verdad Histórica y Nuevo Trato's recommendation to address rights to self-determination, constitutional recognition, territorial rights, or increase Indigenous representation. In an interview, Alejandra Krauss, minister of MIDEPLAN under Lagos, asserted that the Comisión de Verdad Histórica y Nuevo Trato was "the effort by the government to define a project that incorporates the demands of indigenous groups about recognition, as a kind of 'halfway' between national integration and recognition of autonomy and territorial independence" (qtd. in Rodriguez and Carruthers 2008, 14). Reynaldo Mariqueo, a Mapuche activist based in England, went as far as renaming the effort the "commission of historical truth and a new mistreatment (*Comisión de Verdad Histórica y Nuevo Maltrato*)" (qtd. in Ray 2007, 141).

The other cornerstone of Lagos's broad Indigenous policy platform was Programa Orígenes, announced in 2001. The development project promoted community development and entrepreneurship through health, education, community, and development programs, funded in part by a US$140 million loan from the Inter-American Development Bank. Its slogan, *Mira el future desde tu origen* (look towards the future from your origins), reinforced that development would resolve Mapuche demands (Richards 2010). Notably, the program did not allocate money toward land purchases, arguably the most proximate state response to Mapuche territorial demands. The program was critiqued for being created without Indigenous participation, "reproducing classic verticalism" (Rodriguez and Carruthers 2008, 12). The program was further criticized for how it incorporated a number of Indigenous leaders into the program's management; as one author summarized, "This does not contribute to the strengthening of the indigenous organization concerned and, less still, to the strengthening of the movement. On the contrary, it creates mechanisms of division within the communities and conflict within the indigenous organizations, particularly if we consider the large remunerations available" (Ray 2007, 140).

Similar to previous administrations, the Lagos administration also utilized antiterrorism and internal security laws. While the Frei administration charged Mapuche activists under the Ley de Seguridad Interior del Estado, the Lagos administration began applying the Ley Antiterrorista. During Lagos's administration, hundreds of Mapuche activists were charged under this law, prompting many to conclude that militarization took on a more "permanent and systematic character, whose objective exceeded repression and evictions" (Mella Seguel 2007, 173). As during the Frei administration, the Lagos administration also militarized many Mapuche communities. As Mella Seguel (2007, 100) describes, "Police presence in communities became permanent, Chilean prisons admitted hundreds of Mapuche, and protest was responded to with criminalization." This strategy became more explicit as the Lagos administration developed Operación Pacienca (Operation Patience), a police operation requested by the Ministerio Público de la Araucanía in December 2002 to destroy the autonomous Indigenous movement and its mobilization efforts. The operation focused primarily on detaining the activists associated with the attacks on property reported to have been carried out by CAM since 2000 and constructing them as terrorists, both in public opinion and legally (Mella Seguel 2007, 101).

Land policy played an integral role in the Chilean government's efforts to demobilize Mapuche protest. The Lagos administration hoped to provide material incentives, in the form of land transfers, to communities willing to abandon protest in favor of dialogue and negotiation through Article 20B; to this end, the Lagos administration openly and formally prioritized a strategy of negotiating "social peace for land."[2] As Pairican Padilla (2014, 207) summarizes, "The government would not permit—and did not want—new mobilization like that which rocked Eduardo Frei in 1999. . . . it was urgent to reinstate and institutionalize the Mapuche question. The government's proposal for abandoning mobilization seemed to be a threat, or perhaps a political negotiation, towards the organizations." An explicit condition of these negotiations was that the community would abandon the use of violent mobilization. One activist described that "executive officials, to discourage occupations, argued *predio tomado, predio no negociado.*' The [state] organizations were beginning to mark the difference between 'good and bad Mapuches,'" with *predio tomado, predio no negociado* referring to the government's policy that if the community took over a plot of land, the government would not negotiate for that plot of land (Seguel 2007, 65).

Publicly, land-for-peace negotiations demanded demobilization; in practice, however, the government sought demobilization, initiating negotiations with some of the most emblematic organizations and communities that continued to organize in protest after agreements. Alejandra Krauss, minister of MIDEPLAN during the Lagos administration and daughter of a famous former minister, initiated many of these negotiation processes to resolve land demands (Seguel 2007, 66). There are reports of concrete offers to communities associated with CTT (Fundo Alaska), Asociacion Nankuchew de Lumaco, and, after October 2001, communities in Collipulli (Seguel 2007, 66). Victor Ancalaf, former leader of Coordinadora Arauco-Malleco (CAM), publicized that he had participated in a number of secret negotiations with representatives of the Ministry of the Interior in January 2001 over four plots of land in Collipulli that had seen repeated arson attacks, occupations, and armed ambushes. The agreement promised an end to violence in return for 1,625 hectares of land for five communities, including 262 hectares for his community, Choin Lafquenche,[3] but Ancalaf warned that "if the government does not comply with the terms of the agreement, we will break the negotiations and continue with . . . mobilizations and land occupations."[4] Cecilia Perez, minister of MIDEPLAN after Krauss, finalized the agreement. Ancalaf also referred to the case of the Ignacio Quiepul community, who reached a signed agreement with the Ministry of Planning and Cooperation after more than twenty violent confrontations on two of the most emblematic and contested plots of land.

The Chilean government hoped that these working tables and negotiations would effectively demobilize more violent and radical organizations and communities by offering specific incentives. Yet the government became frustrated as these communities broke the land-for-peace agreements and continued mobilizing; in the case of the Ignacio Quiepul community, the community was reported to have broken the agreement fourteen times with land occupations, arson, damage, and hijacking of a bus, prompting Forestal Mininco to present four complaints to the district court.[5] Critiques quickly emerged from within the government. In October 2001 *El Mercurio* reported that anonymous sources within CONADI and MIDEPLAN criticized that negotiations were "altering the logic" of the government's Indigenous policy response.[6] Frequently, allegations emerged that the government used these agreements to protect economic interests in the region. Jaime Andrade, the appointed government negotiator of the Malleco region in 2001 and later director of MIDEPLAN, negotiated deals with forestry companies to protect operations and with Indigenous communities to receive land in other regions (Rodriguez and Carruthers 2008, 15).

This left the government in a complicated situation. Publicly, they called for land-for-peace negotiations while denying their involvement with emblematic communities in unsuccessful negotiations. Minister Krauss denied such agreements took place, repeatedly stating that violent Mapuche groups were never favored while she was responsible for CONADI and reiterating that the ministry would dialogue with Ancalaf and the communities he represented if they respected the rule of law and abandoned violence.[7] Yet there is evidence of exceptions to her insistence. MIDEPLAN subsecretary Andrade confirmed a number of agreements, referring specifically to negotiations with five communities in Collipulli and confirming that Ancalaf participated in the reunions led by MIDEPLAN and CONADI officials.[8] A spokesperson of the Alianza Territorial Mapuche (ATM) said that their organization vaguely knew of these agreements signed in the early 2000s, stating, "Ministers reached an agreement with these communities. I am not sure if it is public, but they did it . . . what is the name of the daughter of Krauss? She came to sign everything with them in Villarica and Traigen. We don't know the details, but they happened" (Interview, November 2013). In January 2002 the Lagos administration officially "closed the doors on the negotiations of 'land in conflict'" (Mella Seguel 2007, 96), and in March the administration made it official policy that communities that used violence as a means of pressure would lose everything they gained.[9] The newly appointed coordinator of Indigenous politics, Jaime Andrade, backtracked, arguing that the agreements were finalized before President Lagos formalized the policy in 2002, and that certain cases were exceptions.

Many of the CONADI officials tasked with implementing the policy were dismissed, as responsibility for failed negotiations jumped between levels of government. National director of CONADI Edgardo Lienlaf was asked to resign in March 2002, when the Lagos administration formally announced it would not negotiate with communities involved in any kind of violence. Lienlaf attributed his resignation to a lack of support from the government; his relationship with MIDEPLAN became strained after he announced that CONADI did not fulfill promises signed by the minister of MIDEPLAN with communities in Lumaco in August 1999.[10] Lienlaf was often accused of prioritizing conversations and negotiations with more radical and violent Mapuche communities, particularly those in conflict with forestry companies in Collipulli and Lumaco. From the perspective of those with economic power in the region, usually on the Right, the prioritization of these relationships was inappropriate. Indeed, Lienlaf was censored by the Chilean government during his term as the director of CONADI for denying his links with communities.[11] In many ways, his resignation was unsurprising. His task was to implement a governance strategy that the central government formally and publicly rejected. Lower-level CONADI officials were similarly trapped. One administrator in FTAI described his departure from office, summarizing that "leaders of the social party, landowners, and indigenous leaders called me. A minister of Lagos tried to force me to give priority to one land purchase and I said no. 'You will have to leave,' they said. 'Yes, I'll leave. No problem'" (Interview, September 2013).

The Lagos administration's response to Indigenous mobilization was, "through the end of his term, characterized by tension and contradiction" (Pairican Padilla 2014, 189). At the start of Lagos's administration, land-for-peace negotiations sought to demobilize violence in the region. Because the Lagos administration could not guarantee demobilization, however, the administration faced allegations of negotiating with violent communities. CONADI officials were situated in the middle, tasked with effecting both negotiated agreements and policy procedures. They acutely understood that policy implementation was part of a broader effort to manage the public demands of the Mapuche; as Richard Mansilla, a CONADI official, described of how criminalization and militarization worked in conjunction with land policy implementation: "Many times we are able to negotiate with communities that are in conflict, establishing what the price of the land will be . . . But many times, we have direct orders from the president that we must keep the noise down in the most conflictive communities . . . We understand that our struggle is permanent, we compete with intelligence agencies . . . we try to take control so that [the conflict] is not addressed with the involvement of police forces" (qtd. in Rodriguez and Carruthers 2008, 11–12). Indeed, as highlighted, an inability by officials to effectively and discretely resolve these tensions resulted in either their resignation or removal from CONADI.

Ultimately, the Lagos administration institutionalized these tensions in Indigenous policy and patterns of Mapuche-state engagement. Radical mobilization strategies were often the expression of more demands that could not be fulfilled by the Chilean government or Article 20B; by institutionalizing yet obscuring land-for-peace agreements, the Lagos administration motivated communities to engage in these land-for-peace agreements, while continuing to rally in pursuit of autonomy and self-determination. As Pairican (2014, 237) summarized of this period, "Lagos, in his symbolic offensive, had managed to institutionalize the discontent of some of the organizations calling for self-determination, but CAM showed it was willing to continue its national liberation project and more strongly assert their actions."

2006–2010: MICHELLE BACHELET

The Bachelet administration (Partido Socialista, Left/center Left) further institutionalized and centralized land-for-peace agreements. Lagos left office with a 70 percent approval rating, facilitating Michelle Bachelet's election and, for the first time since the return to democracy, a Concertación majority in both houses. Bachelet called for a "citizens' government" that would incorporate citizens' demands into policy. While continuing the focus on Indigenous development, Bachelet's administration was successful in advancing Indigenous rights recognitions, ratifying ILO 169 in 2008.

Bachelet's initial indigenous politics platform was characterized by centralization. When Alberto Parra was appointed National Director of CONADI in November 2006, he distanced himself from previous land for peace agreements: "While we certainly have to take care of conflicts and seek solutions, the director of CONADI should not mediating between communities or resolving specific conflicts. As a director I shall advise the Minister and all domestic agencies that require it, but the solution to the conflicts do not go through CONADI, but rather through political dialogue established between the government and Mapuche organizations."[12] Previewing the rest of the Bachelet administration, land-for-peace negotiations fell to offices above CONADI. Accordingly, there was little movement on Indigenous politics during the first portion of Bachelet's administration. When Parra resigned in May 2007, Indigenous counselors criticized that CONADI had only used 6 percent of its budget and failed to purchase any land; everything CONADI had accomplished during this period had been put in place during the Lagos administration.

This dramatically changed in 2008 after the Mapuche activist Matías Catrileo was killed, shot in the back by a *carabinero* (police officer) while participating in a land takeover on January 4, 2008. The Bachelet administration took explicit steps to more actively improve the management of Indigenous policies for the second half of her administration, articulated most broadly in the Re-Conocer: Pacto Social por la Multiculturalidad (Re-Knowing/Recognizing: Social Pact for Multiculturalism) policy. Bachelet justified that "the 1989 Pact [Acuerdo de Nueva Imperial] between the State and indigenous has expired, and the public institutions created in 1993 are in crisis" (Programa Orígenes 2008, 2). The plan called for constitutional recognition of Indigenous peoples within the Chilean state, in pursuit of "the full integration of indigenous peoples, while respecting their differences and particularities, generating cultural changes in all citizens that inhabit *our* territory" (18, emphasis added). While the plan used the language of "indigenous peoples," inferring recognition of collective rights, the scope of these promises was clearly limited, pursuing integration into one nation. The policy also prioritizes development, calling for "a new and productive relationship between indigenous peoples, the State, and the rest of the national community" (13).

The plan also restructured CONADI, institutionalizing the centralization of decision-making and policy implementation. Rodrigo Egaña, an economist and specialist in public management, was appointed presidential commissioner for Indigenous affairs and tasked with improving the management of Indigenous policies by coordinating Indigenous policies among various government offices. Alvaro Marifil was also appointed director of CONADI with the explicit task of executing Re-Conocer.[13] One Indigenous counselor critiqued the new director, noting that as "the right arm of the Presidential Commissioner for Indigenous Affairs Rodrigo Egaña . . . the new director did not come to prioritize commitments and demands of the communities, but rather to bleach, delay, and divert the objectives in the collective interest of indigenous peoples."[14]

These governing trends extended to land purchases. Re-Conocer created a waiting list to specify which communities would benefit from land purchases, prioritizing the land claims of 115 communities whose cases were already documented and approved. The claims of 308 communities, whose documents were submitted, but were yet to be approved, were to be processed after the 115 claims were finalized. The waiting list dramatically changed the dynamics of contention in the region, taking decision-making out of the hands of local bureaucrats and administrators. An administrator at the time described to me, "After *Re-Conocer*, people understood. We didn't process anything for anyone because the procedures did that. The district attorney was always on top of us. That was part of my agenda and, to me, it seemed healthy. . . . there was a level of annoyance because things couldn't be invented" (Interview, October 2013). From the perspective of CONADI officials working to preserve procedures, this centralization shielded them from the critiques and pressures of negotiating land for peace.

Yet land-for-peace agreements, regardless of what level of government they originate, created the same incentives for Mapuche communities to collectively enforce implementation. At the end of the Bachelet administration in 2009, political pressure overwhelmed the policy's capacity. Numerous communities, some organized with ATM and most on the list of 115, mobilized and participated in many visible land takeovers and confrontations with the police. CONADI had already spent the yearly budget for land purchases and the Chilean government faced unwelcome criticism during a campaign year for not meeting its predictions, particularly problematic considering Bachelet's emphasis on Indigenous politics.

To address this mobilization during the presidential campaign, Bachelet further prioritized and centralized Indigenous politics. In 2009 she appointed José Antonio Viera-Gallo, who had served as the minister secretary general of the presidency (Ministerio Secretaría General de la Presidencia, SEGPRES) since 2007, to be coordinating minister of Indigenous affairs. SEGPRES is the cabinet-level administrative office, with the minister of SEGPRES serving in an advisory role equivalent to the US president's chief of staff; the appointment of a high-level official represented the Bachelet government's commitment and preoccupation over the mobilization. In September 2009 Viera-Gallo's first move was to restructure CONADI, removing fourteen employees, including the director of FTAI, in response to allegations of irregularities in the land policy. In October 2009 Viera-Gallo announced that FTAI would function as a land bank, working to "prevent speculation, making purchases more transparent to avoid any suspicion of corruption."[15] These reforms confronted allegations that the land policy was the Concertación's "petty cash" and a "remnant of political clientelism." [16] Explicitly referencing his position on land-for-peace agreements and allegations that the Chilean government negotiated with activists on trial, Viera-Gallo described that "if on trial, the corresponding portions of land will remain pending. If [community members] are declared innocent, they shall have access to their fair share. If convicted, which will surely happen in the next government, our approach is that land will be transferred after they have finished their sentence."[17]

Despite these efforts to insulate the land policy's management, Viera-Gallo continued to use the land policy to negotiate land for peace in direct response to contentious action. In October 2009 Viera-Gallo sought out and signed a number of agreements with the Alianza Territorial Mapuche, one of which appears below. A representative of ATM described to me: "The government insisted on the necessity of talking and talking and then Viera-Gallo arrived. His advisers called us . . . he was fairly explicit with us, explaining that they were at the end of the administration and the budget for the year was gone. But, they would leave it for the next year and it would certainly go through. This lasted five or ten minutes" (Interview, November 2013). The agreements establish that CONADI would buy particular portions of land for eighty-two communities in March 2010, when the new government would take office.[18] Contradicting Viera-Gallo's statement concerning the implementation of land purchases, some of the communities included on this list had community members on trial at the time. Most problematically, the Chilean government agreed to return specific portions of land to communities; because the current landowners were not involved in the agreement and were not obliged to sell their land, they were likely to demand much higher than market value if they knew of the existence of an agreement.

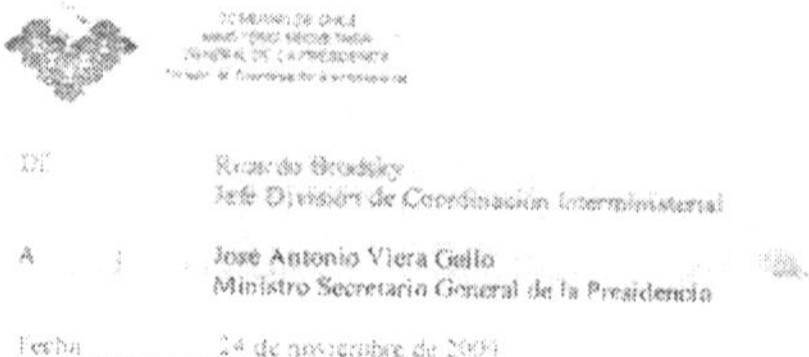

GOBIERNO DE CHILE
MINISTERIO SECRETARÍA
GENERAL DE LA PRESIDENCIA
División de Coordinación Interministerial

DE: Ricardo Brodsky
        Jefe División de Coordinación Interministerial

A: José Antonio Viera Gallo
        Ministro Secretario General de la Presidencia

Fecha   24 de noviembre de 2009

En reuniones sostenidas por el asesor y personal de la Oficina de Asuntos Indígenas de la SEGPRES con diversas comunidades y representantes de organizaciones indígenas de las provincias de Malleco y Cautín, siendo muchas de ellas coordinadas por la Alianza Territorial Mapuche, hemos concluido iniciar procesos para la compra para las comunidades que se indican:

1. *Nivel prioritario:* Es decir, de compra de predios con el número de hectáreas que se indican durante el primer trimestre del año 2010 para diez comunidades (una por territorio o lof) a propuesta de las organizaciones indígenas. Estos territorios y comunidades son las siguientes:

Comuna	Lof o Territorio	Comunidad P.J.	Predios	N° de hectáreas
Ercilla	Temukuykuy	Ignacio Queipul Millanao PJ.828	La Romana, Montenegro, El Manzano, Gelolmaro, Parte de Poluco Pidenco (F. Mininco, Poluco (F. Arauco)	1800
Ercilla	Chacaiko	Huañaco Millao y otros PJ. 232	Predios según detalle ANEXO N° 1	700 aprox
Ercilla	Kollico	Collico PJ 1749	Predios según detalle ANEXO N° 2	800 aprox.
Victoria	Pewenko	Pancho Curamil PJ:624	Fundo Terra Nova / Fundo Los Coyhue	250 / 480
Freire	Xapilwe-Mawizache	Trapilbue PJ 1056	Fundo Maquehue, UFRO / Fundo San Antonio / Fundo Santa Elisa	283 / 700 / 500
I. Schmidt	Budi	Llaguepulli PJ:276	-Sociedad Agricola Chelle (González Olguin María Angélica) / -Sociedad Agricola Chelle (Carlos Baumert Felmer) / -La Parroquia	426 / 534 / 80
Cunco	Wawanko	Mariano Sandoval PJ:1369	Fundo La Bastilla de Beatriz Hinan	846 aprox
Cunco	Xomelafken	Tromelafquen PJ 757	Sucesión Ferrari / Forestal Mininco	230 / 700
P. las Casas	Rufuwe	Rufuwe	Por definir	
Cunco	Werere	Juan José Quidel PJ. 915	Fundo Huerere (Leonardo García) / Fun El Mirador (Mario García)	480 aprox / 700 aprox

2. *Segundo Nivel:* Es decir, comunidades a las cuales se les debe asesorar para que completen sus antecedentes desde el punto de vista técnico-administrativo y jurídico, proceso que concluirá al mes de junio del año 2010, a fin de que puedan contar con aplicabilidad, previa presentación a la CONADI de la documentación correspondiente. Si en este listado existen comunidades con aplicabilidad, se incorporará al proceso de compra en ese mismo plazo. La nómina es en el orden de prioridad que sigue:

Image 2.1. Scan of agreement between José Antonio Viera Gallo, Ministro Secretario General de la Presidencia, and the Alianza Territorial Mapuche, 2009.

By 2009 CONADI heavily regulated land purchase prices, making it nearly impossible for CONADI to pay more than 10 percent over market value. Furthermore, the document gave communities a tool to leverage the government to implement.

Criticism came from all sides. CONADI employees condemned political motivations for eclipsing administrative processes. One employee explained, "We ran out of resources to meet our yearly goal and something had to be done . . . [the agreement had] zero technical accessory. . . . from a technical point of view, how do I say it? It didn't make sense

Nº	Comunidad	PJ	Comuna
1	Antonio Milla	582	Victoria
2	Alex Lemun	1861	Ercilla
3	Santiago Coñoeman	1377	Freire
4	Huilquilao Hueche	1385	Freire
5	Newen Weñe	1379	Freire
6	Epu Francisco Huenchuñir	1189	Freire
7	Coñoñol Epuleo	673	Ercilla
8	Manuel Amuil	1456	Pto. Saavedra
9	Pilquinao Naculman	147	Pto. Saavedra
10	Santa Isabel Newen Mapu	1633	Cunco
11	Antonio Paine de Curileufu	1833	Vilcun
12	Santos Curinao	22	Vilcun
13	Domingo Cario	64	Vilcun
	Eduardo Quilaqueo	586	Vilcun
14	Antonio Pilquiman, Maria Lienqueo	52	Vilcun
15	y Gregorio Ñanco		
16	Juan Añiñir Inaipil	404	Vilcun
17	Juan Segundo Marileo	341	Vilcun
18	Juan Nicolás Catrileo	399	Vilcun
19	Martin Montri	70	Vilcun
20	José Llancao	1375	Vilcun
21	Juan Agustín Purran	425	Vilcun
22	Samuel España	1729	Vilcun
23	Peñas Mapu	1580	Victoria
24	Juan Paillalef	1138	Cunco
25	Cañeta Calfuqueo	744	Ercilla
26	Juan Pinoleo	1133	Ercilla
27	Manuel Calfuil	623	Nva. Imperial
28	Martín Cayuqueo	663	Nva. Imperial
29	Cacique Nicolás Quintrel	443	Temuco
30	Juan Coña	1127	Temuco
31	Juan Cariqueo	1512	Temuco
32	Juan Cayupan	729	Temuco
33	Juan Collinao	1007	Temuco
34	Juan Huilcan	345	Teodoro Schmidt
35	La Araucana Treo Tren	1657	Carahue
36	Domingo Cayuqueo Catrileo	1485	Lonquimay
37	Huallenmapu	198	Lonquimay
38	Huenucal Ivante	4	Lonquimay
39	Pedro Calfuqueo	3	Lonquimay
40	Quecupu Marimenuco	1614	Lonquimay
41	Pehuenco Alto	774	Lonquimay
42	Pehuenco Bajo	784	Lonquimay
43	Wallako Millao Manidinche	En Trámite	Ercilla

Dar la debida prioridad por parte de CONADI a estos procesos supondría reforzar la capacidad de trabajo del equipo de Tierras de la Corporación, con el objeto de no afectar los procesos en marcha.

RICARDO BRODSKY

ALVARO MARIFIL
Recibido el
26/Nov/2009

JOSÉ A. VIERA-GALLO
Recibido el 25/XI/09

Image 2.2. Scan of agreement between José Antonio Viera Gallo, Ministro Secretario General de la Presidencia, and the Alianza Territorial Mapuche, 2009.

and had some other motivation. We were organizing the process; that was populism. . . ." (Interview, October 2013). Another described, "The political objective was to lower the level of conflict. The strategy was to calm the issue, promising benefits that the government was not in the condition to follow through on" (Interview, September 2013). A 2011 congressional investigatory committee concluded that "what the minister did was basically to put out a fire, but he put it out with gasoline" by creating expectations among communities about how the policy was enacted.[19]

The Bachelet administration shifted contention over the implementation of Indigenous land policy from the local to the national level. Yet land-for-peace agreements continued. Scaling land-for-peace agreements to higher levels of government alleviated CONADI of the tension to protect both security and institutional procedures, while continuing to provide Mapuche communities the incentive to mobilize.

2010–2014: SEBASTIÁN PIÑERA

In 2009 Sebastián Piñera was elected, the first right-wing president since the return to democracy (Renovación Nacional, center Right, in the Alianza por Chile coalition). Compared to the previous center Left to left-wing presidents in office from 1990 to 2010, Piñera's Indigenous politics platform was a more explicit form of neoliberal multiculturalism in its focus on recognition of cultural differences and integration into one state and nation. As he summarized: "[In March 2010] we initiated a new deal with our indigenous peoples, based on four pillars. First, a constitutional reform that recognizes various ethnic entities existing within the same nation and territory. Second, replacing the strategy of assimilation with true integration . . . Third, stimulating their economic and social development in order to reduce existing gaps. And fourth, recognition, appreciation and promotion of their history, culture, traditions and language" (qtd. in Alorda 2013). Piñera proposed a constitutional reform that would recognize cultural differences but did not match Bachelet's calls for Indigenous communities to be recognized as peoples. In early 2013 Piñera reasserted that "we believe that Chile is a multicultural country. Among these various cultures, there is one that deserves special recognition: the culture of our indigenous peoples." When discussions of converting CONADI to a cabinet level arose, Piñera's minister of the interior explicitly rejected the possibility, justifying "the existence of a state within another state is impossible."[20]

Specific to land policy governance, the Piñera administration hoped to strengthen CONADI's institutional capacity. From their perspective, this required halting land purchases through Article 20B in order to reevaluate implementation procedures. An advisor to the president on Indigenous Affairs justified, "When the new administration took office, the chaos in the land policy was so severe that it seemed that the least we could do was stop, look inward, and try to solve it" (Interview, August 2013). Indeed, the Piñera administration did not use a significant portion of the 2010 budget for land purchases as they, instead, focused on reviewing how to restructure and institutionalize procedures. As one administrator described of the priorities of this work: "When we restarted the land policy, we bought land under certain parameters: 1: no violence; 2: more than 12.7 hectares per family; 3: per capita should not pass $20 million [Chilean pesos]; 4: 2.5/3 million [Chilean pesos] per hectare" (Interview, August 2013). In hopes of creating a clear list of which communities' claims would be studied, processed, and when, the Piñera administration chose to preserve the list of the 115 communities prioritized by the Bachelet administration, then study the cases of the 308 communities on the waiting list.

Yet the Piñera administration was not aware of the agreement Viera-Gallo had signed with ATM. An administrator at the Indigenous Affairs Division in the Ministry of Social Development described: "We encountered the agreement when we arrived. . . . it was to win votes and was completely part of the political campaign. It was impossible to implement because [the previous administration] did not have the resources; they never had the intention of doing so. We asked those communities to be on the waiting list . . . We have not ratified the agreement" (Interview, September 2013). Formally, the Piñera administration declared that the agreement was a political maneuver that did not have standing in the new administration.

Yet most observers note that the Piñera administration recognized the political importance of land-for-peace agreements and continued the practice outside of formal bureaucratic procedures. One prominent Mapuche academic and activist interpreted to me that, just like previous administrations, in the second year, "They [the Piñera administration] realized that land politics were a political tool to resolve conflicts with the Mapuche community. They realized its potential and radically changed its management, buying land to put out fires (*apagar incendios*). . . . What the state is buying is not really land, but rather a solution to a conflict" (Interview, July 2013). A former administrator similarly concluded, "They realized that this became a highly conflictive situation and changed course. It was the same that Bachelet had done. They did not follow their original program" (Interview, August 2013).

The subsequent administration released evidence corroborating these interpretations of the Piñera administration's use of land-for-peace agreements. In May 2014, three months after the change of government, the new director of CONADI, Alberto Pizarro Chiñalao, announced a number of irregularities in the land purchases finalized during the Piñera administration. He expressed that "in some cases, purchases were just awaiting a final signature, but many of them did not meet minimal, basic procedures . . . Everything was done poorly." Fifty people were placed on administrative leave, although the severity of their infractions was not specified.[21] Fifteen files were handed over to the public prosecutor, ten of which dealt with land purchases; the national public prosecutor of CONADI said the folders showed that ex-national directors of CONADI were involved in tax fraud, incompatible negotiation, and influence peddling in 2011, 2012, and 2013.[22] Senator Eugenio Tuma (PPD) summarized, "Neither the previous nor current government want to make land values or land markets transparent. They always leave it open to hidden negotiations."[23]

CONCLUSIONS

What motivates the implementation of Chile's Indigenous land policy? This chapter highlights how the Chilean government works to demobilize and disarticulate Mapuche mobilization through the implementation of Article 20B of Indigenous Law 19.253. More specifically, this is accomplished through land-for-peace agreements, representing the government's ongoing efforts to negotiate with mobilized Mapuche communities in pursuit of stability in the region. Over time, CONADI gradually shielded itself by institutionalizing implementation procedures, as evaluated in chapter 1, requiring the intervention of higher-level policymakers and politicians who could push for land-for-peace agreements. CONADI officials were no longer able to apply the policy to fulfill political interests and filtered demands through increasingly institutional procedures. Yet land-for-peace agreements informally continued, increasingly masked and complicated by procedures, and only possible when higher-level politicians intervene and push CONADI to do so. The response to Viera-Gallo's 2009 agreements is indicative of this shift. Like many of his predecessors, he signed an agreement to resolve the demands of a group of mobilized Mapuche communities; general consensus, however, found it illegitimate to openly use the policy to respond to political pressure and bypass institutionalized procedures. This response proved the extent to which the policy and procedures had been institutionalized as well as persisting room for exceptions to these policies and procedures. Fransisca de la Maza (2014, 362) similarly observes this tension in Indigenous policy in Chile: "The State, headed by ministers, secretaries, mayors and so on, generates new positions and programmes. The Indigenous population and public employees strengthen identification and organisational processes. These efforts frequently widen the margins to allow greater negotiation for policies and spaces for recognition as well as political control, allowing the replication of state hegemony. Indigenous policy is continually constructed and re-constructed during the tug-of-war between negotiation and conflict (real or potential) and between the value and threat represented by the ethnic element." This fundamental ten-

TABLE 2.1. NATIONAL DIRECTORS OF CONADI, 1993–2013

DIRECTOR	APPOINTED	END OF TERM AND CONTEXT
Jose Bengoa	1993	1994
Mauricio Huenchulaf Cayuqueo	1994	Resigned, April 1997
Domingo Namuncura	April 1997	Government asked for resignation, August 1998
Rodrigo González	September 1998	Resigned, March 2000
Edgardo Lienlaf	March 2000	Government asked for resignation, March 2002
Aroldo Cayún Anticura	April 2002	March 2006
Jaime Andrade	March 2006	Resigned, November 2006
Alberto Parra Salinas	November 2006	Resigned, May 2007
Wilson Reyes Araya	May 2007	Resigned, June 2008
Alvaro Marifil Hernández	June 2008	Resigned (change of government), March 2010
Francisco Painepán	March 2010	Resigned, Jan 2011
Jorge Retamal	Jan 2011	Resigned (change of government), 2014

sion between preserving elite interests or institutionalizing procedures remains unresolved; politicians' efforts to satisfy and accomplish both concerns undermines the significance of the rights recognitions.

As highlighted throughout this chapter, the central government often intervenes in CONADI's implementation procedures to respond to contentious action. Because CONADI's organizational mission was never clearly established, the work of bureaucrats is frequently subsumed into national political interests. As a prominent member of Piñera's administration summarized of these internal contradictions to me: "From a policy perspective policy, CONADI was never prepared for its task because of the way it was conceived. For most indigenous leaders, CONADI should be of the indigenous community. But, it is a state institution, comprised of state representatives. It is not of the indigenous community or of the state. It is an institution cursed by a vital, internal contradiction" (Interview, August 2013). Another observer characterized CONADI's work as having "a fundamental, paralyzing contradiction. The problem is that the law does not clarify whether this institution represents the State against the Indians or Indians against the State" (qtd. in Vergara, Foerster, and Gundermann 2004, 7).

This imposition of national interests is perhaps most evident in the rapid turnover of national directors of CONADI, common when they oppose the direction of the central government or can be blamed for informal patterns of policy implementation documented throughout this chapter. A long-serving CONADI bureaucrat concluded that "there is a big problem with instability in the institution. There is no continuity between directors. They arrive through political connections, spend their first year trying to understand the office, and, when they try to implement changes in their second year, are removed from office" (Interview, November 2012). Table 2.1 documents these turnovers.

Manuel Marileo, the president of the National Association of CONADI Civil Servants in 2009, repeated, "They have changed the director of CONADI five times in two year[s], with every *compadre* in his party adding or removing people. We are fed up of the abuses and that is what we are denouncing."[24] Manuel Namuncura confided: "Our performance is not the best, and irregularities sometimes occur because of the instability. Those who denounce are dismissed and those who commit remain. They cut the thread at its thinnest point."[25] Commenting on the role of the national director, CONADI national communications officer Cecilia Amzamora concluded in 2001:

> When the director is politically close to the President, he has more influence. In such cases he is sometimes not very popular with the Indians. [Eduardo] Frei sacked the previous director, who was against the Ralco Dam. Frei had been an entrepreneur, with links with the companies working in Ralco, so he supported the dam. Rodrigo Gonzalez, who was put in place by Frei, was actually physically attacked, with indigenous women throwing plates and eggs at him. This was very bad for his image, so he in turn resigned. CONADI is current[ly] being investigated by the courts for corruption . . . There is plenty of money at stake, so people are vulnerable . . . you might call it systemic corruption. (qtd. in Ray 2007, 139)

While the central government continued to intervene in particular cases, this institutionalization required higher and higher levels of political actors to make those interventions.

This chapter highlights how government officials navigate often contradictory visions of how to extend the neoliberal project. Institutionalized procedures work to extend neoliberalism to the governance of Mapuche territorial demands, but the preservation of these procedures often comes into tension with efforts to preserve the strength of local market interests. The result, as one expert commented of Indigenous land policy governance, "The issue jumps between levels of the administrations, depending on how hot (*incendiado*) the issue is." Ultimately, the Chilean government subverts institutionalized procedures to preserve elite market interests, while simultaneously working to further institutionalize procedures.

CHAPTER 3

NAVIGATING LAND POLICY

If a community presents their demand, [CONADI] files and archives their paperwork. But if the community takes action with the movement, CONADI feels the community.

—Mapuche activist, Padre Las Casas (Interview, April 2013)

This chapter shifts the focus to the experiences of eight Mapuche communities in the Padre Las Casas district, located just outside the regional capital of Temuco. While previous chapters highlight how bureaucrats rewrote policy procedures to serve their own interests (chapter 1), and understood and implemented the policy process on behalf of particular interests (chapter 2), this chapter documents how Mapuche communities understand, experience, and engage with the policy. When and why do Mapuche communities turn to bureaucrats and politicians as they work to navigate the policy process? What do Mapuche leaders perceive as the most effective ways to pursue territorial demands through Article 20B of Indigenous Law 19.253?

Motivation for this chapter comes via early conversations with members of a Mapuche community working with the Instituto de Estudios Indígenas at the Universidad de la Frontera. They were interested in presenting their territorial demand to CONADI but were unfamiliar with the technical requirements to do so. As many of these relationships start, a community member became familiar with the work of some of the anthropologists, lawyers, and historians affiliated with the institute through one of his university courses. That initial connection grew into a joint meeting to discuss the community's aspirations and opportunities for collaboration. Huddled between electric heaters as extensive amounts of food and mate were passed around the room, community members passionately spoke of the history of their community's territory, laying out a plan to document this history over the next months with the assistance of anthropologists and lawyers; they were kind enough to let me observe these initial conversations.

At the end of the meeting, a young community member approached me, inquiring what past policy trends would predict about if and how CONADI would respond to the community's territorial demand. Exchanging emails, I sent along details about which communities in their district had received land in which years and at what price, using the government data under analysis in this book. At that early point in my field research, I was working backward to understand when, why, and how the Chilean government would purchase land on behalf of a particular Mapuche community, ultimately producing the line in a spreadsheet I had spent hours examining before moving to Chile with information on the community's name, region, number of families in the community, the number of purchased hectares, the price paid for that land, and year of the purchase. Providing some quick analysis of the trends and neighboring communities' experiences most relevant to this community, my email seemed horribly inadequate and raised more questions than it answered. What does it take for that community to show up as one line of data on the government spreadsheet of land purchases? Where could the process stall or end without a land purchase? What resources could the community draw on to increase the likelihood they would acquire land through CONADI?

This chapter tells those stories, documenting the experiences of eight communities in the Padre Las Casas district. These eight communities include communities that acquired land through CONADI as well as those who requested but failed to acquire land. As in previous chapters, these stories reveal concerning inconsistencies in the patterns of policy implementation, driven by the decision-making of politicians and bureaucrats. One community leader described trading votes with a local politician to advance the community's claim, and another made the same argument referencing their community's participation in the occupation of the regional airport. In one of the most publicized cases in the region, a minister signed an agreement with the Juan Catrilaf community to purchase land held by a powerful economic stakeholder. Certainly, these patterns deviate from what appears to be a bureaucratic, technical, and market-driven process expected to be a means of extending neoliberal governance.

While from a different vantage point, these stories reiterate many of the trends documented in prior chapters. By limiting which actors can present which demands to what ends, Chile's interpretation of the territorial turn places the state firmly in control of an extended, protracted interaction in which the burden of proof falls to the community. Most community leaders are aware that the burden of proof falls to them to both prove the applicability of their claim and the community's insis-

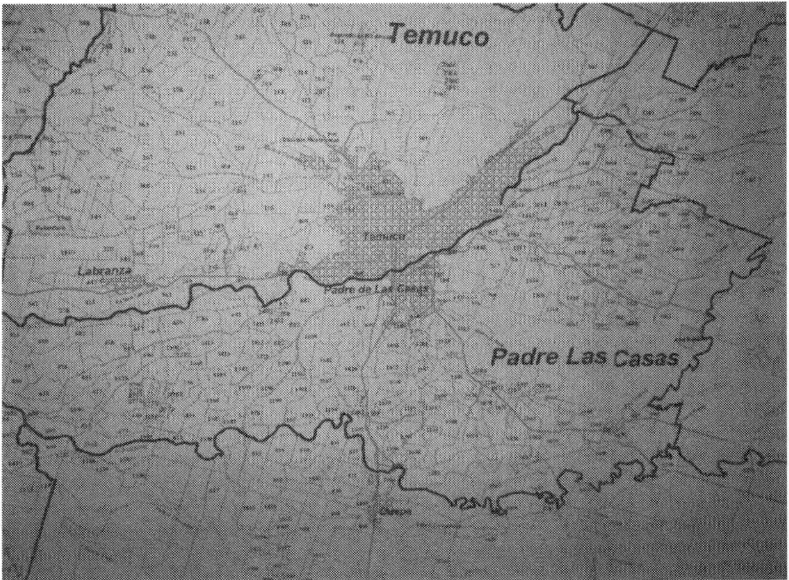

Image 3.1. Map of *títulos de merced* and Mapuche communities in Padre las Casas. Photo by the author, taken at the Archivo General de Asuntos Indígenas in Temuco, Chile, in July 2013.

tence that their claim will be resolved. Communities turn to bureaucrats and politicians, through both formal and informal avenues, to do so. Community leaders note that these connections most often serve to help community members work through the administrative and technical elements of their proposal. But the most politically adept community leaders recognize the need to prove their community's insistence that CONADI process their paperwork. Some communities are able to prove their insistence by directing mobilization toward local bureaucrats and politicians. If a territorial demand confronts the interests of economic or political elite in the region, communities must prove their insistence to high-level politicians, leveraging contention and unrest for a government response. The state often uses repression to demobilize and disarticulate the mobilization of communities that do engage in these levels of contention. While this opens space for some Mapuche communities to instrumentally navigate the policy to access land, these piecemeal, bureaucratic efforts undermine the broader pursuit of territory, both of communities that receive and fail to receive land through Article 20B. Community leaders express significant frustration at the gap between communities' territorial demands and the formal regulations governing the state's bureaucratic, technocratic, piecemeal land policy.

TERRITORIAL DEMANDS IN PADRE LAS CASAS, ARAUCANÍA

The Padre Las Casas (PLC) district is located just outside Temuco, the regional capital of the Araucanía (region IX). The district is often considered to be part of Temuco with approximately 300,000 living in Temuco and surrounding areas, including PLC. In 2012 PLC had 75,000 habitants, 42.7 percent of whom live in rural areas on small plots of land; 52 percent of the land in PLC is in plots of less than 10 hectares, 64 percent of the landowners hold less than 10 hectares, the average landowner holds 5.99 hectares, and only 4.5 percent of the land in PLC is in plots larger than 500 hectares (Instituto Nacional Estadísticas 2002).

PLC contains 102 *títulos de merced* (historic land titles granting Indigenous communities plots of land), shown by the numbered plots in figure 3.1. Mapuche communities or individuals hold title to 73 percent of the rural sectors of PLC (294.51 km^2); because of the history of land tenure in the area and the proximity to Temuco, the majority of these land holdings are small, nontransferable plots of land. The rural economy is largely subsistence farming, partially oriented toward the market and heavily relying on land. The family is the basic unit of production, living on and working on average three hectares per family and relying primarily on the production of wheat, subsistence agriculture, and small livestock. The construction of the regional airport had a significant impact on the region, and is repeatedly referenced in the interviews. Not only did many communities lose access to historically claimed and accessed land and territory, but many neighboring communities protested its construction. Because of the regional significance of the airport, many communities use the airport as the site of their protest, causing disruptions that quickly leverage the attention of local politicians. Furthermore, in 2014 the airport was moved further south of Temuco to the district of Freiere, prompting a new round of protests over the future use of the old airport. As Iván Reyes, president of a local Mapuche organization, contextualized of their participation in the protests, "The authorities have not given us a response since the construction of the airport began; one of [the requests] is the delivery of land for my community, which has been promised, but they have not complied." He also called for the state to compensate the community "for the lands that were taken from us to build the airport," and called for the community to "have greater political participation and in the administration of the airport, so that we can have some form of monetary income."[1] Very much like the demands presented here, these demands fluidly include both the specific—a particular plot of land a community has a territorial claim to, and the broad—degrees of autonomy.

In the following section, I present analysis of interviews with eight community leaders in PLC. Of the eight communities, three land claims were rejected, four were in process, and one was resolved as of 2013. The interviews discussed below lasted between forty-five minutes and two hours and focused on how the community learned about the policy, the steps they took to present their demand, whether the communities have connections to civil servants/politicians/academics/ lawyers/ political parties, if they participated in any type of protest or mobilization while presenting their demand, how they would characterize the government's responsiveness, their challenges and successes navigating the policy, and their perceptions of why some communities were more or less successful. As discussed in the introduction, the names of the presidents and communities are changed. Particularly in this chapter, this decision was motivated by a desire to highlight that the state's patterns of engagement are not specific to the individual, community, or case but rather broader representations of the relationship between Mapuche communities and the Chilean state.

PROVING APPLICABILITY:
NAVIGATING POLICY FORMULATIONS AND REGULATIONS

Article 20B and the accompanying regulations documented in chapter 1 outline the conditions under which Mapuche communities can present their territorial claim to the Chilean government. During an early conversation at the subnational CONADI office in Temuco, an official provided me several documents, which are included here. She explained that these were not formal, regulatory documents but rather were provided to communities for guidance on what documents and reports need to be completed to prove the legitimacy of their claim throughout the various stages of the policy process. The first summarizes the stages of Article 20B; in pen, she bracketed the first (*1° Etapa)* and second (*2° Etapa*) stages of the process, separated by the approval of the legitimacy of the community's demand (*resolución*). The next illustrates additional information given to communities about which documents were needed to complete portions of stage 1; the last specifies the requirements needed for documenting the history of the community (*historia de la comunidad*). These documents are not formal procedure but rather efforts by CONADI to institutionalize procedures to shield themselves from critique of inconsistent implementation.

The list of documents annotated to be part of stage 1 (*1° Etapa*) are those that a community must compile to prove that their demand qualifies for processing through Article 20B and to formally open a folder on their demand. For many communities, these requirements are insurmountable, as the nature of their territorial demand does not meet the policy requirements. One leader explained their frustration with CONADI's requirement that the community prove they lost access to more than five hectares of the land for more than thirty years, as documented in their *título de merced*. The community invested in hiring a topographer to survey the community's territory, who, in turn, concluded that the community only had a two-hectare discrepancy between their currently held land and the boundaries demarcated in the *título de merced*. Another community leader expressed frustration over their claim's rejection, arguing, "I don't have a loss of land, but I do have contamination [from the airport adjacent to the community's land]" (Interview, April 2013).

For communities whose territorial demands do not meet the requirements of Article 20B, CONADI often recommended that the community pursue access to land through Article 20A of Indigenous Law 19.253. In contrast to Article 20B, Article 20A establishes a lottery through which individuals and communities can apply for a subsidy to purchase land; this path responds more directly to situations of poverty and conceptualizes land as an economic resource used to promote development. Often, individuals pursue a subsidy through Article 20A while the community is presenting a claim through Article 20B. For example, as one community struggled to collect all of the documents for Article 20B, two of its community members received subsidies through Article 20A and six more were in the process of applying as the community's demand stalled. CONADI also recommended Article 20A to the community who had lost three hectares of land; the leader responded, "But I have my cemetery here" (Interview, May 2013).

Community leaders unable to use Article 20B to present their territorial demands were frustrated, often framing their frustration with the language and precedence of the International Labour Organization's Convention 169. Leaders frequently pointed to Chile's 2009 ratification of ILO 169 as a turning point in the history of subordination of Indigenous communities in Chile, arguing that the Chilean government should and would enforce territorial rights because of those international protections and recognitions. While ILO 169 establishes the legitimacy of each of the communities' territorial demands, many of these demands fall outside of the narrow scope of Article 20B. Leaders were frequently more familiar with the broad purview of ILO 169 than the limited scope of Chile's land policy, leaving many frustrated and confused that the bureaucrats tasked with implementing Article 20B rejected their claims. As one leader summarized, "The authorities do not understand the necessities of the communities" (Interview, April 2013). When asked why

DOCUMENTOS EN CARPETA
EN MARCO DE ARTICULO 20 LETRA B LEY INDIGENA 19.253
(antecedentes aportados por la comunidad)

Socilicitud de la comunidad

Listado de socios fundadores e incoproración

Listado de grupos familiares

Historia de la comunidad

Plano de división

Título de Merced

Antecedentes administrativos o judiciales (juicios o denuncias)

Carta tipo enviada

Pauta de antecedentes

Certificado de Personalidad Jurídica

Copia RUT de la comunidad

Dirección y/o telefóno:

DOCUMENTOS EN CARPETA
(Antecedentes Técnicos)

Informe Ocupacional

Informe Social

Informe Jurídico

Informe Cultural

Resolución de Fiscalia

Acta de elección del predio

Acta de prenegociación

Estudio de Títulos de predio

Tasaciones

Planos

Resolución Exenta de compra

Escritura de compra y venta

Certificado de Personalidad Jurídica vigente

Image 3.2. Article 20B required documentation (first and second stages written in pen).

the government had not followed through on these international commitments and why there was such a significant gap between international and domestic recognitions, leaders often expressed that politicians *no nos pesca* (do not pay attention to us) and *no tienen voluntad* (are not willing).

For the communities whose demands did meet the conditions of Article 20B, sufficiently documenting their demand poses a significant challenge. The burden of proof falls on the community, requiring documentation of the territorial demand as outlined here and in chapter 1. Each leader emphasized the challenge of understanding and navigating

CONADI
SUBDIRECCIÓN NACIONAL TEMUCO
U.L.T.A

**DOCUMENTOS NECESARIOS PARA LA CONFECCIÓN
DE INFORME N° 1**

¿Qué es el informe N° 1?

Es el primer paso para la postulación al Fondo de Tierras, el cual consiste en realizar un estudio jurídico efectuado por el abogado de la Unidad de Tierras Y Aguas, previo a estudios efectuados en notarias, conservadores, juzgados, archivos de la CONADI y los antecedentes aportados por la comunidad.

De acuerdo a esto complete las siguientes preguntas:

Nombre Comunidad	:
Lugar	:
Comuna	:
Dirección Postal	:
N° Título de Merced	:
Superficie según TM	:
Superficie reivindicada Por la Comunidad	:
Superficie actualmente ocupada Por la Comunidad	:

Image 3.3. Required documents for the completion of the first (juridical) report for Article 20B.

these formal, bureaucratic requirements and procedures. Many communities are geographically isolated, relying on sporadic rural buses or carpools to travel to Temuco. As one president expressed regarding his community, "We are people so, as we say, so basic, that we do not have great technical, professional knowledge" (Interview, April 2013). He explained that some community members were familiar with CONADI and its basic responsibilities because of conflicts over the construction of the regional airport. While he had limited experience working with CONADI, some university-educated aunts "opened my mind about how I had to act." As he explained, "[The government] domesticated us so severely that it confused us. By the time we realized, we were in a bad

Hay ó ha habido juicio?:

SI   ☐   NO   ☐

Estado del Juicio, marque con una Cruz:

Pendiente ☐   Resuelto ☐   Ganado ☐   Perdido ☐

Nombre de los propietarios u ocupantes de terrenos que fueron comprendidos por Título de Merced.

1.- ....

2.- ....

3.- ....

4.- ....

5.- ....

Razones o causas de la ocupación (marque con una X)

Compraventa ☐   Arrendamiento ☐   Ocupación de hecho ☐

Expropiaciones:

SI   ☐   NO   ☐

Antecedentes de Reforma Agraria (si los hubiera):

____

____

Image 3.4. Required documents for the completion of the first (juridical) report for Article 20B.

situation. We have to establish our right and establish our position as well" (Interview, April 2013). Several others described that the decision to proceed with paperwork depends specifically on the community president's knowledge of the policy process. One community had prepared all the paperwork to document the community's demand, but was told they could not apply; the president did not know why or how to proceed, stalling the process until anyone could leverage more resources and information. Local organizations, nearby communities, or outside organizations can help communities to overcome these initial impediments, but many claims do not advance because communities are unfamiliar with technical requirements and bureaucratic procedures.

HISTORIA DE LA COMUNIDAD:

COMUNIDAD:
LUGAR O SECTOR:
COMUNA:
PERSONALIDAD JURIDICA:
TITULO DE MERCED:
SUPERFICIE SEGÚN TITULO DE MERCED:
SUPERFICIE SEGÚN DIVISIÓN:
NUMERO DE FAMILIAS DE LA COMUNIDAD:
NUMERO DE SOCIOS Y PERSONAS DE LA COMUNIDAD:
CONTAR COMO HA SIDO LA HISTORIA DE LA COMUNIDAD DESDE QUE SE
RADICARON CON EL TITULO DE MERCED:
EXPLICAR COMO SE HA PERDIDO LA TIERRA, MEDIANTE QUE
MECANISMOS (COMPRAS, CORRIDAS DE CERCOS,, SANEAMIENTOS, ETC)
EXPLICAR EN MANOS DE QUIEN QUEDO ESA TIERRA, LAS HIJUELAS QUE
ESTARÍAN OCUPADAS Y CUANTO TERRENO INVOLUCRARÍA
INDICAR SI LA COMUNIDAD O MIEMBROS DE ELLA HICIERON GESTIONES
JUDICIALES O DENUNCIAS PARA TRATAR DE RECUPERAR LA TIERRA, SI
ES ASI ADJUNTAR LOS ANTECEDENTES.
POR ÚLTIMO TERMINAR LA CARTA SEÑALANDO QUE EN RAZÓN DE TODO
LO ANTERIOR, LA COMUNIDAD SOLICITA SE OTORGUE APLICABILIDAD
SEGÚN EL ARTICULO 20 LETRA B DE LA LEY 19253 A SU SOLICITUD DE
RECUPERACIÓN DE TIERRAS

Image 3.5. Required documentation of the history of the community for Article
20B.

PROVING INSISTENCE: NAVIGATING UNWRITTEN RULES

While formal policy procedures presented a challenge for many communities, the unwritten rules of policy implementation were frequently
more consequential. A conversation with the bureaucrat who provided
me the guiding documents shown in this chapter was particularly revealing of how crucial it was for communities to understand these unwritten
rules of policy implementation. It was clear that I was not understanding her responses to my questions about when and why certain communities stalled while others advanced. She dug into stacks of files and
randomly pulled out three folders, holding them tight to her chest; as
these were open, active demands, she said she would not share the name
of communities or the details of the case, but she could talk through the
trends using those examples. She tried to recollect the specifics of each
case as she flipped through the folders. Of the first two, she commented
on the status of the file, murmured about which documents they had
submitted, and explained that process was paused until the communities "did something." With a quick glance at the third community's file,
she immediately recognized and recalled the case, commenting that the
community was searching for a plot of land because "of their insistence"
(Interview, November 2012). When I asked if the first two communities
knew CONADI was waiting for them, she shrugged and commented
that CONADI was understaffed and could not possibly follow up on

open files. Furthermore, and more problematically, she explained that CONADI had so many files requesting territory through Article 20B that they could not possibly work on a file without the "insistence" of the community. Whether community leaders understood what "insistence" entailed and how crucial it was to the processing of the community's territorial demand remained unclear.

Many community leaders recognized that formal procedures do not always strictly govern policy implementation, expressing the need to also use extrainstitutional means to prove their "insistence." Often, leaders spoke of the need to *trabajar* (work), *andar* (walk/work/go after), *moverse* (move/activate/put in motion), *luchar* (fight), or *pelear* (fight). While my questions for community leaders were specific to how the community presented their territorial demand through Article 20B, this portion of the conversation always flowed into the abstract, revealing that community leaders situated this pattern of engagement within broader patterns of engagement with the Chilean state. One president concluded, "[Politicians and government officials] have always kept us just over there, placated. Because indigenous policies don't consider us, we have to fight" (Interview, April 2013). Another described that "it is such a bureaucratic system that asks for this document and that document that, in the end, forces the Mapuche to fight (*obligan a los Mapuches a luchar po*)" (Interview, April 2013). Another reflected that the policy process "almost fulfills the saying that only a crying baby gets milk" (*la wawa que no llora, no mama*, similar to the expression "the squeaky wheel gets the grease") (Interview, May 2013). Some leaders recognized the need to engage in these processes, yet acknowledged that their community struggled to do so. As one leader described, "[Government officials] do not worry much about us, so we have to work. We also delay because we do not have vehicles. We are not well known" (Interview, May 2013). Communities that perceive the process to advance according to bureaucratic procedures most frequently stalled; those that saw and utilized other strategies advanced as they demonstrated their insistence.

Many leaders referenced specific events that increased their awareness about the necessity of engaging in these informal forms of pressure. These references were to the region of Ercilla, approximately ninety kilometers north of Temuco and were often referred to as the "red zone" of conflict between Mapuche communities and the state. One community leader explained, "Maquehue [part of PLC] is not a community like in Ercilla. We are all Mapuches, but we are more domesticated. It was difficult to wake up . . . If the people from Ercilla lived here there wouldn't be an airport" (Interview, April 2013). Referencing the killing of young Mapuche activist Matías Catrileo by police during an occupation in

2008, one leader described, "When they killed *peñi* (Mapuche brother), I woke up. I stood up . . . we are part of them" (Interview, April 2013). These events made communities aware of the limitations the state and how it would respond to territorial demands.

Most often, communities generated this pressure on formal procedures by developing connections with a range of local politicians and bureaucrats. As noted by the bureaucrat who provided me the documents discussed in this chapter, an outside push was necessary to continue moving the community's claim forward. This came from a variety of relationships with the bureaucrats themselves, their superiors, and politicians related to the process. These relationships form for a variety of reasons; one community leader described a close relationship the community fostered with the assistant to the director of the subnational CONADI office "because of the protests about the airport. We didn't need many people—ten was sufficient" (Interview, April 2013). These connections served to give the community additional information about how to complete the requirements on the necessary documents and also to elicit promises that CONADI would continue to complete their requirements. Reflecting on one meeting with the director of CONADI, one leader described, "Then the director said that when we had a meeting, he would give the first applicability to [our community]. So, the director gave the priority to our community" (Interview, May 2013).

If community members allied with a particular political party, they often relied on those politicians' connections to make phone calls to CONADI on their community's behalf. Interestingly, though, community leaders brought up these connections in reference to generating technical knowledge about completing portions of the stages listed on the required documents, not about leverage to move a community's folder from one stage to the next. As one member described of Andres Matta and Ana Llao, two Mapuche representatives on the National Council to CONADI, "We have a good relationship with them. Yes, they help the process. They also search and recommend where there is terrain (*terreno*). They know which communities have the right to buy and help motivate those communities" (Interview, May 2013). While this information is valuable assistance to help communities complete their requirements, it has much less influence than communities who were able to leverage associations with politicians to push CONADI on their requirements.

Other communities recognized the importance of political connections but struggled to develop these connections as they approached higher-level politicians that heard multiple, similar requests about territorial demands in the region. One leader explained, "We have talked with [the politicians], but they, particularly the *intendente*, don't leave the record straight. They delay and demand so much" (Interview, April 2013). References to politicians making promises for political benefit were common. Another expressed, "All the politicians pass through here, but they just pass through. We haven't connected ourselves to them. Their purpose is to confuse the people" (Interview, April 2013). Another noted that these connections are fleeting, reflecting on communities that had worked out some sort of agreement to advance through the policy process, but a change in government administrations undid that work and progress.

One leader stood out for his ability to navigate the process. Two years after becoming community president, CONADI approved the community's claim, allowing the community to start searching for a plot of land to buy. He outlined his approach by sharing:

> I . . . quickly began to meet workers at CONADI so they knew who I was and how I wanted to work with them. They opened their doors and wanted to talk with me. In that way I got to know the people, the authorities. After, I laid out the needs of our community, and occasionally brought up the issue of the land recovery. So, I explained that I was new in the leadership position but the community had waited six years. Why haven't they given us a solution? In that way, I got to know the civil servants, who told me to talk to a particular person, who directed me to another. Now, when I go to the office and they see me, "Hola Don Manuel!" That's how it went. . . . I don't know if that was why [the process moved fast] . . . I don't understand much about why . . . The documents were sleeping [in the CONADI office] in the trunk. I went to wake them up. Well, and a little of persistence because I didn't leave them alone.
>
> First, I asked Consejo Maquehue. The leaders have been on this path for more time and they explained how things work. They asked me: "Why don't you locate such and such person in CONADI or the municipality?" Because politically, things work like that. The mayor is of the same party of the subdirector of CONADI so I went to a public employee. She is also Mapuche and I expressed the anxieties, the necessities, of our community. Very kindly, she recommended me to another civil servant. . . . We invited the mayor to the community. . . . We asked for a hearing with the mayor. "Ask for a meeting with the national director of CONADI," he told me. "You talk to him but I'll speak to him as well." See? Politics.
>
> We promised to support the mayor in his new campaign with a big *but*. I said, "If you agree that you will take out projects for us in the future, we will agree for you to be mayor again." "I agree," he said. "You have to sign," we said. And he won. We asked him, "Did you notice our support?" Now, when

we arrive they attend to us well because we have power. That is how we advanced. Politics. (Interview, May 2013)

While other community leaders struggled to find both the support to complete their application requirements and the political leverage to keep CONADI advancing on their requirements, this leader merged both.

Some communities utilized direct action to advance their land claim. In PLC, most mobilization is targeted and local, in the form of land occupations, roadblocks, and, occasionally, occupation of the regional airport. Several leaders explained that mobilization forced local politicians to hear and respond to their demands. One leader illuminated, "We occupied the highway, the airport, and then they listened. . . . We occupied CONADI and then they had to attend to us. One person in CONADI helps us because of the mobilization and the airport" (Interview, April 2013). This community received the right to buy land; of the eight communities included here, two advanced their demands by engaging in this small-scale, targeted direct action. Other communities were quick to avoid the visibility that often came with mobilization. One leader described: "We don't want [a land takeover] because we are passive. We want things to be passively resolved with the authorities. We don't want to show up fighting on TV. Often, everyone pays for what one person does. Because of that, we are slow because we are passive. It is not useful for us to make . . . that is not our reality" (Interview, May 2013). In most instances, these strategies operate at very local levels.

When communities are facing a powerful stakeholder, however, they indicated that local politicians and bureaucrats are extremely hesitant to act on a claim that confronts that stakeholder. In these instances, communities must work to attract the attention of higher-level political elites who can intervene in institutional procedures to diffuse the tension. One community leader described his community's strategy of working through a stalled policy process:

Our community developed a formula, a strategy, to get the government to return our lands to us. We occupied the estate, which accelerated the process—some communities have waited ten years. We arrived to a working negotiating table with the government to deal with the issue of applicability [the first stage of the policy process], the bureaucratic issues. It was the only way the government could buy land for us from the gringos. We continued negotiating with the government while the community continued mobilizing. The government called us to La Moneda [seat of the executive in Santiago] and said they wanted an agreement that would stop the mobilizations by finalizing the land purchase. We talked, and the government accepted the conditions we presented. They started a series of processes, bureaucratic formalities . . . to make the agreement legally acceptable. They bought three estates (Interview, December 3013).

For this community, local actions were insufficient for CONADI to respond to their land demand. Remarkably, their petition was only addressed when the community escalated their mobilization to the point that it reached powerful political elites, who intervened in the local, bureaucratic procedures to resolve the demand and deescalate the pressure generated by the community's mobilization. Perhaps most notably, the community drew on these strategies throughout the policy process. While stage 1 is the responsibility of the community to document and present to the government the demand, the community engaged with the government to work through even these bureaucratic requirements of the policy process. Certainly, this community's experience is exceptional for the levels of government it was able move the demand through; but the case simultaneously reveals the necessity of proving their insistence throughout the policy process.

As is hopefully evident throughout this discussion, communities face numerous, overwhelming challenges to prove the seriousness of their territorial claim, despite their awareness of the necessity of doing so. One constant frustration among community presidents were the ways in which CONADI worked against their efforts to prove both their applicability and insistence. Like other conversations, these comments often flowed into abstractions with comments like, "CONADI adds many difficulties." One leader complained that CONADI was "prejudiced because we [his community] are very big" (Interview, May 2013). Another criticized that CONADI lost the folder documenting their claim twice. Many communities noted that CONADI discourages working with a local organization or lawyer in helping with the presentation of their territorial demand, commenting that CONADI predicts that external assistance will ultimately raise the price of the land the community is requesting. Another leader remarked that their community divided into two in order for CONADI to respond to part of the community's demand, stating: "When CONADI came [to the community headquarters], we were not on their list of prioritized communities. Priority is when the community already has the money to buy. But the money arrived, opinions changed . . . Now, the community is divided. There are neighbors who don't greet another. And it's understandable because they say, '*Puta*, why him and not me?'" (Interview, April 2013). While the bureaucrat who provided the documents in this chapter suggested that

CONADI was passively slowing down the policy process because of workload and resource constraints, these comments from community leaders suggest that CONADI is more actively working to undermine the successful resolution of territorial demands through Article 20B.

EXTRAPOLATING

To what extent are the experiences of communities in PLC similar to those of communities in other regions? And how do these experiences relate with other communities involved in some of the most public presentations of territorial claims? This section recounts the experiences of two communities in PLC that have very publicly engaged with the Chilean state in the presentation of their territorial claims, as reported by local newspapers.

The territorial demands of the Juan Catrilaf II community are among the most publicized. The community recovered nearly five hundred hectares of ancestral land in 2009 after one of the most emblematic processes of negotiations with the Chilean state. The plot of land was owned by the prominent Luchsinger family, known for calling for a *mano duro* (hard line on crime) response to Mapuche mobilization. Jorge Luchsinger argues: "These [land takeovers, protests, mobilization] are the exact same as what happened between 1970 and 1973! It could be that military authorities will not act like they did in 1973, but we are going to face them because there is no other solution. If the authorities do not fulfill their duty, if there is no rule of law, if there is no protection of public or private property . . . this has to end badly" (qtd. in Correa and Mella Seguel 2010). The disputed plot of land was one of the most historically conflictive in the region; the Ayjarewe Xuf-Xuf coordinating organization first occupied the plot of land in 1999, there were several arson attacks in 2000, and the plot was placed under police surveillance in 2005. Ayjarewe Xuf-Xuf presented a formal petition on behalf of thirteen neighboring communities in 2001, and, in 2005, CONADI declared the community met the policy requirements. As mobilization continued, Matías Catrileo was shot in the back by police officers during a land occupation in January 2008. Afterward, Minister Viera-Gallo traveled to the Araucanía region, announcing the purchase of 458 hectares for approximately US$4.3 million on October 8, 2009, the highest price per hectare CONADI ever paid in the region (Observatorio Social de America Latina 2009).

As expected, there was strong opposition from agricultural interests to the Chilean government's appeasement of the community's demands. Gastón Caminondo, president of the Agricultural Development

Society of Temuco (Sociedad de Fomento Agrícola de Temuco, Sofo), questioned Minister Viera-Gallo's decision, stating: "If we are talking about terrorism, this sends the wrong signal. What has to be done, and what the government has always said, is that anyone involved in terrorism or violence will have no chance of accessing land or benefits."[2] Andrés Molina, president of CorpAraucanía, an organization representing the main business associations and promoting entrepreneurship and productive development with Mapuche associations, argued, "You cannot reward violent communities under any situation."[3] While these economic interests usually limit the ability of certain communities to acquire land, the communities' ability to escalate their demand subverted these interests.

Certainly not all communities are able to attract the attention of elites of this level. Many of these communities report similar patterns of engagement with the state and state officials. The Juan Quintremil community claims territory held by the Masisa Forestry Company (prior to 2007, Millalemu Forestry Company and later Terranova SA, owned by the prominent Swiss businessman and philanthropist Stephan Schmidheiny). In 1999 the Masisa Forestry Company reached a "peace agreement" with the community in hopes of preempting conflict. The community agreed to allow the company to develop and extract pine and eucalyptus, in exchange for having permission and access to a *rehue* (ceremonial site) on company land, until CONADI finalized the land purchase from the company.[4] In August 2007 the Masisa Forestry Company deviated drastically from this agreement, asking the police to block community members from entering the land, destroy the *rehue*, and replace it with a police checkpoint. Aucan Huilcaman, one of the most prominent Mapuche activists, denounced the company's shift before the Office of the United Nations High Commissioner for Human Rights:

> We were surprised when *Masisa*, as other forestry companies have done, requested police protection last November to protect land that was on loan, provoking the community's reaction. The Chilean government mobilized 200 police, militarizing the conflict . . . [the company's decision] changed the course of this relationship, reopening the clashes and a continuing conflict. We think it has to do with the national interests . . . because adjacent to the forestry company are the properties of Hernán Büchi, another businessman of Swiss origin and former Pinochet minister, the property of Angel Delano, another former Pinochet minister, and the estate of Luisa Durán, the wife of former President Ricardo Lagos. We think that is where the

pressure comes from, because they are powerful families in the country. If *Masisa* transferred land to the communities, the land of these families could be part of the same recovery process later.[5]

Again in 2009, four community members were denied entrance to the Masisa Forestry Company for driving a truck without the correct paperwork. One community member stated, "The police have known us for two years. They know that we have the company's authorization . . . but, they denied us passage in such an intolerant way."[6] The community wrote a letter to the *intendente* Nora Barrientos and the company's management, but "we have no answer. Nobody wants to hear us. We denounce that the agreements, reached over 8 years of talks, have not been met and our land continues to be usurped."[7] Considering the interests of powerful political and economic elites at stake in the community's demand, the community has been unable to leverage a land purchase.

The state often responds to communities presenting demands confronting the interests of a powerful economic stakeholder with significant repression, regardless of if their land claim advanced or not. Victor Marileo, *lonko* (chief) of the Juan Quintremil community, describes:

> We were preparing to prevent them from replanting and that was when they accused me of stealing wood, but that was staged. The forestry company and the police are always looking for ways to imprison me and they have carried out operations against my life. It is satanic. They bribed another *peñi* to testify against me, but as *lonko*, who is a respected guide and man of confidence with a vision for the community, those allegations could not be true. I was arrested again on October 30, 2007, when a forestry company truck was passing through the dirt road where we were protesting. The police threw bombs and bullets. I moved towards the police to mediate, but they ran over me with their two cars and shouted "You deserve to die. Indians like you should be killed.". . . They tortured me in the police station to disorient me, leaving me with head injuries and cuts on the face. Then they said, "We'll have to kill a Mapuche," and, shortly after, January 3, 2008, they killed Matías Catrileo.

> I have been threatened and beaten by police. They tortured me in the second police station in Temuco, handcuffed me and ignored my status as *lonko*. They twisted me by the arm, the highest-ranking office Cristian Llévenes ordered a policeman to put a loop around my neck, so that my arms fell. They beat me with a stick and broke three ribs. . . . I want to make clear that the community where I live is militarized. I'm condemned to an injunction,

I am banned from entering the land we claim on the *Roble Huacho* estate of the Masisa forestry company, and I cannot leave the country. I'm always controlled by police, they are installed 100 meters from my house. There is a tear gas tank, police presence, and they film everything I do. From the perspective of the forestry company, I am a threat. But they are the ones who take resources of my family and leave a desert in the community.[8]

Other communities faced very similar repression. After the government agreed to purchase land for the Juan Catrilaf II community, special police forces (Fuerzas Especiales de Carabineros de la Tercera Comisaría de Padre Las Casas) violently raided the community. Twenty were injured and six were detained under the antiterrorism law for involvement with a July 28 attack on a bus (Observatorio Social de America Latina 2009). One community member described being shot in the leg three times at close range, operated on under police presence, handed over to the correctional system, and released without any charges.[9] Several other community members remained in preventative detention—one, Sergio Catrilaf, relates: "They set up me up. Special Forces came to my house, pulled me out, threw me to the ground and left me face down while others entered the house. According to them, they found weapons including thick calibrated bullets with high destructive power, fuses, cartridges, shotguns, and high-tech equipment such as GPS."[10]

As evidenced, community leaders perceive nuanced and often violent ways in which informal forms of governance interact with or usurp formal governance. In addition to the limited scope and purview of Chile's Indigenous land policy and the onerous requirements of communities, as discussed, the Chilean government is hesitant to implement the policy in ways that conflict with the interests of powerful economic stakeholders in the region, working to preserve the strength of established markets in the region. This interaction of formal and informal governance pushes communities to operate over and above institutions through local connections and mobilization. In response, the state governs with combinations of patronage, appeasement, and repression.

CONCLUSIONS

The patterns of engagement documented in this chapter point to the ways the Chilean government strategically engages with Mapuche communities through Article 20B of Indigenous Law 19.523. The experiences of the eight Mapuche communities discussed reiterate how post-Pinochet administrations worked to demobilize and disarticulate Mapuche mobilization through, around, and behind the façade of bureaucratic policies.

Not only do communities face significant challenges to understand and work through the stages of the policy process, but they must prove their insistence to CONADI, while CONADI bureaucrats slow down the policy process knowing the limitations of their workload and resources. The result is a complicated contradiction; while some communities can present their territorial demands to the Chilean government, the written and unwritten requirements of the policy process pose significant and often repressive hurdles to completing each stage, sometimes to the point of fully stalling their claim.

Perhaps unsurprisingly, these patterns of engagement extend far beyond the experiences shared by these eight community leaders in PLC. While there is limited systematic documentation of Mapuche communities' territorial claims through Article 20B beyond what is documented here and in the memories of those working in or through CONADI, the experience of the Nicolás Ailío Mapuche community near the coast in the IX region is documented in Florencia Mallon's 2005 book, *Courage Tastes of Blood*. In 1997 the community received a subsidy through Article 20A to purchase land. While the technical procedures of Article 20A are different from those of Article 20B, leaders of Nicolás Ailío faced the same tension over how strategically and instrumentally the community should engage with CONADI bureaucrats and politicians. Choosing to enter into these processes, the community was left with a series of insufficient policy responses. First, the community found out they had purchased 37.5 hectares less than they thought they did. As Mallon (2005, 209–10) described, "The leadership blamed CONADI for its poor technical assistance; some of CONADI's officials, they said, are wolves in sheep's clothing who care only about their salaries . . . In a random sample of twenty such properties (CONADI purchased), eighteen were found to have measurement errors." Second, community leaders clearly articulated the gap between their demands and CONADI's response. In a grant application to develop the new plot of land, the community summarized the gap between their needs and the government's policy responses: "Even though communities like Nicolás Ailío have the ability to make proposals that can be turned into programs for sustainable development, they have no one at the national level to hear or support these ideas and programs, and on the contrary, the public agricultural extension agencies already work from a 'Green Revolution' perspective, offering the communities a previously formulated package that includes technology and credit and cannot be modified by the peasants who receive it" (qtd. in Mallon 2005, 207). Ultimately, Mallon (2005, 227) concludes, "In order to survive, [community members] have to play by the rules the government sets. But the state attempts to dilute all processes of mobilization and confrontation while creating expectations it can at best only partially fulfill." This rhetoric is remarkably like that articulated to me by a leader in Padre Las Casas, who concluded, "Our struggle is legitimized," citing the existence of bureaucratic resources and bureaucrats tasked with responding to resolve territorial demands as evidence of the state-recognized legitimacy of Mapuche territorial demands (Interview, April 2013). But that glimmer of recognition served a broader policy goal, which the leader acutely recognized: "[Our struggle] is stretching, stretching to such a point . . . It is policy for the Mapuche to tire of making demands of CONADI" (Interview, May 2013).

CHAPTER 4

QUANTIFYING MOBILIZATION AND LAND PURCHASES

They realized that the land policy was a political tool to resolve conflicts with the Mapuche community. They realized its potential and radically changed its management, buying land to *apagar incendios* (put out fires). . . . the state is not really buying is not really land, but a solution to a conflict.

—Mapuche activist and academic (Interview, July 2013)

Previous chapters demonstrate how successive administrations, officials, and communities work to influence how particular land demands are processed through Article 20B of Indigenous Law 19.253. What are the outcomes of this contestation? Whose efforts are successful in shaping policy implementation? How consistently are certain actors able to influence or direct policy implementation?

To most abstractly generalize the outcomes of contestation over the implementation of Chile's Indigenous land policy, this chapter distances the conversation from the efforts of specific communities, bureaucrats, and politicians. Instead, this chapter presents a quantitative analysis documenting broad patterns of policy implementation, using an original data set of land purchased through Article 20B for 266 Mapuche communities between 1994 and 2013. Four concerning trends emerge, highlighting the ongoing effectiveness of the strategies of different actors. Community mobilization, the extent to which each community was associated with narratives of Mapuche demands as radical and violent, and the presence of forestry companies all influence the likelihood of a community receiving a land purchase; each of these effects is mediated by degrees of policy institutionalization.

This analysis reiterates that much of how the Chilean government carries out Indigenous land policy serves to extend expected narratives

TABLE 4.1. MODEL ESTIMATIONS OF LIKELIHOOD OF A LAND PURCHASE BY CONADI

VARIABLES	FIRST PURCHASE	SUBSEQUENT PURCHASES
Perception of community's association with radical, violent Mapuche mobilization	0.00987** (0.00492) hr: 1.01	-0.000681 (0.00781) hr: 0.999
Number prior instances of mobilization by community	-0.266*** (0.0370) hr: 0.766	0.113 (0.0870) hr: 1.119
Number of Mapuche families involved in the land purchase	0.0315*** (0.00269) hr: 1.032	0.0575*** (0.0113) hr: 1.059
Percent rural in district	0.0367 (0.0323) hr: 1.037	1.655*** (0.0264) hr: 5.232
Percent Mapuche in district	-0.126*** (0.0420) hr: 0.882	-2.782*** (0.0269) hr: 0.062
Percent vote for the Right in district	-0.0491*** (0.00849) hr: 0.952	-0.0102 (0.0137) hr: 0.990
Percent of forestry land in district	0.478** (0.200) hr: 1.613	13.81*** (0.0525) hr: 993541.5
Observations	2,972	2,348
Robust standard errors in parentheses *** p <0.01, ** p <0.05, * p <0.1		

of consistent neoliberal governance through policy. Indeed, many land purchases serve to demobilize and disarticulate Mapuche mobilization by protecting investments and economic stability in the region. Yet the Chilean government also uses the policy to mediate both contradictory and complementary political interests. Working to protect stability in the region demands exceptions to policy regulations and creates space for actors to influence implementation, as is evidenced by the ongoing impact of local political interests on policy outcomes. This quantitative analysis reveals that both efforts to extend the scope and strength of the neoliberal project influence policy implementation.

DATA COLLECTION AND ANALYSIS

To explain the outcomes of contestation over the land purchase policy process, I developed an original data set on the 266 Mapuche communities who received land from CONADI between 1994 and 2013. This includes original data on the community's history of mobilization and national perceptions of if the community is associated with radical, violent Mapuche mobilization; I discuss the complications of collecting this data in the sections that follow. This original data was integrated with existing data on the presence of forestry companies, and institutional procedures, in addition to political and economic differences between districts. These variables are summarized in table A.1, and discussed in more detail in the appendix.

Survival analysis, which analyzes the predicted time until an event, was used to statistically evaluate the impact of these variables on the likelihood that a Mapuche community received a land purchase, data available from CONADI's published records on what land was purchased for which Mapuche communities in which years. Table 4.1 reports the results of this model. A positive coefficient indicates the variable increases the likelihood that CONADI purchases land on behalf of a Mapuche community. The interpretations that follow in the text are based on hazard ratios (hr), which report the percentage increase (above 1.00) or decrease (below 1.00) in the likelihood of a land purchase caused by a one unit shift in one variable, all other variables held constant. A more detailed description of the model specification and estimation are available in the appendix. To ease interpretation and to highlight broader patterns of significance, I discuss the results and significance of the results table 4.1 thematically in the sections that follow.

HOW DO CONADI PROCEDURES INFLUENCE LAND PURCHASES?

First, this analysis reveals the difference between first and subsequent purchases for a particular Mapuche community. Some Mapuche communities receive multiple land purchases from the Chilean government, particularly when the government is unable to purchase a contiguous plot of land, or is negotiating multiple land purchases from different land holders. Different dynamics drive the likelihood of first and subsequent purchases, as is shown in the shifting effects in table 4.1, highlighting shifting government preferences on how to most strategically utilize policy implementation. First land purchases appear to be quick responses to newer mobilization, and to communities associated with more radical expressions of Mapuche demands, while subsequent land purchases seem to work towards long-term governance solutions. This suggests that the government expects contentious action to be most significantly demobilized by the first purchase; subsequent purchases have a much smaller impact, shifting the government's focus to prioritizing regional political and economic interests.

This shift in decision-making is also evident when comparing the effect of regional variation. The stronger the support for the Right in a region and the greater the Mapuche population in the district, the less likely the government is to make a first purchase for a community. Successive purchases are more likely in rural districts with fewer Mapuche individuals and more forestry companies. Considering the greater influence of communities, the presence of forestry land, and the influence of district-level variables, the government appears to be more strategic in its considerations of which land and communities are prioritized for first purchases. For all purchases that follow, however, mobilization has a much less substantive impact on the government's response compared to the presence of extractive industries and other regional variables.

HOW DO NATIONAL PERCEPTIONS OF MAPUCHE MOBILIZATION IMPACT LAND PURCHASES?

As is highlighted throughout this book and in broader conversations, Mapuche communities and organizations frequently turn to extra-institutional strategies, frustrated by the lack of institutional responsiveness. Mella Seguel (2007, 136–36) concluded, "Mapuche communities and organizations see mobilization and direct land takeovers as the way to force the State to expand their land." Interviews with politicians and bureaucrats discussed in previous chapters highlighted how mobilization pushes politicians to change specific policy regulations (chapter 1) and negotiate land for peace (chapter 2). Interviews with leaders of Mapuche communities reiterated that communities strategically mobilize to move their land claim forward (chapter 3). Yet each of these conversations reiterated that this mobilization often occurs at very local levels and in specific instances; to what extent do these trends more broadly characterize the full history of CONADI's land purchases?

To answer this question, I first distinguished between known instances of Mapuche mobilization and perceptions of Mapuche mobilization. Most national conversations in Chile about Mapuche protest focus on radical protest; headlines warn: "Alert in Arauco, Fearing Wave of Mapuche Violence," "The Mapuche Intifada: The Indigenous Uprising Worsens," "Mapuches Threaten," and "Indigenous Communities on the War Path" (Richards 2010, 75). Part of the movement is certainly willing and able to use more radical strategies, which Pairican Padilla (2014, 23) references as the *via rupturista a la autodeterminación* (disruptive path toward self-determination), or the *movimiento Mapuche de Resistencia* (Mapuche resistance movement). And many of these actions are linked with the evolution of how the Chilean government implements Article 20B.

Several recent events highlight the need to problematize if and how perceptions of radical mobilization can be accurately attributed to particular Mapuche individuals, communities, and/or organizations. In prominent court cases, the state was unable to substantiate its charges against Mapuche activists, raising significant doubts about culpability. Perhaps most problematically, in 2014 a Mapuche individual revealed that he had acted as an undercover agent since 2009. Raul Castro Antipan was active in the Mapuche movement and became close with CAM in 2007 but was recruited as a secret informant for the Dirección de Inteligencia Policial de Carabineros (DIPOLCAR, Police Intelligence Service) in exchange for leniency on charges of the possession of marijuana and the misappropriation of war material related to his military service. Tasked with infiltrating and disarticulating Mapuche activist groups, Castro later admitted to carrying out four arson attacks with other Mapuche activists, including the 2009 TurBus and Peaje Quino cases (see chapter 2 for further discussion). Castro also revealed that he informed DIPOLCAR of activists' plans for the TurBus attack the day before. His anonymous testimony was used in more than thirty trials of Mapuche activists, resulting in the incarceration of fourteen since 2009, raising concerns about the validity of the testimony and convictions. This testimony was released during the trial of two Mapuche activists accused of involvement with the 2009 attacks, and, despite being minors at the time of the attacks, were being detained under Chile's controversial antiterrorism legislation.[1] Courts threw out the cases based on Castro's testimony, including charges against Rodrigo Melinao, who was found shot dead in August 2013. His younger brother sought diplomatic protection in Venezuela, reporting that his life was repeatedly threatened by paramilitaries and police.[2] Castro's testimony documented the state's efforts to infiltrate and provoke conflict from within Mapuche communities and organizations, corroborating allegations of police infiltration by leaders from several emblematic Mapuche communities, including Victor Quiepul, *lonko* of the Temucuicui community and uncle of one of the activists.[3] Pedro Cayuqueo, a prominent Mapuche journalist, concluded, "We have a clear violation of due process, a type of Olympic gymnastics by the prosecutors to twist the law and use it to secure convictions against leaders who, in many cases, have no responsibility in these acts of violence."[4] These and similar stories highlight the complications of attributing certain events to certain individuals, particularly when drawing on national news coverage, and the importance of understanding the construction of these narratives.

To capture which Mapuche communities are perceived to be associated with this narrative about Mapuche mobilization as violent and radical, I recorded the number of times *El Mercurio* reported on each of the 266 communities that received land through Article 20B between 1994 and 2013. *El Mercurio* is Chile's largest and oldest national newspaper, with a reputation of having well-established ties to the Right (Moulian 2002; Monkeberg 2009; Navia and Osorio 2015; Navia, Osorio, and Valenzuela 2013). The historian Fernando Pairican Padilla (2014, 16, 28) summarized how *El Mercurio*'s reporting constructs the Mapuche movement as violent; noting: "By drawing the subaltern as an aggressive oddball who is creating an unexplained and unilateral conflict, public opinion—and often the colonized subject themselves—has the repulsive image that the Mapuche movement is the mad, primitive, criminal, and terrorist enemy of the rule of law, social peace, civilization, and progress. . . . [*El Mercurio*'s reporting is] predominantly political and in opposition to the fundamental rights of the Mapuche. The newspaper has been important in reconstructing the historical processes that it narrates, sometimes overemphasizing acts of violence. For years, *El Mercurio* has essentially presented a vision of violent, non-rational subjects, inherited from the 19th century."

Effectively, this coding takes advantage of documented biases in *El Mercurio*'s reporting. Because *El Mercurio* is more likely to report exclusively more radical and violent instances of mobilization and conflict, I use their reports to capture which communities are associated with this portrayal and these perceptions. For example, *El Mercurio*'s reporting on the Ancapi Nancucheo community between 1994 and 2013 is documented below. The thirteen reports on the community, over twenty years, highlights a near exclusivity of stories about violent mobilization and conflict by Mapuche communities or individuals.

EL MERCURIO REPORTING ON ANCAPI NANCUCHEO COMMUNITY
(THIRTEEN TIMES OVER TWENTY YEARS)

1. Violent house raids concern to the residents of Ercilla.

   Violentos asaltos a viviendas preocupan a los vecinos de Ercilla, September 2011.

2. Investigations into the death of a young Mapuche found with a gunshot wound in Ercilla.

   Investigan la muerte de un joven mapuche hallado con herida de bala en Ercilla, October 2011.

3. Investigations into responsibility for the fire to a farm of René Urban's daughter in Ercilla.

   Investigan intencionalidad en el incendio a un fundo de la hija de René Urban en Ercilla, January 2013.

4. Attack on the house of district PPD president in Ercilla.

   Atacaron a balazos la casa del presidente comunal del PPD en Ercilla, April 2012.

5. Attack on the house of district PPD president in Ercilla.
   Atacan a balazos vivienda de presidente comunal del PPD en Ercilla, April 2012.
6. Appeal ruling declared a fugitive Mapuche free.
   Apelarán fallo que dejó libre a mapuche prófugo, August 2008.
7. Quintana and Tohá dialogue with the Mapuche community of Ercilla
   Quintana y Tohá dialogan con comunidad mapuche de Ercilla, April 2011.
8. Government buys land from attacked farmers attacked to stop violence
   Gobierno compra tierras vecinas a las de agricultores atacados para detener violencia, March 2009.
9. Mapuche linked to attack arrested.
   Detienen a mapuche vinculado a atentado, August 2008.
10. CONADI paid up to $15 million per hectare in Araucanía
    Hasta $15 millones por hectárea ha pagado la Conadi en la Araucanía, August 2009.
11. Attack on former Mapuche activist who left violent resistance to work with a forestry company.
    Atentan contra ex activista mapuche por dejar la vía violenta y trabajar con empresa forestal, August 2008.
12. Operation in Mapuche community leaves at least two policemen wounded.
    Operativo en comunidad mapuche deja al menos dos carabineros heridos, August 2008.
13. Mapuches denounce desecration of Rehue.
    Mapuches denuncian profanación de Rehue, August 2000.

Considering this focus, *El Mercurio* does not report on the vast majority of Mapuche communities. Between 1994 and 2013, 86 percent of the 266 communities that received land through Article 20B did not appear in *El Mercurio* reports. Table 4.2 lists the number of times each of the 266 communities are mentioned in *El Mercurio* as well as the names of the communities mentioned more than ten times. Effectively, these reporting trends highlight that the national narrative about the security concerns posed by radical Mapuche mobilization is only associated with a small number of particular communities. The names and stories of most Mapuche communities drop out of the national narrative.

Statistical analysis, summarized in table 4.1, indicates that the perceived intensity of a community's mobilization has a small, statistically significant impact on the first plot of land purchased through Article 20B procedures overseen by CONADI. For each additional mention of a community in *El Mercurio*, the likelihood of a first land purchase increases by 1 percent; however, these perceptions do not have a statistically significant impact on subsequent land purchases. To a very limited

TABLE 4.2. PERCEPTIONS OF MAPUCHE COMMUNITIES, AS CAPTURED BY *EL MERCURIO* REPORTING

NUMBER OF MENTIONS IN *EL MERCURIO*	NUMBER OF COMMUNITIES	COMMUNITY NAME
0	228 (85.7 percent)	—
1	3	—
2	2	—
3	6	—
4	7	—
5	3	—
7	3	—
8	2	—
10	4	Antonio Nirripil, Huanaco Millao Chacaico, Huanaco Millao y Otros, Juana Millahual
13	3	Pancho Curamil, Caunicu, Ancapi Nancucheo
23	1	Juan Catrilaf II
26	1	Didaico
32	1	Tricauco
39	1	Juan Collio
105	1	Ignacio Queipul

degree, the Chilean government prioritized land purchases for emblematic communities who are often sensationalized in national press as posing a threat to security, stability, and governability of the region. Nevertheless, this is the smallest substantive effect, compared to the other variables, and only applies to a first purchase for a community.

HOW DOES MAPUCHE MOBILIZATION IMPACT LAND PURCHASES?

Importantly, many Mapuche individuals, communities, and organizations reject radical mobilization strategies, but still mobilize to assert demands. Unless these actions raise concerns about security or stability, most of these actions are unlikely to appear in national news but are still reported in a number of websites and blogs that publicize Mapuche communities' demands and actions. Relying on the new stories available at http://paismapuche.org/ (site discontinued January 2019) and Mapu Express.org, I documented which of the 266 communities engaged in mobilization along with the corresponding years it occurred. As expected, this broader measure captures many more instances of mobilization; 67 out of 266 (25 percent) communities that received land through CONADI between 1994 and 2013 mobilized at least once between 1994

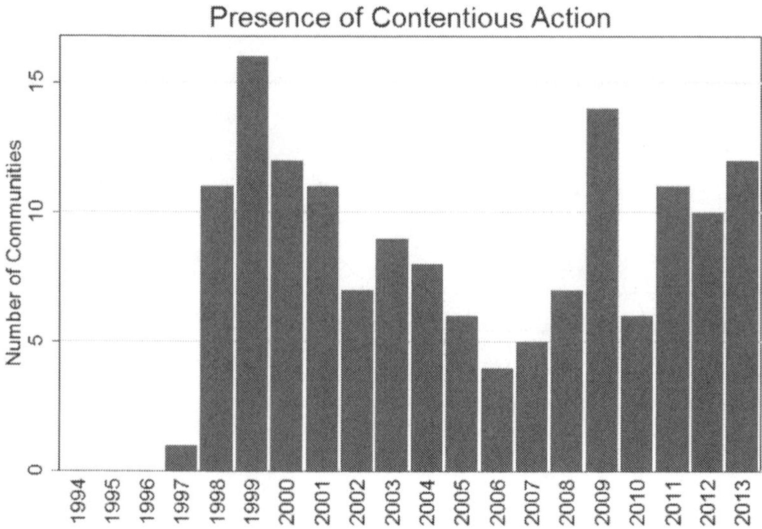

Figure 4.1. Mobilization by Mapuche communities, 1994–2013, based on El Mercurio reporting.

and 2013, and seven communities had documented evidence of contentious action in five or more of the twenty years.

As evidenced, there are significant differences between perceptions of Mapuche mobilization in local sources reports and those reported in national sources. While *El Mercurio* only reported on thirty-eight communities between 1994 and 2013, the broader coding of mobilization recorded instances of mobilization in sixty-seven communities. In fact, there is only weak correlation (0.30) between the number of times a Mapuche community is mentioned in *El Mercurio* and the broader measure of the mobilization, as captured in local reports. For example, table 4.4 contrasts local reports of mobilization with national reporting on the Ancapi Nancucheo community from 1994 to 2013, in addition to the years in which the community received a land purchase from CONADI.

Statistical analysis highlights that a community's current and past mobilization has a much greater impact than perceptions of mobilization on the likelihood a community receives their first land purchases. Specifically, communities with a longer history of mobilization are less likely to receive a land purchase from CONADI; each additional prior year of mobilization decreases the likelihood of a first purchase by 23.4 percent. This history of contentious action does not, however, have a significant impact on subsequent land purchases.

TABLE 4.3. MOBILIZATION IN MAPUCHE COMMUNITIES

COMMUNITY	NUMBER OF YEARS WITH EVIDENCE OF MOBILIZATION IN LOCAL SOURCES, 1994–2013	YEAR(S) OF LAND PURCHASES
Huanaco Millao y Otros	5	2003, 2006, 2012
Ignacio Queipul	5	1998, 2002
Antonio Paillacoi	5	2006, 2009
Juan Ahilla Varela	7	2002
Antonio Nirripil	16	1999, 2000, 2005, 2011
Didaico	16	2003, 2011, 2012
Juana Millahual	17	2013

TABLE 4.4. CODING OF INSTANCES OF MOBILIZATION FOR ANCAPI NANCUCHEO COMMUNITY

YEAR	DID CONADI PURCHASE LAND FOR THE COMMUNITY?	DID LOCAL SOURCES REPORT MOBILIZATION BY THE COMMUNITY?	NUMBER OF REPORTS BY *EL MERCURIO*?
1994	—	—	—
1995	—	—	—
1996	—	—	—
1997	X	—	—
1998	—	—	—
1999	—	—	—
2000	—	—	1
2001	—	—	—
2002	—	—	—
2003	—	—	—
2004	—	X	—
2005	—	—	—
2006	—	—	—
2007	—	X	—
2008	X	X	4
2009	X	—	2
2010	—	—	—
2011	X	X	3
2012			2
2013	X	X	1

The Ancapi Nancucheo community is located in the Araucanía region, Malleco province, Ercilla district. Sixty-six families received a total of 391 hectares, bought for a total of $1.8 million USD. The community was reported on by *El Mercurio* thirteen times between 1994 and 2013.

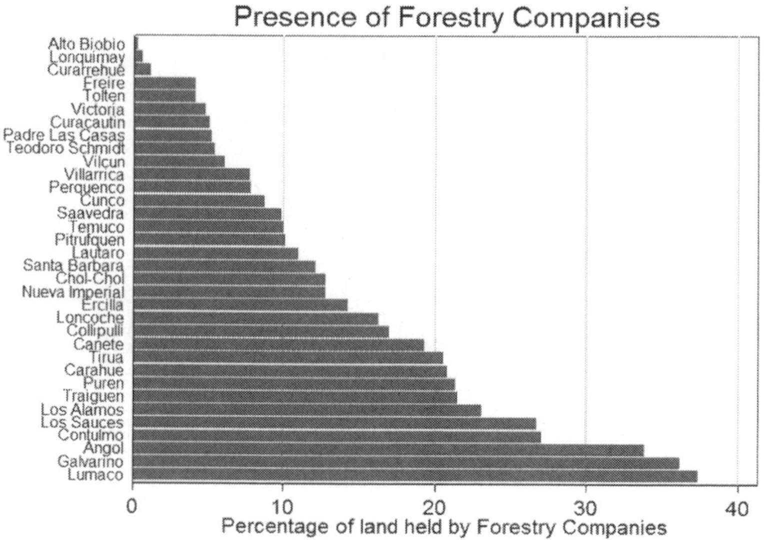

Figure 4.2. Presence of forestry companies, by district.

The difference between instances of mobilization and perceptions of mobilization reiterates that understanding national, security-focused narratives about Mapuche communities is necessary, but not sufficient, to understand patterns of policy implementation—local, nonviolent mobilization has a more substantial and statistically significant influence on policy implementation. Government officials are aware of and responding to broad range of locally publicized, nonviolent mobilization by Mapuche communities. Importantly, the Chilean government responds to mobilization differently, contingent on if the community has already received a land purchase; while mobilization impacts the likelihood of a first purchase, it has no effect on communities' subsequent purchases.

HOW DO FORESTRY COMPANIES IMPACT LAND PURCHASES?

Forestry companies have the most powerful influence on the likelihood a Mapuche community receives a land purchase through CONADI. As shown in figure 4.2, there is significant regional variation in the presence of forestry companies. While large-scale agriculture has been a key development strategy for the region since the nineteenth century, the Pinochet dictatorship shifted to focus on commercial forestry (Klubock 2014, 18–9). As discussed in chapter 2, Decree 701 (1974) facilitated the rapid expansion of forestry companies in the region, which, in conjunction with the privatization of the largest state-owned forestry companies, Celulosa Arauco and Celulosa Constitucion, in 1977 and 1979, structure the industry's current influence in the region. After the return to democracy, an influx of international investment resulted in the further expansion of agricultural, mining, forestry, and fishing industries, aided by ongoing subsidies for planting costs. These companies maintained expansion during the 1990s, buying land from small farmers and Indigenous communities (Meza 2009). By the middle of the 1990s, logging was the third largest export (after mining and agriculture), accounting for an estimated 10 percent of Chile's total export revenues, after exports of forest products tripled from 1989 to 1997 (Klubock 2014, 270). In the Araucanía region, as much as 87 percent of sown land is tree plantations.

This strategic expansion of the forestry industry concentrated land ownership in the region. Reyes and Nelson (2014, 4, 7) summarize: "Three large companies own 64% of plantations, 100% of pulp mills, 81% of paper and cardboard plants, 75% of wood-panel factories, 37% chip production, 26% of sawmills, and 36% of nurseries (UDEC 2009). . . . 67% of native forests and less than 10% of plantation forests are in hands of thousands of small and medium landowners (indigenous communities and farmers), while 64% of plantation forests and less than 4% of native forests are in hands of only three transnational corporations: ARAUCO, CMPC and MASISA." This concentration of wealth is accompanied with political power. Forestry companies are some of the largest landholders in southern Chile; the Angelini Group (ARAUCO) and the Matte Family (CMPC) were included in *Forbes*'s 2005 World's Richest People (Meza 2009). The percentage of landholders owning less than ten hectares of land increased from 47.9 percent in 1997 to 60.4 percent in 2007 (Torres et al. 2015, 116), and the presence of tree plantations correlates with increased incidences of poverty (Andersson et al. 2016).

This extractive model of development in the region is often at the root of contention between Indigenous communities and the state, and many development projects are the "flashpoints for the sharpest conflict" (Carruthers and Rodriguez 2009, 8). As CAM described: "The decision to carry out a struggle for territory and autonomy is because, of all our lands, private forestry companies have our wealth from poverty and oppression . . . We propose, first, Mapuche resistance to the capitalist system and oligarchy in our ancestral territory, seen in forestry investments, hydroelectric companies, tourism" (qtd. in Mella Seguel 2007, 85).

In ancestral Mapuche territory, forestry companies hold 1.5 million hectares, three times what is held by Mapuche communities. One company alone, Forestal Mininco, holds 350,000 hectares, the majority of which Mapuche communities claim as ancestral land (Aylwin Oyarzún

2000, 286). In the Arauco province, an estimated 60,000 hectares held by forestry companies are in conflict (286–87).

How does this economic and political power impact the implementation of Article 20B? Land purchases for Mapuche communities are significantly more likely in districts where forestry companies have a greater presence. For the first land purchase, each additional percentage of forestry land in a district increases the probability the government purchases land for a Mapuche community by 61 percent, exerting more influence over policy implementation than any other factor. While instances of or perceptions of Mapuche mobilization have no influence on subsequent purchases, the presence of forestry companies has an exponentially greater impact on the likelihood of subsequent purchases. The Chilean government strongly prioritizes land purchases in districts where forestry companies have a prominent presence, particularly when CONADI has already purchased land on behalf of a particular community.

These results highlight the somewhat counterintuitive conclusion that forestry companies are often in favor of land purchases by CONADI on behalf of a Mapuche community. For a company, CONADI land purchases can protect investments and profits, offering to appease communities and prevent potentially costly future mobilization by the same or neighboring community, and allowing the company to sell off less productive land. As the CAM activist Hector Llaitul (2014) summarizes of the strategy, "Usurper farmers or forestry companies, after having profited for years from Mapuche lands, are compensated with millions by the State so that they can continue to invest." Informal conversations during my fieldwork in southern Chile suggested that forestry companies are aware, or suspect, that significant portions of their land could be claimed by Mapuche communities. One employee of Mininco corroborates this argument when discussing how Mapuche territorial demands impact companies: "Did we commit a sin? No. Should we have cared about everything related to this? No, probably no. And when the indigenous communities claim their ancestral rights and things like that, the State declares that it is a problem between private entities. It is an assertion against the State. However, we are close to them [Indigenous] and we are the first to suffer the attacks" (qtd. in Meza 2009, 154). For forestry companies, demobilizing local conflict works to expand and preserve their investments and profitability for an export-driven market. Indeed, recent research finds that tree plantations are expanding, with more relative growth in districts where Mapuche individuals and communities hold less land, as companies avoided areas with "high levels of conflict or social complexity, as this is likely to increase the costs of firms' operations" (Andersson et al. 2016, 131).

HOW DO CONSTITUENCIES IMPACT LAND PURCHASES?

Finally, land purchases are influenced by the characteristics of affected constituencies. While research has only recently begun to explore subnational variation in Chilean politics, research suggests that local leaders, particularly in rural areas, maintain strong clientelistic relations with voters (Barozet 2003; Durston 2005a, 2005b; Espinoza 2006; Toro Maureira and Jaramillo-Brun 2014). For example, a 2012 survey found that in Araucanía, party affiliations are stronger (25 percent of people claim strong party affiliations in Araucanía, compared to 14 percent in Chile), protest participation is lower (4.3 percent Araucanía, 11.1 percent in Chile), confidence in local government is higher (60.8 percent Araucanía, 58.4 percent Chile), and interpersonal confidence is higher (88.7 percent Araucanía, 63 percent Chile) (Selligson et al. 2012). Similar assumptions are used to explain the ties between Mapuche individuals and politicians. Often, research and public opinion assumes that the Mapuche community is conservative, but research repeatedly finds that "the indigenous and poor peasantry, tend to be politically linked with those they believe can best solve their problems" (Toro Maureira and Jaramillo-Brun 2014, 12). Marimán (1990) argues that these links with conservative parties are not the result of political allegiances but rather a useful and tactical vote for political parties capable of delivering resources; Cayuqueo (2006) argues that this stems from a series of historic alliances between Mapuche organizations and conservative parties. This relationship may stem from cultural and political norms of, as Toro Maureira and Jaramillo-Brun (2014, 586) summarize of Marimán's argument, of "reciprocity towards those who help, and personal relationships that do not distinguish between political divides, but rather recognize authority and mutually beneficial relationships."

Research also finds that patterns of societal exclusion and discrimination extend outside of the formal political realm. The 2012 survey concluded that political culture of the region is strongly shaped by how ethnic and urban/rural divides interact. For example, 36 percent of people in Araucanía agree that people with dark skin are not good leaders, compared to 34 percent in Chile, the highest in Latin America (Americas Barometer 2013). Finally, there is skepticism over policy perceived to prioritize Mapuche individuals and communities. When surveying Chilean elites about discrimination against the Mapuche community, de Cea, Heredia, and Valdivieso (2016, 343) found:

> The interviewees have a fairly negative perception of this type of policy [positive discrimination], and this cuts across all the elite groups interviewed.

The arguments given against this type of positive discrimination measure are that they do not contribute to the construction of an integrated Chilean society and a single nation, and that in the end they exacerbate differences because those who do not receive the benefits consider them unjust. We immediately find universalist views like "we're all equally Chilean" and "we must all abide by the legal framework existing in Chile." This paradox cannot be ignored by those who, as party members or experts, wish to increase the respect for and advocate for indigenous peoples. In a society in which the public and a significant part of the elite perceive there to be a high level of discrimination, public debate is called for to address the most appropriate ways to recognize differences and step towards dialog between the different cultures sharing the same territory.

These demographic and political trends highlight the persistence of a clientelistic logic.

Quantitative analysis of the implementation of Article 20B confirm many of these trends. Purchases are more likely for larger Mapuche communities, with each additional family increasing the likelihood of a land purchase by 3 percent for the first purchase and 6 percent for subsequent purchases. Communities in rural districts are much more likely to receive subsequent purchases, while first purchases are less likely for communities in districts with more support for right-wing politicians. Communities in districts with a smaller Mapuche population, as a percentage of the district population, are less likely to receive both first and all subsequent purchases.

CONCLUSIONS

The quantitative analysis presented here shows that Mapuche communities, forestry companies, and broader political calculations influence policy implementation in nuanced and shifting ways. Chile's policy response to Mapuche territorial demands is dynamically adapted to both appease Mapuche communities, protect economic interests, and extend political interests, particularly after a community has received their first land purchases. These patterns highlight that the Chilean government is aware of and responding to local, nonviolent instances of contentious action as well as to regional economic and political interests; in southern Chile, those policy objectives center on stabilizing economic productivity in the region, reiterating that "land tenure regulation is contested at the level of policy *implementation*, that is, how regulation at different levels in society undoes or reworks state efforts to regulate land tenure in accordance with policy objectives" (van der Haar 2000, 285). The national-level perception of the intensity of contentious action in certain communities has little impact on policy implementation, in contrast to frequently made allegations that the government prioritizes particular emblematic Mapuche communities. While these patterns of policy implementation strongly highlight the protection of economic investments and regional stability, this comes at the expense of preserving transparent patterns of policy implementation.

CONCLUSIONS

The nation-state does not negotiate its project—it denies legitimacy and rights.

Time and again, under the most difficult and painful conditions, the community manages to transform and establish ownership over state discourse and practice.

In the process of preparing and discussing the ideas presented in *Negotiating Autonomy*, many have expressed a desire for the book to be many things it is not. Most often, scholars and activists want this book to tell the story of the limitations and risks of pursuing Indigenous rights through institutional strategies. Policymakers often want this book to serve as a tool documenting how a state should appropriately and efficiently respond to Indigenous territorial demands, highlighting outcomes and successes. Certainly, those stories of both mobilization and policy outcomes emerge within these pages, but the study interrogates the space in the middle. What and whose work happens within this context? And what is the significance of the work that happens at the negotiated nexus of Indigenous resistance and state domination? Under what conditions do particular strategies produce particular outcomes in particular contexts? Inevitably, these middle spaces offer consequential space for both resistance and domination.

Negotiating Autonomy: Mapuche Territorial Demands and Chilean Land Policy reveals how policy is a negotiated, contested, contradictory, and consequential middle space through which territorial demands are both made and unmade in neoliberal contexts. While Indigenous rights recognitions certainly offer the potential to construct a more inclusive, participatory democracy, the meaningful exercise of these rights depends on if and how those recognitions are implemented. Insufficient implementation is not merely the result of vague political indifference or limits in bureaucratic capacity but rather the result of local dynamics of contention operating within specific implementation procedures with degrees of institutionalization. Therefore, this book highlights the need to theorize how states govern Indigenous demands through policy; this concluding chapter summarizes what is learned from this focus and analyzes the significance of these conclusions for understanding Chilean politics and the politics of recognition in neoliberal contexts.

In southern Chile, focusing on policy reveals consequential negotiations over the shape of Indigenous territorial demands and neoliberal governance. Avoiding broader conversations about the significance of Mapuche demands for governance, territory, and autonomy, Chile's formal interpretation of the territorial turn is best interpreted as an intended effort to preserve and extend both the strength and scope of neoliberal governance in southern Chile. The Chilean government actively works to control the definition and expansiveness of Mapuche communities' territorial demands, processing them as if they were piecemeal demands for property that can be resolved with buyer-willing, seller-willing land transfers; in doing so, the policy works to make Mapuche territorial demands legible to the state's broader efforts to bring Mapuche communities into a market logic of governance, production, and recognition. Pulling discussions of territorial rights and autonomies into the government limits the potential for Indigenous communities to acquire territory from the state, undermining the potential for a more radical reconfiguration of the relationship between place and space. Yet these intended, ideal, and expected efforts by the Chilean government to extend neoliberal governance to Mapuche communities in southern Chile immediately start to unravel at the local level; indeed, attempts to study neoliberalism as a utopian project mandate exploring "actually existing neoliberalisms" (Ferguson and Gupta 2002), as specific policies and paperwork are processed by specific government officials. After the central government hesitantly created Article 20B of Indigenous Law 19.253, responsibility for the implementation of these rights recognitions of these rights shifted to the local level, situating policy implementation between national priorities for the region and local power dynamics. So, does CONADI preserve formal, bureaucratic regulations that extend the scope of neoliberalism by furthering a neoliberal interpretation of territorial demands as property, enforcing the neoliberal logic that individuals should pursue the resolution of their demands through policies and paperwork that required market resolutions? Or does CONADI quickly respond to Mapuche territorial demands and mobilization perceived to threaten the economic, political, and social interests and stability of the region?

As demonstrated throughout this book, the results of this contestation within the façade of bureaucratic policy implementation shifts across space and time, conditioned by the interests and actions of local and national actors, and the work of bureaucrats. Usually, the result reveals the strength of the Chilean government to pursue a neoliberal logic that both protects elite interests and funnels Mapuche demands into market mechanisms. But occasionally, these negotiations produce the uneven, contradictory governance in which communities receive land outside of bureaucratic policies and regulations. This stems from the potential schism between the government's interests in extending the scope of the neoliberal project, in the form of disciplining Mapuche demands into market-motivated policy regulations, from its interest in extending the strength of the neoliberal project, in the form of favoring the market interests of the elites and corporations who are self-actualized neoliberal subjects. The stories highlighted throughout this book reveal that when pressured on this potential schism, the Chilean government will sacrifice efforts to extend the scope of the neoliberal project to new subjects in order to protect elite interests. Four successive administrations (1994–2013) from across the political spectrum used Indigenous land policy to *apagar incendios* (put out fires), as is often described of the threat perceived to be posed by Mapuche mobilization, sacrificing policies intended to pull Mapuche demands into a neoliberal logic. Communities that attempt to subvert these processes face militarization and criminalization, and rhetoric that the Chilean government will not respond to these forms of engagement. Because the internationally recognized collective demands of the Mapuche community are perceived to threaten both governing efforts, Mapuche communities and individuals are able to occasionally pit these governing logics against each other, revealing moments in which neoliberal governance serves to extend state strength, and moments in which extending state strength overrules neoliberal governance. And because the government actions described throughout this book are relatively shielded from public view, there is limited documentation of these governance patterns that preserve and reinforce the perception of Chilean governance as centralized, technocratic, and neoliberal.

While living in Temuco, I frequently felt caught between contradictory assumptions about the reality of Chilean governance: the public or the hidden, and the expected or the unexpected. Both are true, and insufficient. I opened *Negotiating Autonomy* sharing a story about attending a planned but avoided march in Temuco in 2013. In some ways, the events of the day were public and expected: the government distributed resources through institutionalized policies and programs in public ceremonies in Mapuche communities. This explanation of transparent and technocratic policy implementation became the public account, neatly mapping onto expected narratives of Chilean governance. Yet that public version of the story hid the fuller, more accurate explanation of when, how, and why those events transpired. Only a few knew that those ceremonies were the result of the Chilean government's scramble to prevent Mapuche communities from traveling to the march, efforts that indeed undermined the size and power of the march. This work was never formally recorded, only existing in the memories of those directly involved and the networks they shared the information with. The façade of policy, and assumptions of how and why policy is implemented in Chile, upheld expected understandings of Chilean governance and obscured the hidden, unexpected stories of contestation over policy implementation.

A series of interviews I conducted with politicians, administrators, and activists connected to the list of 115 communities further captures these contradictions of which patterns of governance are known and unknown, and by whom. As discussed in chapter 2, the Bachelet government named 115 communities to a waiting list in 2008, working to prioritize cases already approved through the requirements of Article 20B and giving those communities some assurance their claim would be processed. Naming this list was an effort by the Chilean government to undo prior informal and hidden patterns of implementation that only occasionally and problematically became public and controversial. The publicity of the informality of prior implementation patterns, as one CONADI bureaucrat described to me, was "generating problems for the government," so the list of 115 communities intended to rework those incentives so that "the government could work distinctly in the two remaining years [of the Bachelet administration] to decrease conflict levels and politically face the issues most effectively" (Interview, September 2013). A CONADI administrator described, in relation to how the list changed policy implementation, "If you are demanding land, it is best to have clear rules. It is not that if I claim more and do something, I will be first. That was the previous logic: if I go and occupy CONADI and it does not work, then we go to Santiago. People understood these clear, powerful signals" (Interview, November 2013). In naming a list of 115 communities, however, the Chilean government opened avenues for those communities to more quickly resolve their demands outside of market-motivated policy mechanisms regulated through Article 20B, particularly because of the potential publicity offered by the ongoing presidential campaign and communities' ability to mobilize in ways that call attention to, depending on someone's political persuasion, insufficient recognition of Mapuche rights, or the perceived threat that Mapuche mobilization posed to economic interests and security in the south. One Mapuche activist described how keenly aware the 115 communities were of the potential of that political moment: "The demand was to meet with the president. Everyone had that clear- no mobilization without a compromise. No one believes in words, *cachai*?" (Interview, November 2013). Indeed, Minister Viera-Gallo stepped in, signing an agreement that worked around the bureaucratic procedures to more immediately resolve the issue and deescalate tensions during the presidential campaign season. One CONADI administrator rebuked Viera-Gallo's intervention during our conversation: "The system fails when everything depends on one person. There was never a conversation. I never spoke with [Viera-Gallo]. My communities called me and said they had signed an agreement. I said, 'You know, I'm glad for you, because we always understood, and that was law, that an agreement signed with an authority had to be fulfilled'" (Interview, October 2013). All involved in the fallout over Viera-Gallo's intervention were frustrated, but not surprised. As happens through the history of Article 20B, policy outcomes occasionally represent efforts to divert Mapuche demands and deescalate mobilization. And in doing so, those outcomes establish incentives for Mapuche communities to pursue future mobilization to activate the same political motivations, knowing that there is potential to separate the state's interest in extending both the scope and strength of the neoliberal project. Certainly, some individuals and communities are less willing and/or able to navigate these informal norms and the risks associated with mobilization, but the vast majority of Mapuche leaders and relevant government officials knew the trends and how, at least in theory, to negotiate policy to their advantage. Paradoxically, the resulting signed agreements represented both the subversion of policy institutionalization, and an aspiration that the negotiated agreement would be upheld on the basis of its institutionalization.

These paradoxes emerged repeatedly during my time in southern Chile. To those unfamiliar with the land policy, stating that a land transfer was the result of an institutionalized policy procedure was sufficient to claim that there were no intervening motivations, influences, or contestation, preserving the expectations of post–Pinochet Chilean governance as technocratic, centralized, and neoliberal. And indeed, public policy was a crucial element in the design and implementation of Chile's return to democracy. As the Chilean sociologist Gonzalo de la Maza (2010, 2) summarizes, "Public policies were not simply a consequence of the political agreement, but one of the central ways the transition was designed and carried out." Civil society was largely folded into this transition, with the intention of directing mobilization toward the state so that "demands can be neutralized and depoliticized by process-ing them in a selective, piecemeal, and particularistic fashion" (Prevost, Oliva Campos, and Vanden 2012, 111). One government official stated the Chilean government's objective to "mobilize popular organizations, not to transform the neoliberal system, but rather to mobilize them to support and deepen the neoliberal system . . . We didn't create spaces so that they could penetrate and change the state, those spaces were cre-ated in order to rebuild linkages, to penetrate their networks, and to provide a platform through which to transform them" (101). A leader of an urban neighborhood council describes of the effect of this work: "The government's strategy is to divide and conquer the working class and the poor. It has been this way ever since the dictatorship. This is why popular movements seem to have disappeared. In reality, popular move-ments did not disappear. Many were absorbed into municipalities, which turned them into small organizations that chase after the little projects that are offered by the government, and that really doesn't change our reality. Those few who continue to resist or who don't play by the rules are marginalized and either worn down or repressed" (109). Effectively, policymaking was isolated from political pressures and worked to divide popular demands, despite discourses from successive administrations that public policy undid legacies of the dictatorship, restored participa-tion, and expanded the quality of democracy.

Problematically, that discourse of policy implementation as democra-tizing and transparent served to marginalize and delegitimize Mapuche individuals and leaders articulating a different narrative and experience with policy; they were often dismissed as not knowing or understand-ing how to follow bureaucratic procedures. Yet all my interviews with government officials directly responsible for processing a portion of the policy pointed to the necessity of seeing policy as an arena of contesta-tion and negotiation, with policy procedures and outcomes representing the tangible, observable outcome of this contestation and negotiation. Indeed, these interviews started with conversations about formal pro-cedures, but quickly flowed into language of exceptions, conditions, and unevenness of those procedures. In merging these narratives of the ex-pected and the unexpected, the hidden and overt, I hope that *Negotiating Autonomy* validates and complicates the narrative on this often-shielded view post–Pinochet neoliberal governance in Chile.

This understanding of policy offers new insight into when and why neoliberal multiculturalism and territorial rights recognitions fail to meet their promise. Scholars have extensively documented the ways in which neoliberal multicultural Indigenous rights recognitions are un-done as they are translated into policy, noting the unexpected creativity of Indigenous communities navigating around these neoliberal contexts (Postero and Zamosc 2006; Gustafson 2010; Anthias 2018). For example, Penelope Anthias and Sarah Radcliffe (2015, 259) find that "governmental aspirations for indigenous territories unraveled in practice, producing hybrid, double-edged and 'not-quite-neoliberal' spaces—spaces which have, paradoxically, emerged as key sites for the construction of more radical indigenous projects." Evolving contradictions over the shape of governance in the region created space for resistance and creation. As Anthias (2018, 7) concludes of the results of these dynamics in Bolivia, "Following waves of state-backed colonization, the Guaraní of Itika Guasu today share their ancestral territory with a heterogeneous population of non-indigenous land claimants. During the land titling process, these competing claimants mobilized threats of violence, clientelistic networks, and racialized discourses of rights to defend their property claims and obstruct the implementation of indigenous land rights. Their interests were supported by the arrival of oil companies in the territory, which made land use agreements with private land claimants and created incentives to prevent the implementation of indigenous land rights." And in Chile, these same dynamics have certainly pushed some Mapuche communities to pursue more radical demands and mobilization strategies outside of the constraints of the state; as one Mapuche activist described, "Through direct action, break the institutionalization that [the Chilean state] wants to impose on us" (Llaitul and Arrate 2012, 123).

Yet this narrative about working around policy overlooks the extent to which communities work through policy, and this is where *Negotiating Autonomy* most directly contributes to our understandings of neoliberalism, neoliberal multiculturalism, and Indigenous territorial rights recognitions. This analytical space reveals how both resistance and domination, negotiated within policy constraints, explain the persisting *brecha de implementación* between the recognition and exercise of Indigenous rights. Indigenous demands exist and develop within these spaces, building on research on Indigenous ontologies challenging the assumption that Indigenous demands exist separate from colonialism, capitalism, and modernity; rather, Indigenous demands are structured within these governing structures (Coulthard 2014; Simpson 2014; Anthias 2017; Postero and Fabricant 2019). As the Aymara sociologist Silvia Rivera Cusicanqui's (2012, 105) work on the concept of *ch'ixi* documents, "Ch'ixi combines the Indian world and its opposite without ever mixing them," creating the effect of "parallel coexistence of multiple cultural differences that do not extinguish but instead antagonize and complement each other." Sarah Hunt similarly demands that "these sites of resurgence and recognition are not separate, but unfold in the same spaces, within our territories, in relation to the same people, on the same bodies" (Hallenbeck et al. 2016, 113), and Kevin Bruyneel situates that "indigenous resistance tends to happen in a political 'third space' through which Native activists attempt to politically exploit the 'inconsistencies, contingencies, and fissures in the practices of colonization and decolonization'" (Bruyneel 2007, xviii). In southern Chile, Mapuche territorial demands are similarly structured by policies that define which demands can be processed through the state.

Chile, where neoliberalism "reached highest levels of influence and greatest success" (Leiva 2008, xxxi), is particularly useful for this task of uncovering the internal inconsistency of neoliberal governance, precisely because of the façade of consistency of policy and governance in post-Pinochet Chile. In contrast to work that finds that neoliberal reforms of the 1980s and 1990s inadvertently reduced both the scope and strength of the state (Fukuyama 2004), *Negotiating Autonomy* highlights the tensions that emerge when state efforts to pursue the extension of the scope of the neoliberal project are tied up in efforts to extend state strength. Neoliberalism is not evenly extended, and the strategic decisions of how to "best" extend neoliberalism are conditioned by prejudicial assumptions of which subjects can be quickly and most productively pulled into the neoliberal project. From 1994 to 2013, successive presidential administrations in Chile attempted to respond to Mapuche territorial demands by extending both the strength and scope of neoliberalism in the region through land policy. While "neoliberalism would seem paradoxically to govern without governing" (Read 2009, 29), the Chilean government's response to Mapuche territorial demands exposes how actively and unevenly the state governs while appearing it is not.

Certainly, the strategies documented here firmly require Indigenous individuals and communities to engage with the state, and, effectively, engage with the hegemonic structures of neoliberalism and elitism embedded within Chilean governance. There are severe limitations and costs of this strategy—Mapuche communities that pursue territorial rights through this space face incredible risks. Working within this space has provided some communities with specific, incremental land acquisitions, to the extent that Indigenous communities articulate demands appropriate to be addressed in the middle space of policy. Communities' demands for self-determination and autonomy cannot be resolved within the constrained conceptualization of territory preserved and extended through the patterns of policy implementation described here. Also, pursuing territorial rights and autonomies through the state has been accompanied by violent criminalization and militarization, and undermines potential demands for more radical reconfigurations of territoriality and governance in Chile.

What does this mean for the potential for Mapuche communities to acquire and exercise territorial rights through this land policy? Positioning policy as a double-edged arena of both resistance and domination suggests that it is too simple to classify participating in policy as exclusively a hegemonic or counterhegemonic strategy; rather, policy is an arena of contestation within which to engage demands. As Rosamel Millaman (2001, 12), a Mapuche anthropologist, summarizes of this tension:

> The Mapuche organizations are facing a great dilemma: On the one hand, they can participate actively in the spaces made available to them by civil society and the state, such as the municipalities. In this way, by positioning themselves to participate in the top-down dialogue imposed by the state, they can struggle to ensure that state policies take account of the interests and cultural particularities of the Mapuche people. On the other hand they can engage in more outright autonomous action and wage constant struggle against any state control of their territories. For the present, it seems the communities and their leaders have chosen to combine the two strategies.

Wainwright and Bryan (2009, 169) similarly find that using cartographic-legal strategies to map Indigenous territory "is neither useless nor futile," and Charles Hale (2011, 197) concludes, "We know how power works; what activists portray as resistance is best understood as constrained maneuverings, which at best yield a range of unstable, fluid and ambiguous effects." Hegemony is also negotiated within the constraints of this policy—policy continues to be remade by the bureaucrats overseeing the policy, reiterating that "being 'irreducibly utopian,' governmental interventions can never achieve all they seek" (Li 2007, 18). Kymlicka (2013, 99) similarly states that "if neoliberalism has shaped social relations, it is equally true that those relations have shaped neoliberalism, blocking some neoliberal reforms entirely while pushing other reforms in unexpected directions, with unintended results." Effectively, as these structures evolve, they create space for new negotiations with the state that are worthy of investigation.

While Indigenous rights recognitions promised to more radically transform territoriality and governance in other Latin American countries, the Chilean state's exercise of power through its institutionalized response to Mapuche territorial demands facilitates analysis of the internal inconsistencies in the "uses of neoliberalism" (Ferguson 2010). Responding to Gramsci's call to start "from where we are" (Santos and Rodríguez-Garavito 2005, 18), *Negotiating Autonomy* documents the middle space of the policy conditions and processes through which Mapuche communities have acquired land through Article 20B, occasionally at the expense of powerful competing interests. The result are frustratingly limited yet significant; 3 percent of land in the regions under analysis transferred to Indigenous communities through Article 20B of Indigenous Law 19.253 from 1994 to 2013, 20 percent of the land the Chilean state originally titled to Mapuche communities in the late nineteenth and early twentieth centuries. The middle space of public policy consequentially structures contestation between Mapuche territorial demands and Chilean land policy.

EPILOGUE

As I finish writing from a steamy, contentious Santiago in December 2019, it seems inappropriate to finish this analysis without considering the significance of the ongoing protests for patterns of post–Pinochet Chilean governance. In October secondary school students coordinated a fare-evasion campaign (#evasionmasiva, #evacionmasiva) in response to a thirty-peso increase (about US$0.04) in the Santiago metro fare, a protest that quickly escalated to shut down the full metro system after seventeen stations were burned down and the rest were damaged on October 18. The government response was swift and harsh. President Sebastian Piñera declared a state of emergency and military curfew on October 19, declaring, "We are in a war against a powerful and relentless enemy that respects nothing and no one" and "democracy has a right to defend itself."[1] He deployed tens of thousands militarized national police (*carabineros*) and criminalized protest by applying the state security law (Ley de Seguridad del Estado). The law has been nearly exclusively applied to Mapuche activists since the return of the democracy; minister of the interior Andrés Chadwick justified that terrorist acts are those intending to "eliminate or inhibit resolutions from the authorities or to impose demands on them," echoing similar justifications made when trying Mapuche activists.[2] From October 18 to December 6, domestic sources documented 26 deaths, 12,652 injuries, 2,808 hospitalizations, 283 eye injuries from the use of pellet guns and teargas, 20,645 arrests, and 2,670 reports of human rights violations.[3] Protests spread throughout the country, expanding to critique the persistence of neoliberalism and the 1980 constitution and resulting vast inequalities and immobilities in Chilean society. Protesters demanded dramatic structural change to programs, including education, social security, health, and pension, and a new constitution.

Considering the strength through which the neoliberal project permeated Chilean society, eviscerating the provision and quality of government services while empowering privately run corporations to pass costs to consumers, the eruption of protests was unsurprising. Critiques of neoliberalism permeated rhetoric in and about the protests. Protest signs declared, "Neoliberalism started in Chile and will die here" and "It's not about 30 pesos; it's about 30 years," referencing continuities in the Chilean governance since Pinochet. International headlines were also quick to frame the protests as a critique of the neoliberal project, declaring "Chile's Protests are a Reject of the Excesses of Neoliberalism," "Chile in Flames: The Neoliberal Model in Crisis throughout the Region," and "Chile Learns the Price of Economic Inequality."[4] Yet as *Negotiating Autonomy* highlights, this neoliberal frame insufficiently captures how state governance efforts to preserve elite interests create inequalities in citizenship that also translated into the protests. Uneven, strategic, and often contradictory, the Chilean neoliberal project interacts with other governing priorities. This nuance has received limited international news coverage, but protesters were and are acutely aware of how the Chilean state prioritizes preserving the hegemony of a particular vision of the nation-state to the exclusion of those constructed to be outside of this imagined entity. And they are calling attention to which patterns of Chilean governance were known and unknown to which Chilean citizens and which points in time, declaring, "Mapuche community, forgive us for not believing you. Now we know who the real terrorists are" and "the Mapuche were telling the truth."[5] Indeed, for many Mapuche communities and individuals, the criminalization and militarization of protest was not new but rather made visible to new audiences as the government exported this policing to Santiago.

Three images most prominently highlighted these more nuanced and evolving understandings of the interaction of identity politics interact with neoliberalism in Chile. First, the image of Camilo Catrillanca, a Mapuche community leader and activist killed by police officers on November 14, 2018, featured prominently in 2019 protest signs and graffiti. Catrillanca was shot in the back of the head and killed by a member of the Comando Jungla, a tactical special operations unit of the *carabineros*, in Temucuicui. Police officers justified their actions by stating they suspected Catrillanca of car theft and were ambushed, but a police video was later released verifying that Catrillanca was unarmed and fleeing, as the fifteen-year-old witness on the tractor with Catrillanca had testified. The death—and reports of government efforts to misrepresent or cover-up evidence—sparked outrage and protests throughout Chile. While Ma-

Image E.1. Protest art from Universidad Católica metro station in Santiago, December 2019. Photo by the author.

puche communities and activists saw the event as another in the state's long history of the repression and criminalization of Mapuche demands, many Chileans had long supported the state's heavy-handed response, believing the state's justifications of their use of violence against Mapuche communities and activists. Yet the details of Catrillanca's murder and subsequent actions of the *carabineros* and Piñera administration marked a point of departure, with many Chileans first questioning the state's justifications of their actions. The prevalence of Catrillanca's image in the protests highlights that protesters conceptually linked state actions surrounding Catrillanca's murder with the severe criminalization and militarization of the October protests.

Second, Mapuche flags were often more prevalent than Chilean flags at protests. In casual conversations about the protests in December, many Chileans shared with me how proud they were to have bought and waved the Mapuche flag at protests; prior to the protests, I more often heard suspicion and curiosity about my work and the Mapuche community than expressions of pride of and support. The Mapuche academic and activist Miguel Melin analyzed this same point of departure in October 2019, concluding: "The Chilean people now realized what the Mapuche having been living for the past 200 years. The Mapuche people have always been fighting, compared to the Chilean society where discontent appears every so often but was sleeping. Today there is an important awakening; it is their turn to live what the Mapuche have lived for a long time, which is perpetuated by the elite. That is why I hope this marks an opportunity towards understanding of our demands."[6] The Mapuche journalist Pedro Cayuqueo similarly offered: "Thousands of Mapuche flags crowned the marches and protest days, as, by far, the main identifying sign of the protesters who see in it an emblem of rebellion and resistance to the neoliberal model. . . . The Mapuche, for decades, have been questioning the Chilean model and we have paid a high price for it: jail, death, political persecution. The new generations of Chileans know it and maybe that's why they chose us as a symbol."[7] Rather than broadly and ambiguously pointing to neoliberalism as the root cause of protesters demands, Melin and Cayuqueo conceptually highlight the persistence of elitism in Chilean governance, and the ways that elitism creatively and strategically interacts with identity politics and neoliberalism.

Finally, protestors throughout the country translated this understanding of the current moment into reconciliations of Chile's historical memory, visible in the destruction of statues. In Temuco, protestors pulled down the statue of the Spanish conquistador Pedro de Valdivia, and hung the decapitated head of the statue of Chilean military aviator Dagoberto Godoy from the arm of a statue of Mapuche military leader Caupolicán, who lead Mapuche resistance to the Spanish. As one protestor summarized, the act "is the perfect demonstration that history is written wrong, and the wrong people are celebrated."[8]

These emerging images and discourses leave me cautiously optimistic about the potential for Chile to move past the governance patterns documented in *Negotiating Autonomy*. Protesters are calling attention to the limitations of the neoliberal model but also to how neoliberalism interacts with the preservation of elitism in Chilean governance and exclusionary access to the full exercise of Chilean citizenship. The critique is about more than neoliberalism. It is a damning condemnation of who the state acts on behalf of, highlighting how those with power deploy neoliberal governance to the exclusion of others. In this critique, Mapuche demands would no longer be isolated and Othered but rather representative and constitutive of broader set of critiques of and for Chilean governance and citizenship. The upcoming votes about a constitutional convention will be particularly consequential in translating these demands into more inclusive, equitable rights recognitions and exercise. Yet as Mapuche communities have learned to navigate the governing processes and procedures of Chilean governance, so too has the state learned to navigate efforts to preserve both hegemony and neoliberalism through those administrative processes and procedures. *Mapuche Territory and Chilean Land* provides some vision into the tools the Chilean government will turn employ to both extend neoliberalism and state hegemony through militarization, criminalization, and policy; my hope is that this work facilitates communities' abilities to unmake these governance patterns in favor of a more broadly inclusive and plurinational understanding of Chilean citizenship.

APPENDIX

DATA SET

The data set analyzed in this book includes all the Mapuche communities in the Araucanía and Bíobío regions of Chile that received a land purchase, data publicly available through the CONADI website. For each land purchase, government records include the location of the request (district, province, and community), the location of the land granted (in some circumstances the government acquires land separate from the community's current location, requiring the community to move to receive the land), the name of the community actors requesting the land, the number of hectares of land received, the number of families associated with the particular request, and the amount paid for the land (in 2008 constant USD, averaged to be 590.75 Chilean pesos = 1 USD). This data was restructured as discrete time duration data to capture if each of the 266 communities received a land purchase in each year (266 communities over 20 years for a total of 5,320 observations).

I rely on protest-event analysis to code instances of mobilization, which I broadly defined to include "nonroutine, collective, and public acts that involve claims on behalf of a larger collective" (Olzak 1994, 53; see also Paige 1975; Tilly 1978). Content analysis, usually of newspaper reports, translates "words to numbers" to capture characteristics of the event (Crist and McCarthy 1996; Rucht and Neidhardt 1999; Klandermans and Staggenborg 2002; Oliver, Cadena-Roa, and Strawn 2003; Franzosi 2004; Hutter 2014). With all three sources, I used a half-automated selection strategy, searching the website's online search engine for the name of the Mapuche community, and reviewing each of the results to eliminate results that were not related to mobilization.

While protest-event analysis of newspaper accounts is a common method of studying contentious action, it is important to note potential biases that stem from collection strategies, characteristics of the news

TABLE A.1: SUMMARY OF VARIABLES

LAND PURCHASE?	BY YEAR, DID THE COMMUNITY RECEIVE A LAND PURCHASE? NO: 0, YES: 1	CONADI[1]
Number of prior instances of mobilization by community	Count of the number of years, since 1994, with evidence of community mobilization or conflict Min: 0, Max: 17, Mean: 0.26	Various online searches, secondary resources as described in text
Perception of community's association with radical, violent Mapuche mobilization	By community, count of the number of times the community's name appears in *El Mercurio* between 1994 and 2013. Min: 0, Mean: 105, Mean: 1.54	*El Mercurio*, emol.com
Percent support for the Right	By district, percent of vote in congressional races for candidate(s) on the Right (1994, 1998, 2002, 2006, 2010, 2012) Min: 3.48, Max: 61.42, Mean: 32.45	Servicio Electoral de Chile[2]
Percent of forestry land in district	By district, percent of land in district held by forestry company Min: 0.3, Max: 37.39, Mean: 16.64	Instituto Nacional de Estadísticas, 2007 Survey[3]
Percent rural	By district, percent of people residing in rural areas Min: 5.22, Max: 83.6, Mean: 47.28	Instituto Nacional de Estadísticas, 2002 Census[4]
Percent Mapuche	By district, percent of people who self-identify as Mapuche Min: 4.8, Max: 64.7, Mean: 29.55	Instituto Nacional de Estadísticas, 2002 Census
District	Thirty-four districts across the Araucanía (IX) and Bíobío (IIX) provinces, dummy variable	—

1. Base de Datos DTAI, 2013. "Subsidio a la Aplicación del Artículo 20 letra b) de la Ley Indígena." https://docplayer.es/14516001-Subsidio-a-la-aplicacion-articulo-20-letra-b-de-la-ley-indigena.html.

2. "Elecciones a Diputados 1989–2013," https://www.servel.cl/elecciones-de-diputados-1989-al-2013-por-circunscripcion-electoral/.

3. "SUPERFICIE DE LAS EXPLOTACIONES AGROPECUARIAS CON TIERRA POR USO DEL SUELO, SEGÚN REGIÓN, PROVINCIA Y COMUNA," http://webanterior.ine.cl/estadisticas/economicas/estad%C3%ADsticas-agropecuarias.

4. "Censo 2002," Instituto Nacional de Estadísticas, http://www.inearaucania.cl/contenido.aspx?id_contenido=13.

agency (space limitations, reporting norms, and editorial concerns), and characteristics of the issue and the event (Franzosi 1987; Olzak 1989; Rucht and Neidhardt 1999; Koopmans and Rucht 2002; Earl et al. 2004). Chapter 4 highlights the complexity and uncertainty surrounding attributing responsibility for specific events to specific people. Not only are instances of contentious action often attributed to a unitary "Mapuche movement," but it is unclear if the state is inaccurately attributing blame to Mapuche activists. In response to these limitations, I collected the entire population of events for each community under analysis from 1994 to 2013, rather than making decisions about how to sample from newspapers. Second, I used news reports to capture the "hard news" (the when, what, where, and why details of an event), which research has found to be relatively unbiased in comparison to "soft news" based on journalists' perceptions of the event. Finally, I took advantage of the biases of various sources. To capture instances of contentious action, I relied on multiple sources; to capture the perceived intensity of the contentious action, I relied on reporting by *El Mercurio*.

To account for regional variation, I treat this data as hierarchical, with communities clustered within thirty-three districts. Treating *district* as the level-two unit situates the plot of land within the district, hypothesizing that district-level political, economic, and social contexts influence the likelihood of land purchases. The number of land purchases per district ranges from one to fifty-two, and I include data on the percentage of the population that voted for a right-wing candidate per congressional election, the percentage of the population that self-identify as Mapuche, the percentage of the district that is rural, the concentration of land by district, and included fixed effects for the district. Several district-level variables control for political, economic, and social variables, including the percentage of the population that voted for a right-wing candidate, per congressional election, the percentage of people that self-identify as Mapuche, and the percentage of the district that is rural. Fixed effects for the district are also included.

MODEL SPECIFICATION AND ESTIMATION

I use survival analysis to statistically evaluate the impact of mobilization, narratives about mobilization, and the presence of forestry companies on the likelihood that a Mapuche community receives a land purchase. This data is treated as time-duration data, allowing for evaluation of the likelihood a community will receive a purchase in one of the twenty years under analysis. Survival models allow for analysis of repeated events, explicitly testing if first and subsequent land purchases are similarly determined. I estimate separate models for the first and all subsequent purchases, testing if the regulations and procedures governing the first purchases limit the impact of external actors, including Indigenous communities and forestry companies, on patterns of implementation.

These data are modeled using a conditional gap time, or conditional risk set, survival model (Prentice, Williams, and Peterson 1981; Kelly and Lim 2000; Box-Steffensmeier and Zorn 2002). The event of interest is a land purchase on behalf of a Mapuche community through Article 20B, coded as zero if the community "survives" the year (does not receive a land purchase) or one if the community "fails" (receives a land purchase).

The stratified Cox model is a semiparametric Cox model that does not make an assumption about the shape of the hazard ratio over time. It also directly analyzes repeated events; while conventional event history models drop observations after the first failure, this approach preserves subsequent observations to model multiple failures. Some communities received multiple purchases in a particular year—these are collapsed into one year. Because second and subsequent purchases are likely to be influenced by, yet in different ways, from the first, treating repeated events as independent would incorrectly estimate standard errors and assume the effects of the covariates to be constant regardless of the event number (Box-Steffensmeier and Jones 2004; Cleves 2008). This model assumes that repeated events affect the variance of the estimates (rather than biasing the estimates themselves), correcting the variance estimates after model estimation (variance-correction models). Allowing the baseline hazard to vary, the estimates of the covariates vary by strata, or the event a community is likely to receive, allowing for heterogeneity for the different events (Barai and Teoh 1997; Beck, Katz, and Tucker 1998; Box-Steffensmeier, De Boef, and Joyce 2007).

The dependent variable is the time until the event, introducing variation on the dependent variable. In this data, the policy was first implemented in 1994, so communities fall in strata one before they have received their first purchase. After receiving a first purchase, communities fall into the second strata, meaning the model estimates the likelihood that a community receives its second purchase. Because there are very few observations for higher ranked events, standard errors are larger for subsequent purchases, making the estimates more unstable and imprecise; conceptually, I distinguish between first and subsequent land purchases rather than separately considering estimates at each strata. Neither the key independent variables nor the full model violate the Cox model's proportional hazards assumption. I use the Efron method to address potential tied durations, in which communities have the same duration (particularly common as several communities receive land purchases in two or more subsequent years). I also include dummy variables for thirty-three of the thirty-four *comunas* (districts) and cluster standard errors by community to account for potential heteroskedasticity.

ACRONYMS AND ABBREVIATIONS

ATM	Alianza Territorial Mapuche
CAM	Coordinadora Arauco Malleco (Arauco Malleco Coordinating Committee)
CEPI	Comisión Especial de los Pueblos Indígenas (Special Commission for Indigenous Peoples)
CONADI	Corporación Nacional de Desarrollo Indígena (National Corporation for Indigenous Development)
CTT	Aukiñ Wallmapu Ngulam or Consejo de Todas las Tierras (Council of All the Lands)
DIPOLCAR	Dirección de Inteligencia Policial de Carabineros (Police Intelligence Service)
FTAI	Fundo de Tierra y Agua Indígena (Fund for Indigenous Land and Water)
IACHR	Inter-American Court of Human Rights
ILO 169	Indigenous and Tribal Peoples Convention of the International Labor Organization
INDAP	Instituto de Desarrollo Agropecuario (Agricultural Development Institute)
MIDEPLAN	Ministerio de Planificación (Ministry of Planning and Cooperation)
PACMA	Pacto Mapuche por la Autodeterminación (Mapuche Pact for Self-Determination)
PLC	Padre Las Casas
PDC	Partido Demócrata Cristiano (Christian Democratic Party)

NOTES

INTRODUCTION

1. Coverage of these events is from "CONADI entregó aparejos de pesca y buceo a pescadores lafquenche de Chiloé," 2015, CONADI, accessed April 10, 2017, http://www.conadi.gob.cl/index.php/noticias-conadi/980-conadi-entrego-aparejos-de-pesca-y-buceo-a-pescadores-lafquenche-de-chiloe (article removed); "CONADI lanzó concursos por \$680 millones para apoyar la productividad de las tierras mapuche de La Araucanía," 2015, CONADI, accessed April 10, 2017, http://www.conadi.gob.cl/index.php/2-noticias/975-conadi-lanzo-concursos-por-680-millones-para-apoyar-la-productividad-de-las-tierras-mapuche-de-la-araucania/ (article removed); "La Conadi entregó \$1.740 millones en subsidios de tierra a familias Mapuche," 2013, https://www.soychile.cl/Valdivia/Politica/2013/04/12/167034/La-Conadi-entrego-1740-millones-en-subsidios-de-tierra-a-familias-mapuche.aspx .

2. Throughout this book I generally use the word *land* to describe what the Chilean government is processing and as an economic commodity that can be sold, transferred, and owned; I use the word *territory* to describe what communities most often demand: recognition of and rights to economically, socially, politically, and historically constructed spaces representative of deeper, mutually constitutive relationship between Indigenous peoples and spaces. These categories are not mutually exclusive; some communities recover land that overlaps with their territorial demand. Chapter 1 further discusses the conceptual differences between land and territory, and analyzes how a policy response to Mapuche territorial demands evolved into a land policy.

3. Unless otherwise noted, all translations are the author's.

4. The international coordination of distinct Indigenous movements was first evident in the 1982 United Nations Working Group on Indigenous Populations, Decade of Indigenous Peoples (1993–2003). Two key international conventions on Indigenous rights set minimum standards (the 1989 International Labor Organization Convention 169 and the 2006 United Nations Declaration on the Rights of Indigenous Peoples). Most Latin American countries have signed on to ILO 169.

5. There is significant variation in the adoption of multicultural reforms; Van Cott (2006) characterizes Bolivia, Colombia, Ecuador, Panama, and Venezuela as strong; Argentina, Brazil, Costa Rica, Guatemala, Honduras, Mexico, Nicaragua, Paraguay, and Peru as modest; and Belize, Chile, El Salvador, Guyana, and Suriname as weak.

6. Before Spanish colonialism, the Mapuche community lived on the band of land spanning across Southern Cone through Patagonia, including significant portions of Argentina and Chile. Today, approximately 10 percent of the Chilean population (1.7 million people) consider themselves to be Indigenous; the Mapuche community comprises 88 percent of the Indigenous population in Chile, and the focal point of Indigenous policy and Indigenous-state relations (INE 2012).

7. CONADI is located within the Ministry of Planning and Cooperation (Ministerio de Planificación y Cooperación, MIDEPLAN) converted to the Ministry of Social Development (Ministerio de Desarollo Social) in 2011.

8. Calculated from data publically available from CONADI and the 2007 Survey by the Chilean National Institute of Statistics (INE), discussed in further detail in chapter 4 and the appendix.

CHAPTER 1. BUREAUCRATIZING TERRITORY INTO LAND POLICY

1. This distinction between territorial demands of highland and lowland Indigenous communities is argued to be linked to the history of land tenure and agrarian reform in the respective regions. See Lucero (2008), Assies (2000), and Zuniga (1998) for a discussion of the construction of territorial demands and the potentially exclusionary and inappropriate "territorial model" of recognition.

2. Similarly, Articles 25 and 26 of the 2007 United Nations Declaration on the Rights of Indigenous Peoples (UNDRIP), establishes that "Indigenous peoples have the right to maintain and strengthen their distinctive spiritual relationship with their traditionally owned or otherwise occupied and used lands, territories, waters and coastal seas and other resources and to uphold their responsibilities to future generations in this regard. . . . (1) Indigenous peoples have the right to the lands, territories and resources which they have traditionally owned, occupied or other-wise used or acquired. (2) Indigenous peoples have the right to own, use, develop and control the lands, territories and resources that they possess by reason of traditional ownership or other traditional occupation or use, as well as those which they have otherwise acquired. (3) States shall give legal recognition and protection to these lands, territories and resources. Such recognition shall be conducted with due respect to customs, traditions and land tenure systems of the indigenous peoples concerned."

3. This has been confirmed by the Inter-American Court of Human Rights in the Mayagna (Sumo) Community of Awas Tingni v. Nicaragua 2001, and by ILO supervisory bodies that concluded, "The fact that land rights have originat-

ed more recently than colonial times is not a determining factor. The Convention was drafted to recognize situations in which there are rights to lands which have been traditionally occupied, but also may cover other situations in which indigenous peoples have rights to lands they occupy or otherwise use under other conditions." Governing Body, 276th Session, November 1999, Representation under Article 24 of the ILO Constitution, Mexico, GB.276/16/3, para. 37. Also relevant are Committee of Experts, 73rd Session, 2002, Observation, Peru, 2003, para. 7; and Governing Body, 276th Session, November 1999, Representation under Article 24 of the ILO Constitution, Mexico, GB.276/16/3, para. 37. For further discussion, see ILO 2009, 94.

4. For additional discussion, see Correa, Molina, and Yáñez (2005); Haughney (2006); Marimán et al. (2006); Richards (2013); Crago (2015).

5. Yet as the Chilean government worked to bring Indigenous Law 19.253 into compliance with ILO 169, it undermined many of the principles of ILO 169. For example, Supreme Decree 124 (Decreto Supremo 124, 2009) addressed the requirements for consultation and participation of Indigenous communities. The National Institute of Human Rights argued that Supreme Decree 124 only described the mechanisms though which Indigenous communities could present demands to the government, rather than establishing the responsibility of the government to consult with and facilitate the participation of Indigenous communities. For additional information, see Instituto Nacional de Derechos Humanos (2010).

6. While I focus specifically on the Mapuche Indigenous community, the policy does not exclude other Indigenous communities in Chile from acquiring land through the policy. A number of plots of land have been transferred to other Indigenous communities in the north and far south, yet the land policy was written in a way that prioritized the types of land recognitions historically granted to Mapuche communities. Other Indigenous communities' land was often recognized through legal tools that Indigenous Law 19.253 does not recognize; for additional information, see Aylwin Oyarzún (2003). Of the 499 plots of land that have been transferred to such communities through Article 20B, only 6 of those plots of land were transferred to non-Mapuche Indigenous communities in Chile.

7. For additional information on the different types of land claims based on these different documents, see Gonzalez Palominos et al. (2007, 21–22).

CHAPTER 2. NEGOTIATING LAND FOR PEACE

1. Here, I understand technocrats as "individuals with a high level of specialized academic training which serves as a principal criterion on the basis of which they are selected to occupy key decision-making or advisory roles in large complex organizations- both public and private" (Cardoso 1979, 403), and technocratic governance as the positioning of technocrats at higher levels of

decision-making with more autonomy over policy creation and implementation (Centeno 2010, 34–36). The isolation of decision-making from the influences of popular participation or political negotiation, often presumed to be "depoliticization," is argued to be effective for facilitating administrators and bureaucrats to implement cohesive and consistent policy decisions based on professional expertise and experience to improve policy efficiency and effectiveness. It is largely assumed that technocratic rule requires particular political alliances in order to avoid resistance to policy decisions from those most affected by economic restructuring. In fact, literature on technocratic governance in the 1970s focused on how the link between technocratic rule and authoritarianism facilitated dramatic economic restructuring. Since the third wave of democratization, technocratic rule has been decoupled from authoritarianism and more frequently associated with neoliberal economic policy reform. For technocrats to be effective, however, they still frequently rely on political alliances to provide relative political stability and limit the potential for social conflict to impede policy implementation (Domínguez 2010).

2. Iván Fredes, "El premio del Gobierno a los mapuches rupturistas," *El Mercurio*, June 18, 2002, http://www.mapuche.info/news/merc020618.html.

3. Fredes, "El premio del Gobierno."

4. *El Mercurio*, October 25, 2001.

5. Fredes, "El premio del Gobierno."

6. Fernando Rivas and Iván Fredes, "Politica indigena beneficios estatales: Mapuches le doblan la mano al Gobierno." *El Mercurio*, October 18, 2001, http://www.mapuche.info/news02/merc011018.html.

7. Rivas and Fredes, "Politica indigena beneficios estatales."

8. Rivas and Fredes, "Politica indigena beneficios estatales."

9. Fredes, "El premio del Gobierno."

10. Alejandra Muñoz. "Denuncia nuevas irregularidades en compra de tierras," *La Tercera*, March 12, 2002, http://www.mapuche.info/news/terc020312.html.

11. "¡CONADI demanda a uno de sus ex directores!" Tiro al Blanco, March 11, 2002, http://tiroalblanco.cl/index.php?not=14054&do=muestra.

12. Pedro Cayuqueo, "Entrevista a Director Nacional de la Conadi," *Azkintuwe*, December 18, 2006, http://www.mapuexpress.net/content/publications/print.php?id=516 (article removed).

13. "Álvaro Marifil fue designado director nacional de Conadi," *El Mercurio*, June 12, 2008, http://www.emol.com/noticias/nacional/2008/06/12/308352/alvaro-marifil-fue-designado-director-nacional-de-conadi.html.

14. Daniel Sandoval, "Acusan de irresponsabilidad a nuevo director de CONADI, Alvaro Marifil," *La Opinion*, June 19, 2008, http://www.laopinon.cl/admin/render/noticia/15828.

15. Arnaldo Pérez Guerra, "Cheques prueban pago de millonarias comisiones por compra de tierras a comunidades," La Opinion, September 30, 2009, http://www.laopinon.cl/admin/render/noticia/21718.

16. Pérez Guerra, "Cheques prueban pago de millonarias."

17. *El Mercurio*, July 25, 2010.

18. "Comisión Investigadora Conadi: 'Ex Ministro Viera Gallo actuó con irresponsabilidad,'" *La Opinion*, January 8, 2011, http://www.laopinon.cl/admin/render/noticia/26196.

19. "Edwards e irregularidades en la Conadi: 'Viera-Gallo apagó el incendio con bencina,'" *La Tercera*, January 7, 2011, https://www.latercera.com/noticia/edwards-e-irregularidades-en-la-conadi-viera-gallo-apago-el-incendio-con-bencina/.

20. Charlotte Méritan. "Government to Prioritize Constitutional Recognition of Indigenous, *I Love Chile*, January 22, 2013 (article removed).

21. Hugo Oviedo, "Entrevista: Alberto Pizarro, Director Nacional de CONADI," *Austral Temuco*, May 2, 2014.

22. Hugo Oviedo, "Fraude al interior de la Conadi sería de $10 mil millones," *El Austral*, May 26, 2014, https://www.soychile.cl/temuco/sociedad/2014/05/26/251524/fraude-al-interior-de-la-conadi-durante-el-gobierno-de-pinera-seria-de--10-mil-millones.aspx.

23. Viviana Candia, "Tierras mapuche en conflicto: Gobierno dejará 166 comunidades en 'lista de espera,'" *La Segunda*, October 14, 2013, http://www.lasegunda.com/Noticias/Impreso/2013/10/885591/tierras-mapuches-en-conflicto-gobierno-dejara-166-comunidades-en-lista-de-espera.

24. Pérez Guerra, "Cheques prueban pago de millonarias."

25. Constanza Fuentes and Maximiliano Martínez, "Las razones del fracaso de Conadi y la política indígena en la Araucanía," *El Periodista*, November 8, 2009.

CHAPTER 3: NAVIGATING LAND POLICY

1. F. Palomera and V. Ríos, "Retrasan apertura de aeropuerto en Temuco por conflicto con mapuches," July 22, 2014, http://www2.latercera.com/noticia/retrasan-apertura-de-aeropuerto-en-temuco-por-conflicto-con-mapuches/.

2. "Agricultores de La Araucanía critican posible entrega de tierras a violentistas," *El Mercurio*, December 5, 2009, http://www.mapuche.info/?kat=1&sida=157.

3. "Agricultores de La Araucanía."

4. Alberto Dufey, "Dirigente indígena lamenta que forestales suizas hayan roto su compromiso en Chile," Swisslatin, December 10, 2007, http://www.swisslatin.ch/reportajes-0711.htm.

5. Dufey, "Dirigente indígena lamenta que forestales."

6. J. Fando Serey, "Intolerancia y Excesos de Violencia Policial," *Enlace Mapuche Internacional*, November 29, 2009, http://www.mapuche-nation.org/espanol/html/noticias/ntcs-392.htm.

7. Serey, "Intolerancia y Excesos de Violencia Policial."

8. Lucía Sepúlveda Ruiz, "El general de Carabineros Cristián Llévenes, involucrado en una denuncia por tortura del lonko Víctor Marilao," *Rebelión*, February 25, 2009, http://www.rebelion.org/noticia.php?id=92634.

9. "Graves consecuencias en Allanamiento en Comunidad Catrilaf," *liberar.cl*, November 30, 2009, http://aureliennewenmapuche.blogspot.com/2009_11_01_archive.html.

10. "Graves consecuencias en Allanamiento en Comunidad Catrilaf."

CHAPTER 4: QUANTIFYING MOBILIZATION AND LAND PURCHASES

1. Joel Keep, "Terror Case Collapses as 'Activist' Witness Admits Being Informant" *Santiago Times*, accessed March 20, 2015. http://santiagotimes.cl/terror-case-collapses-activist-witness-admits-informant/ (article removed); Oriana Miranda, "Quién es y cómo actuó Raúl Castro Antipán, el 'terrorista mapuche' infiltrado por Carabineros," *DiarioUChile*, February 13, 2014, http://radio.uchile.cl/2014/02/13/raul-castro-antipan-el-joven-mapuche-infiltrado-por-carabineros-para-inculpar-a-su-pueblo.

2. "Exclusivo: hermano de Mapuche Rodrigo Melinao pide asilo a Venezuela tras recibir amenazas de muerte," *Verdad Ahora*, November 7, 2013, http://verdadahora.cl/exclusivo_hermano_de_mapuche_rodrigo_melinao_pide_asilo_a_venezuela_tras_recibir_amenazas_de_muerte.html.

3. Jorge Molina and Ivonne Toro, "Caso infiltrado: La dura declaración en que Raúl Castro Antipán implica a la Dipolcar en atentados incendiarios," *Clinic*, February 14, 2014, http://www.theclinic.cl/2014/02/14/caso-infiltrado-la-dura-declaracion-en-que-raul-castro-antipan-implica-a-la-dipolcar-en-atentados-incendiarios/.

4. Miranda, "Quién es y cómo actuó Raúl Castro Antipán."

EPILOGUE

1. "Chile in Flames: The Neoliberal Model in Crisis throughout the Region," *OpenDemocracy*, October 23, 2019, https://www.opendemocracy.net/en/democraciaabierta/chile-en-llamas-el-modelo-neoliberal-en-crisis-en-toda-la-regi%C3%B3n-en/.

2. Camila Vergara, "The Meaning of Chile's Explosion," *Jacobin*, October 29, 2019, https://www.jacobinmag.com/2019/10/chile-protests-sebastian-pinera-constitution-neoliberalism.

3. Organization of American States, "CIDH condena el uso excesivo de la fuerza en el contexto de las protestas sociales en Chile, expresa su grave preocu-

pación por el elevado número de denuncias y rechaza toda forma de violencia," December 6, 2019, https://www.oas.org/es/cidh/prensa/comunicados/2019/317.asp.

4. Nicolás Saldías, "Chile's Protests Are a Rejection of the Excesses of Neoliberalism," *World Politics Review*, November 4, 2019, https://www.worldpoliticsreview.com/articles/28316/chile-s-protests-are-a-rejection-of-the-excesses-of-neoliberalism; "Chile in Flames"; "Chile Learns the Price of Economic Inequality," *New York Times*, October 22, 2019, https://www.nytimes.com/2019/10/22/opinion/chile-protests.html.

5. Paula Huenchumil, "El protagonismo de la bandera mapuche en la gran marcha, un símbolo político de las protestas," *Interferencia*, October 27, 2019, https://interferencia.cl/articulos/el-protagonismo-de-la-bandera-mapuche-en-la-gran-marcha-un-simbolo-politico-de-las.

6. Huenchumil, "El protagonismo de la bandera mapuche."

7. "La 'liberación de la nación mapuche,' de la mano de la chilena," *Público*, October 29, 2019, https://www.publico.es/internacional/protestas-chile-liberacion-nacion-mapuche-mano-chilena.html.

8. Johanna Watson, "Temuco: Más justicia, menos monumentos," *el Desconcierto*, November 29, 2019, https://www.eldesconcierto.cl/2019/11/29/temuco-mas-justicia-menos-monumentos/.

BIBLIOGRAPHY

Acuña, Roger Merino. 2015. "The Politics of Extractive Governance: Indigenous Peoples and Socio-environmental Conflicts." *Extractive Industries and Society* 2 (1): 85–92.

Agnew, John. 1994. "The Territorial Trap: the Geographical Assumptions of International Relations Theory." *Review of International Political Economy* 1 (1): 53–80.

Agnew, John. 2005. "Sovereignty Regimes: Territoriality and State Authority in Contemporary World Politics." *Annals of the Association of American Geographers* 95 (2): 437–461.

Agnew, John, and Ulrich Oslender. 2010. "Territorialidades superpuestas, soberanía en disputa: lecciones empíricas desde América Latina." *Tabula Rasa* 13:191–213.

Alorda, Rocio. 2013. "Indigenous Peoples View Chilean Government with Deep Distrust." Lima: LatinAmerica Press.

American Anthropological Association. 1980. "1980 Annual Business Meeting." *Anthropology Newsletter* 22 (1).

Andersson, Krister, Duncan Lawrence, Jennifer Zavaleta, and Manuel R. Guariguata. 2016. "More Trees, More Poverty? The Socioeconomic Effects of Tree Plantations in Chile, 2001–2011." *Environmental Management* 57 (1): 123–36.

Anthias, Penelope. 2017. "Ch'ixi Landscapes: Indigeneity and Capitalism in the Bolivian Chaco." *Geoforum* 82:268–75.

Anthias, Penelope. 2018. *Limits to Decolonization: Indigeneity, Territory, and Hydrocarbon Politics in the Bolivian Chaco*. Ithaca, NY: Cornell University Press.

Anthias, Penelope, and Sarah A. Radcliffe. 2015. "The Ethno-Environmental Fix and Its Limits: Indigenous Land Titling and the Production of Not-Quite-Neoliberal Natures in Bolivia." *Geoforum* 64:257–69.

Assies, Willem. 2000. "Land, Territory, and Indigenous Peoples' Rights." In *Current Land Policy in Latin America: Regulating Land Tenure under Neo-*

liberalism, edited by E. B. Zoomers and Gemma van der Haar, 93–110. Amsterdam: Royal Tropical Institute.

Aylwin, José. 2001. *Políticas públicas y pueblo mapuche*, Concepción, Chile: Instituto de Estudios Indígenas, Ediciones Escaparate.

Aylwin Oyarzún, José. 2000. "Los conflictos en el territorio mapuche: antecedentes y perspectivas." *Revista Perspectivas en Política, Economía y Gestión* 3:277–301.

Aylwin Oyarzún, José. 2003. *Los derechos de los pueblos indígenas en Chile*. Santiago: LOM Ediciones/Universidad de la Frontera.

Barai, Usha, and Nick Teoh. 1997. "Multiple Statistics for Multiple Events, with Application to Repeated Infections in the Growth Factor Studies." *Statistics in Medicine* 16 (8): 941–49.

Barozet, Emmanuelle. 2003. "Movilización de recursos y redes sociales en los neopopulismos: hipótesis de trabajo para el caso chileno." *Revista de Ciencia Política* 23 (1): 39–54.

Bauer, Kelly. 2016. "Land versus Territory: Evaluating Indigenous Land Policy for the Mapuche in Chile." *Journal of Agrarian Change* 4 (16): 627–45.

Beck, Nathaniel, Jonathan N. Katz, and Richard Tucker. 1998. "Taking Time Seriously: Time-Series-Cross-Section Analysis with a Binary Dependent Variable." *American Journal of Political Science* 42 (4): 1260–88.

Bengoa, José. 2000. *Historia del pueblo mapuche (siglo XIX y XX)*. 6th ed. Santiago: LOM Ediciones.

Bengoa, José. 2004. *La memoria olvidada. Historia de los pueblos indígenas de Chile*. Santiago: Publicaciones del Bicentenario.

Bengoa, José. 2014. *Mapuche, colonos y el Estado Nacional*. Santiago: Editorial Catalonia.

Bidegain, Germán. 2017. "From Cooperation to Confrontation: The Mapuche Movement and Its Political Impact, 1990–2014." In *Social Movements in Chile: Organization, Trajectories, and Political Consequences*, edited by Sofia Donoso and Marisa von Bülow, 99–129. New York: Springer.

Boccara, Guillaume. 2002a. "The Mapuche People in Post-Dictatorship Chile." Études rurales 163:283–303.

Box-Steffensmeier, Janet M., Suzanna De Boef, and Kyle A. Joyce. 2007. "Event Dependence and Heterogeneity in Duration Models: The Conditional Frailty Model." *Political Analysis* 15 (3): 237–56.

Box-Steffensmeier, Janet M., and Bradford S. Jones. 2004. *Event History Modeling: A Guide for Social Scientists*. Cambridge: Cambridge University Press.

Box-Steffensmeier, Janet M., and Christopher Zorn. 2002. "Duration Models for Repeated Events." *Journal of Politics* 64 (4): 1069–94.

Brenner, Neil, Jamie Peck, and Nik Theodore. 2010. "Variegated Neoliberalization: Geographies, Modalities, Pathways." *Global Networks* 10 (2): 182–222.

Brown, Wendy. 2003. "Neo-Liberalism and the End of Liberal Democracy." *Theory & Event* 7 (1).

Bruyneel, Kevin. 2007. *The Third Space of Sovereignty: The Postcolonial Politics of US-Indigenous Relations*. Minneapolis: University of Minnesota Press.

Bryan, Joe. 2012. "Rethinking Territory: Social Justice and Neoliberalism in Latin America's Territorial Turn." *Geography Compass* 6 (4): 215–26.

Burchardt, Hans-Jürgen, and Kristina Dietz. 2014. "(Neo-)Extractivism: A New Challenge for Development Theory from Latin America." *Third World Quarterly* 35 (3): 468–86.

Burdick, John, Philip Oxhorn, and Kenneth M. Roberts. 2009. *Beyond Neoliberalism in Latin America?: Societies and Politics at the Crossroads*. New York: Palgrave Macmillan.

Calderón, Fernando, Alejandro Piscitelli, and José Luis Reyna. 1992. "Social Movements: Actors, Theories, Expectations." In *The Making of Social Movements in Latin America: Identity, Strategy, And Democracy*, edited by Arturo Escobar and Sonia E. Alvarez, 19–36. New York: Routledge.

Cardoso, Fernando Henrique. 1979. *The New Authoritarianism in Latin America*. Princeton, NJ: Princeton University Press.

Carrière, Jean. 1975. "Conflict and Cooperation among Chilean Sectoral Elites." *Boletín de Estudios Latinoamericanos y del Caribe* 19:16–27.

Carruthers, David, and Patricia Rodriguez. 2009. "Mapuche Protest, Environmental Conflict and Social Movement Linkage in Chile." *Third World Quarterly* 30 (4): 743–60.

Cayuqueo, Pedro. 2006. "Participación y voto mapuche en las Municipales. Relaciones Internacionales." Paper presented at the III Taller de Formación Política de Wallmapuwen conference, April 2006, Padre Las Casas, Chile, https://www.mapunet.org/documentos/mapuches/mapuches_municipales.pdf.

Cayuqueo, Pedro. 2012. *Solo por ser indios y otras crónicas mapuches*. Santiago: Editorial Catalonia.

Cayuqueo, Pedro. 2014. *Esa ruca llamada Chile y otras crónicas mapuches*. Santiago: Editorial Catalonia.

Cayuqueo, Pedro. 2017. *Historia secreta mapuche*. Santiago: Editorial Catalonia.

Centeno, Miguel Angel. 2010. *Democracy within Reason: Technocratic Revolution in Mexico*. University Park: Pennsylvania State University Press.

Centro EULA. 2004. "Proyecto catastro de tierras, aguas y riego para indígenas: Informe final modelo de oferta-demanda de tierras, aguas y tiego." Universidad de Concepción, Chile.

CEPAL, and Alianza Territorial Mapuche. 2012. *Desigualdades territoriales y exclusión social del pueblo mapuche en Chile: Situación en la comuna de Ercilla desde un enfoque de derechos*. Santiago: United Nations.

Chihuailaf, Elicura. 1999. *Recado confidencial a los chilenos*. Santiago: LOM Ediciones.

Cleves, Mario. 2008. *An Introduction to Survival Analysis Using Stata*. College Station, TX: Stata Press.

Correa, Martín, and Eduardo Mella Seguel. 2010. *Las razones del illkun/enojo memoria despojo y criminalización en el territorio mapuche de Malleco*. Santiago: LOM Ediciones, Observatorio de Derechos de los Pueblos Indígenas.

Correa, Martín, Raúl Molina, and Nancy Yáñez. 2005. *La reforma agraria y las tierras mapuches: Chile 1962–1975*. Santiago: LOM Ediciones.

Correia, Joel E. 2019. "Unsettling Territory: Indigenous Mobilizations, the Territorial Turn, and the Limits of Land Rights in the Paraguay-Brazil Borderlands." *Journal of Latin American Geography* 18 (1): 11–37.

Coulthard, Glen. 2014. *Red Skin, White Masks: Rejecting the Colonial Politics of Recognition*. Minneapolis: University of Minnesota Press.

Course, Magnus. 2011. *Becoming Mapuche: Person and Ritual in Indigenous Chile*. Urbana: University of Illinois Press.

Courville, Michael, and Raj Patel. 2006. "The Resurgence of Agrarian Reform in the Twenty-First Century." In *Promised Land: Competing Visions of Agrarian Reform*, edited by Peter Rosset, Raj Patel, and Michael Courville, 3–22. Oakland, CA: Food First Books.

Crago, Scott. 2015. "Plan Perquenco and Chile's Indigenous Policies under the Pinochet Dictatorship, 1976–1988." PhD diss., University of New Mexico.

Crist, John T., and John D. McCarthy. 1996. "'If I Had a Hammer': The Changing Methodological Repertoire of Collective Behavior and Social Movements Research." *Mobilization: An International Quarterly* 1 (1): 87–102.

Crow, Joanna. 2013. *The Mapuche in Modern Chile: A Cultural History*. Gainesville: University Press of Florida.

Cusicanqui, Silvia Rivera. 2012. "Ch'ixinakax utxiwa: A Reflection on the Practices and Discourses of Decolonization." *South Atlantic Quarterly* 111 (1): 95–109.

Davis, Shelton H., and Alaka Wali. 1994. "Indigenous and Tenure and Tropical Forest Management in Latin America." *Ambio* 23 (8): 485–90.

de Cea, Maite, Mariana Heredia, and Diego Valdivieso. 2016. "The Chilean Elite's Point of View on Indigenous Peoples." *Canadian Journal of Latin American and Caribbean Studies/Revue canadienne des études latino-américaines et caraïbes* 41 (3): 328–47.

De Janvry, Alain. 1981. *The Agrarian Question and Reformism in Latin America*. Baltimore: Johns Hopkins University Press.

de la Maza, Francisca. 2014. "Between Conflict and Recognition: The Construction of Chilean Indigenous Policy in the Araucanía Region." *Critique of Anthropology* 34 (3): 346–66.

de la Maza, Gonzalo. 2010. "Construcción democrática, participación ciudadana y políticas públicas en Chile." PhD diss., Leiden University.

Deininger, Klaus. 1999. "Making Negotiated Land Reform Work: Initial Experience from Colombia, Brazil and South Africa." *World Development* 27 (4): 651–72.

Deininger, Klaus. 2003. *Land Policies for Growth and Poverty Reduction.* Washington, DC: World Bank and Oxford University Press.

Deininger, Klaus, and Hans Binswanger. 1999. "The Evolution of the World Bank's Land Policy: Principles, Experience, and Future Challenges." *World Bank Research Observer* 14 (2): 247–76.

Del Anaquod, Margaret Thomas, and Kenneth I. Taylor. 1984. "Report on the Present Situation of the Mapuche in Chile." Center for World Indigenous Studies. https://www.cwis.org/wp-content/uploads/documents/premium/280dp00130.pdf.

Di Giminiani, Piergiorgio. 2012. *Tierras ancestrales, disputas contemporáneas: Pertenencia y demandas territoriales en la sociedad Mapuche rural.* Santiago: Ediciones Universidad Católica de Chile.

Di Giminiani, Piergiorgio. 2018. *Sentient Lands: Indigeneity, Property, and Political Imagination in Neoliberal Chile.* Tucson: University of Arizona Press.

Domínguez, Jorge I. 2010. *Technopols: Freeing Politics and Markets in Latin America in the 1990s.* University Park: Pennsylvania State University Press.

Dorner, Peter. 1992. *Latin American Land Reforms in Theory and Practice: a Retrospective Analysis.* Madison: University of Wisconsin Press.

Durston, John. 2005a. *Comunidades campesinas, agencias públicas y clientelismos políticos en Chile.* Santiago: LOM Ediciones.

Durston, John. 2005b. "El clientelismo político en el campo chileno (primera parte): La democratización cuestionada." *Ciencias Sociales Online* 2 (1): 1–30.

Earl, Jennifer, Andrew Martin, John D. McCarthy, and Sarah A. Soule. 2004. "The Use of Newspaper Data in the Study of Collective Action." *Annual Review of Sociology* 30:65–80.

Eaton, Kent. 2004. "Designing Subnational Institutions: Regional and Municipal Reforms in Postauthoritarian Chile." *Comparative Political Studies* 37 (2): 218–44.

Eaton, Kent. 2017. *Territory and Ideology in Latin America: Policy Conflicts between National and Subnational Governments.* Oxford: Oxford University Press.

Eckstein, Susan. 2006. "Urban Resistance to Neoliberal Democracy in Latin America." *Colombia Internacional* 63:12–39.

Eisenstadt, Todd A. 2013. *Latin America's Multicultural Movements: The Struggle between Communitarianism, Autonomy, and Human Rights.* New York: Oxford University Press.

Erazo, Juliet S. 2013. *Governing Indigenous Territories: Enacting Sovereignty in the Ecuadorian Amazon.* Durham, NC: Duke University Press.

Espinoza, Vicente. 2006. "Los nuevos agentes políticos locales: Revisión estructural de la tesis de Arturo Valenzuela ¿Cómo se articulan el nivel de representación local con el nacional en la arena local y qué papel juegan el gobierno central y las políticas públicas?" *Revista Mad* 14:8–18.

Fabricant, Nicole, and Bret Darin Gustafson. 2011. *Remapping Bolivia: Resources, Territory, and Indigeneity in a Plurinational State.* Santa Fe, NM: School for Advanced Research Press.

Ferguson, James. 1990. *The Anti-Politics Machine: 'Development,' Depoliticization and Bureaucratic Power in Lesotho.* Cambridge: Cambridge University Press.

Ferguson, James. 2010. "The Uses of Neoliberalism." *Antipode* 41 (1): 166–84.

Ferguson, James, and Akhil Gupta. 2002. "Spatializing States: Toward an Ethnography of Neoliberal Governmentality." *American Ethnologist* 29 (4): 981–1002.

Fernandez, Adriela, and Marisol Vera. 2012. "The Bachelet Presidency and the End of Chile's Concertacion Era." *Latin American Perspectives* 39 (4): 5–18.

Ferraro, Agustín. 2008. "Friends in High Places: Congressional Influence on the Bureaucracy in Chile." *Latin American Politics and Society* 50 (2): 101–29.

Finley-Brook, Mary. 2016. "Territorial 'Fix'? Tenure Insecurity in Titled Indigenous Territories." *Bulletin of Latin American Research* 35 (3): 338–54.

Foerster, Rolf. 2004. "¿Pactos de sumisión o actos de rebelión?: una aproximación histórica y antropológica a los mapuches de la costa de Arauco, Chile." PhD diss., Leiden University.

Foucault, Michel. 1982. "The Subject and Power." *Critical Inquiry* 8 (4): 777–95.

Foucault, Michel. 2008. *The Birth of Biopolitics: Lectures at the Collège de France, 1978–1979.* Translated by Graham Burchell. New York: Palgrave MacMillan.

Foucault, Michel, and Mark Blasius. 1993. "About the Beginning of the Hermeneutics of the Self: Two Lectures at Dartmouth." *Political Theory* 21 (2): 198–227.

Franzosi, Roberto. 1987. "The Press as a Source of Socio-Historical Data: Issues in the Methodology of Data Collection from Newspapers." *Historical Methods: A Journal of Quantitative and Interdisciplinary History* 20 (1): 5–16.

Franzosi, Roberto. 2004. *From Words to Numbers: Narrative, Data, and Social Science.* Vol. 22. Cambridge: Cambridge University Press.

Fukuyama, Francis. 2004. "The Imperative of State-Building." *Journal of Democracy* 15 (2): 17–31.

Galvis Patiño, María Clara, and Ángela María Ramírez Rincón. 2013. *Digesto de jurisprudencia latinoamericana sobre los derechos de los pueblos indígenas a la participación, la consulta previa y la propiedad comunitaria.* Washington, DC: Fundación para el Debido Proceso.

Garretón, Manuel Antonio. 2003. *Incomplete Democracy: Political Democratization in Chile and Latin America.* Translated by R. Kelly Washbourne and Gregory Horvath. Chapel Hill: University of North Carolina Press.

Garretón Merino, Manuel Antonio. 1989. *The Chilean Political Process*. Boston: Unwin Hyman.

Gil, Federico Guillermo. 1966. *Political System of Chile*. Boston: Houghton Mifflin.

Giraudy, Agustina, and Juan Pablo Luna. 2017. "Unpacking the State's Uneven Territorial Reach: Evidence from Latin America." In *States in the Developing World*, edited by Miguel A. Centeno, Atul Kohli, and Deborah J. Yashar, 93–120. Cambridge: Cambridge University Press.

Gonzalez Galvez, Marcelo Ignacio. 2012. "Personal Truths, Shared Equivocations: Otherness, Uniqueness, and Social Life among the Mapuche of Southern Chile." PhD diss., University of Edinburgh.

Gordon, Edmund T., and Charles R. Hale. 2003. "Rights, Resources, and the Social Memory of Struggle: Reflections and Black Community Land Rights on Nicaragua's Atlantic Coast." *Human Organization* 62 (4): 369–81.

Government of Chile, Ministerio de Agricultura. 1979. "Decreto Ley 2568 modifica Ley N° 17.729, sobre protección de indígenas, y radica funciones del instituto de deasrrollo agropecuario."

Government of Chile, Ministerio de Planificación y Cooperación (MIDE-PLAN). 1993a. "Decreto 395: Aprueba reglamento sobre el Fondo de Tierras y Aguas Indígenas. Temuco, Chile."

Government of Chile, Ministerio de Planificación y Cooperación (MIDE-PLAN). 1993b. "Ley 19253: Establece normas sobre proteccion, fomento y desarrollo de los indígenas, y creas la Corporación Nacional de Desarrollo Indígena."

Government of Chile, Ministerio de Planificación y Cooperación (MIDE-PLAN). 2003. "Resolución 878: Manual para la aplicación de procedimiento para la compra de tierras a través del Programa Subsidio Artículo letra b) del Fondo de Tierras y Aguas Indígenas de la CONADI."

Gregory, Gillian, and Ismael Vaccaro. 2015. "Islands of Governmentality: Rainforest Conservation, Indigenous Rights, and the Territorial Reconfiguration of Guyanese Sovereignty." *Territory, Politics, Governance* 3 (3): 344–63.

Gupta, Akhil. 2012. *Red Tape: Bureaucracy, Structural Violence, and Poverty in India*. Durham, NC: Duke University Press.

Gustafson, Bret. 2002. "Paradoxes of Liberal Indigenism: Indigenous Movements, State Processes, and Intercultural Reform in Bolivia." In *The Politics of Ethnicity: Indigenous Peoples in Latin American States*, edited by David Maybury-Lewis, 267–306. Cambridge, MA: Harvard University Press.

Gustafson, Bret. 2010. "When States Act like Movements Dismantling Local Power and Seating Sovereignty in Post-Neoliberal Bolivia." *Latin American Perspectives* 37 (4): 48–66.

Haarstad, Håvard. 2012. *New Political Spaces in Latin American Natural Resource Governance*. New York: Palgrave Macmillan.

Hagopian, Frances. 1992. "The Compromised Consolidation: the Political Class in the Brazilian Transition." In *Issues in Democratic Consolidation: The New South American Democracies in Comparative Perspective*, edited by Scott Mainwaring, Guillermo O'Donnell, and J. Samuel Valenzuela, 243–93. Notre Dame, IN: University of Notre Dame Press.

Hale, Charles R. 2002. "Does Multiculturalism Menace? Governance, Cultural Rights and the Politics of Identity in Guatemala." *Journal of Latin American Studies* 34 (3): 485–524.

Hale, Charles R. 2006. *Más que un indio: Racial Ambivalence and the Paradox of Neoliberal Multiculturalism in Guatemala*. Santa Fe, NM: School of American Research Press.

Hale, Charles R. 2011. "Resistencia para que? Territory, Autonomy and Neoliberal Entanglements in the 'Empty Spaces' of Central America." *Economy and Society* 40 (2): 184–210.

Hallenbeck, Jessica, Mike Krebs, Sarah Hunt, Kanishka Goonewardena, Stefan Andreas Kipfer, Shiri Pasternak, and Glen Sean Coulthard. 2016. "Red Skin, White Masks: Rejecting the Colonial Politics of Recognition." *AAG Review of Books* 4 (2): 111–20.

Hanson, Rebecca, and Patricia Richards. 2017. "Sexual Harassment and the Construction of Ethnographic Knowledge." *Sociological Forum* 32 (3): 587–609.

Harvey, David. 2007. *A Brief History of Neoliberalism*. Oxford: Oxford University Press.

Haughney, Diane. 2006. *Neoliberal Economics, Democratic Transition, and Mapuche Demands for Rights in Chile*. Gainesville: University Press of Florida.

Healy, Kevin. 2001. *Llamas, Weavings, and Organic Chocolate: Multicultural Grassroots Development in the Andes and Amazon of Bolivia*. Notre Dame, IN: University of Notre Dame Press.

Hindery, Derrick. 2013. *From Enron to Evo: Pipeline Politics, Global Environmentalism, and Indigenous Rights in Bolivia*. Tucson: University of Arizona Press.

Horst, Bettina. 2009. "Fuentes de financiamiento para gobiernos subnacionales y descentralización fiscal." In *Pensando Chile desde sus regiones*, edited by Heinrich von Baer, 255–68. Temuco, Chile: Universidad de la Frontera.

Hull, Matthew S. 2012. "Documents and Bureaucracy." *Annual Review of Anthropology* 41:251–67.

Hutter, Swen. 2014. "Protest Event Analysis and Its Offspring." In *Methodological Practices in Social Movement Research*, edited by Donatella Della Porta, 335–67. Oxford: Oxford University Press.

IACHR. 2010. "Indigenous and Tribal Peoples' Rights over Their Ancestral Lands and Natural Resources: Norms and Jurisprudence of the Inter-American Human Rights System." OEA/Ser.L/V/II, Doc. 56/09.

Instituto de Estudios Indígenas. 2003. *Los derechos de los pueblos indígenas en Chile*. Edited by Universidad de la Frontera. Santiago: LOM Ediciones/ Universidad de la Frontera.

Instituto del Medio Ambiente, Universidad de la Frontera. 2011. "Estudio evaluación socio-productiva de tierras adquiridas por el Fondo de Tierras y Aguas de CONADI."

Instituto Nacional de Derechos Humanos. 2010. "Informe Anual 2010: Situación de los Derechos Humanos en Chile."

Instituto Nacional Estadísticas. 2002. "Censo 2002."

International Labor Organization. 2009. *Indigenous & Tribal Peoples' Rights in Practice: A Guide to ILO Convention No. 169*. Geneva: International Labor Organization.

James, Matt. 2013. "Neoliberal Heritage Redress." In *Reconciling Canada: Critical Perspectives on the Culture of Redress*, edited by Pauline Jennifer Henderson and Wakeham, 31–46. Toronto: University of Toronto Press.

Johnston, Michael. 1997. "Public Officials, Private Interests, and Sustainable Democracy: When Politics and Corruption Meet." *Corruption and the Global Economy* 83:67.

Kaufman, Robert R. 1972. *The Politics of Land Reform in Chile, 1950–1970: Public Policy, Political Institutions, and Social Change*. Cambridge, MA: Harvard University Press.

Kay, Cristóbal. 1998. "Latin America's Agrarian Reform: Lights and Shadows." *Land Reform, Land Settlement and Cooperatives* 2:9–31.

Kelly, John H., Peter H. Herlihy, Derek A. Smith, Aida Ramos Viera, Andrew M. Hilburn, and Gerardo A. Hernández Cendejas. 2010. "Indigenous Territoriality at the End of the Social Property Era in Mexico." *Journal of Latin American Geography* 9 (3): 161–81.

Kelly, Patrick J., and Lynette L-Y Lim. 2000. "Survival Analysis for Recurrent Event Data: An Application to Childhood Infectious Diseases." *Statistics in Medicine* 19 (1): 13–33.

Klandermans, Bert, and Suzanne Staggenborg. 2002. *Methods of Social Movement Research*. Vol. 16. Minneapolis: University of Minnesota Press.

Klubock, Thomas Miller. 2014. *La Frontera: Forests and Ecological Conflict in Chile's Frontier Territory*. Durham, NC: Duke University Press.

Koopmans, Ruud, and Dieter Rucht. 2002. "Protest Event Analysis." *Methods of Social Movement Research* 16:231–59.

Kowalczyk, Anna Maria. 2013. "Indigenous Peoples and Modernity: Mapuche Mobilizations in Chile." *Latin American Perspectives* 40 (4): 121–35.

Kurtz, Marcus J. 2004. "The Dilemmas of Democracy in the Open Economy: Lessons from Latin America." *World Politics* 56 (2): 262–302.

Kymlicka, Will. 2013. "Neoliberal Multiculturalism?" In *Social Resilience in the*

Neoliberal Era, edited by Peter A. Hall & Michèle Lamont, 99–125. Cambridge: Cambridge University Press.

Larson, Anne M., Fernanda Soto, Dennis Mairena, Edda Moreno, Eileen Mairena, and Jadder Mendoza-Lewis. 2016. "The Challenge of 'Territory': Weaving the Social Fabric of Indigenous Communities in Nicaragua's Northern Caribbean Autonomous Region." *Bulletin of Latin American Research* 35 (3): 322–37.

Laserna, Roberto. 2009. "Decentralization, Local Initiatives, and Citizenship in Bolivia, 1994–2004." In *Participatory Innovation and Representative Democracy in Latin America,* edited by Andrew D. Selee and Enrique Peruzzotti, 126–55. Washington, DC: Woodrow Wilson Center Press.

Laurie, Nina, Robert Andolina, and Sarah Radcliffe. 2003. "Indigenous Professionalization: Transnational Social Reproduction in the Andes." *Antipode* 35 (3): 463–91.

Leiva, Fernando Ignacio. 2008. *Latin American Neostructuralism: The Contradictions of Post-Neoliberal Development.* Minneapolis: University of Minnesota Press.

Lemke, Thomas. 2002. "Foucault, Governmentality, and Critique." *Rethinking Marxism* 14 (3): 49–64.

Lemke, Thomas. 2007. "An Indigestible Meal? Foucault, Governmentality and State Theory." *Distinktion: Scandinavian Journal of Social Theory* 8 (2): 43–64.

Levitsky, Steven, and Kenneth M. Roberts. 2011. "Latin America's 'Left Turn': A Framework for Analysis." In *The Resurgence of the Latin American Left,* edited by Steven Levitsky and Kenneth M Roberts, 1–28. Baltimore: Johns Hopkins University Press.

Li, Tania Murray. 2007. *The Will to Improve: Governmentality, Development, and the Practice of Politics.* Durham, NC: Duke University Press.

Llaitul, Hector. 2014. "¡El territorio no se compra, se recupera . . . ! ¿ Compraventa, expropiación o control territorial?" *Le Monde Diplomatique,* https://www.lemondediplomatique.cl/2014/10/compra-venta-expropiacion-o-control-territorial.

Llaitul, Hector, and Jorge Arrate. 2012. *Weichan, conversaciones con un weychafe en la prisión política.* Santiago: CEIBO Ediciones.

López, Emiliano, and Francisco Vértiz. 2014. "Extractivism, Transnational Capital, and Subaltern Struggles in Latin America." *Latin American Perspectives* 42 (5): 152–68.

Loveman, Brian, and Thomas M. Davies Jr., eds. 1997. *The Politics of Antipolitics: The Military in Latin America.* Lincoln: University of Nebraska Press.

Lucero, José Antonio. 2008. *Struggles of Voice: The Politics of Indigenous Representation in the Andes.* Pittsburgh: University of Pittsburgh Press.

Madrid, Sebastián. 2012. "Elites in Their Real Lives: A Chilean Comment on Robinson." *Critical Sociology* 38 (3): 389–93.

Mallon, Florencia. 2005. *Courage Tastes of Blood: The Mapuche Community of Nicolás Ailío and the Chilean State, 1906–2001*. Durham, NC: Duke University Press.

Marimán, José A. 2012. *Autodeterminación: ideas políticas Mapuche en el albor del siglo XXI*. Santiago: LOM Ediciones.

Marimán, Pablo, Sergio Caniuqueo, José Millalén, and Rodrigo Levil. 2006. ¡ . . . *Escucha, winka* . . . ! Santiago: LOM Ediciones.

Marimán, Pedro. 1990. "Algunas consideraciones en torno al voto mapuche." *Revista Liwen* 2:25–32.

Martínez, Miguel Alfonso, Erica-Irene A. Daes, and Ribot Hatano. 1999. "Final Report of the Study on Treaties, Agreements and Other Constructive Arrangements between States and Indigenous Populations." United Nations Digital Library, https://digitallibrary.un.org/record/276353?ln=en.

McNeish, John-Andrew. 2008. "Beyond the Permitted Indian? Bolivia and Guatemala in an Era of Neoliberal Developmentalism." *Latin American and Caribbean Ethnic Studies* 3 (1): 33–59.

McNeish, John-Andrew. 2013. "Extraction, Protest and Indigeneity in Bolivia: The TIPNIS Effect." *Latin American and Caribbean Ethnic Studies* 8 (2): 221–42.

Mella Seguel, Eduardo. 2007. *Los mapuche ante la justicia la criminalización de la protesta indígena en Chile*. Santiago: LOM Ediciones, Observatorio de Derechos de los Pueblos Indígenas.

Meza, Laura E. 2009. "Mapuche Struggles for Land and the Role of Private Protected Areas in Chile." *Journal of Latin American Geography* 8 (1): 149–63.

Milkman, Ruth. 1997. *Farewell to the Factory: Auto Workers in the Late Twentieth Century*. Berkeley: University of California Press.

Millaman, Rosamel. 2001. "Mapuches Press for Autonomy." *NACLA Report on the Americas* 35 (2):10–12.

Ministerio de Planificación y Cooperación. 1999. "La política de tierras de la Corporación Nacional de Desarrollo Indígena." Santiago, Chile.

Monkeberg, Maria Olivia. 2009. *Los magnates de la prensa: Concentración de los medios de comunicación en Chile*. Santiago: Random House.

Morales Urra, Roberto. 2002. *Territorialidad mapuche en el siglo XX*. Concepción: Instituto de Estudios Indígenas/Universidad de la Frontera/ Escaparate Ediciones.

Moulian, Tomás. 2002. *Chile actual: anatomía de un mito*. Santiago: LOM Ediciones.

Namuncura, Domingo. 1999. *Ralco, represa o pobreza?* Santiago: LOM Ediciones.

Navia, Patricio, and Rodrigo Osorio. 2015. "El Mercurio Lies, and La Tercera Lies More. Political Bias in Newspaper Headlines in Chile, 1994–2010." *Bulletin of Latin American Research* 34 (4): 467-485.

Navia, Patricio, Rodrigo Osorio, and Francisca Valenzuela. 2013. "Sesgo político en las lunas de miel presidenciales: El Mercurio y La Tercera, 1994–2010." In *Intermedios. Medios de comunicación y democracia en Chile*, edited by A. Arriagada and P. Navia, 35–58. Santiago, Chile: Ediciones Universidad Diego Portales.

Núñez, Rodrigo Míguez. 2013. "Estado chileno y tierras mapuche: entre propiedades y territorialidad." In *Derecho y pueblo mapuche: aportes para la discusión*, edited by H. Olea Rodríguez, 21–50. Santiago: Centro de Derechos Humanos de la Universidad de Diego Portales.

O'Donnell, Guillermo A. 1993. "On the State, Democratization and Some Conceptual Problems: A Latin American View with Glances at Some Postcommunist Countries." *World Development* 21 (8): 1355–69.

O'Donnell, Guillermo A. 1994. "Delegative Democracy." *Journal of Democracy* 5 (1): 55–69.

O'Donnell, Guillermo A. 1999. *Counterpoints: Selected Essays on Authoritarianism and Democratization*. Notre Dame, IN: University of Notre Dame Press.

Observatorio Social de America Latina. 2009. *Documento de trabajo* Nº 441: *Cronología del conflicto social*. Edited by Comité de Seguimiento del Conflicto Social y la Coyuntura Latinoamericana de Chile. Buenos Aires, Argentina, Consejo Latinoamericano de Ciencias Sociales.

Offen, Karl H. 2003. "The Territorial Turn: Making Black Territories in Pacific Colombia." *Journal of Latin American Geography* 2 (1): 43–73.

Oliver, Pamela E., Jorge Cadena-Roa, and Kelley D. Strawn. 2003. "Emerging Trends in the Study of Protest and Social Movements." *Research in Political Sociology* 12 (1): 213–44.

Olzak, Susan. 1989. "Analysis of Events in the Study of Collective Action." *Annual Review of Sociology* 15:119–141.

Olzak, Susan. 1994. *The Dynamics of Ethnic Competition and Conflict*. Stanford, CA: Stanford University Press.

Ong, Aihwa. 2000. "Graduated Sovereignty in South-East Asia." *Theory, Culture & Society* 17 (4): 55–75.

Ong, Aihwa. 2006. *Neoliberalism as Exception: Mutations in Citizenship and Sovereignty*. Durham, NC: Duke University Press.

Ong, Aihwa. 2007. "Neoliberalism as a Mobile Technology." *Transactions of the Institute of British Geographers* 32 (1): 3–8.

Ortega, Roque Roldán. 2004. *Models for Recognizing Indigenous Land Rights in Latin America*. Washington, DC: World Bank, Environment Department.

Paige, Jeffrey. 1975. *Agrarian Revolution*. New York: Free Press.

Pairicán, Fernando, and Rolando Álvarez. 2011. "La nueva guerra de Arauco: La Coordinadora Arauco Malleco en el Chile de la Concertación de Partidos por la Democracia (1997–2009)." *Revista Izquierdas* 10:66–84.

Pairican Padilla, Fernando. 2014. *Malon: la rebelión del movimiento Mapuche, 1990–2013*. Santiago: Pehuén Editores.

Pairican Padilla, Fernando. 2017. *La biografía de Matías Catrileo*. Santiago: Pehuén Editores.

Peck, Jamie, Nik Theodore, and Neil Brenner. 2010. "Postneoliberalism and its Malcontents." *Antipode* 41 (1): 94–116.

Peck, Jamie, and Adam Tickell. 2002. "Neoliberalizing Space." *Antipode* 34 (3): 380–404.

Petras, James F. 1969. *Politics and Social Forces in Chilean Development*. Berkeley: University of California Press.

Pinto Rodríguez, Jorge. 2003. *La formación del estado y la nación, y el pueblo mapuche. De la inclusión a la exclusión*. Santiago: Dibam.

Posner, Paul W. 2004. "Local Democracy and the Transformation of Popular Participation in Chile." *Latin American Politics and Society* 46 (3): 55–81.

Postero, Nancy. 2007. *Now We Are Citizens: Indigenous Politics in Postmulticultural Bolivia*. Stanford, CA: Stanford University Press.

Postero, Nancy. 2017. *The Indigenous State: Race, Politics, and Performance in Plurinational Bolivia*. Berkeley: University of California Press.

Postero, Nancy, and Nicole Fabricant. 2019. "Indigenous Sovereignty and the New Developmentalism in Plurinational Bolivia." *Anthropological Theory* 19 (1): 95–119.

Postero, Nancy Grey, and Leon Zamosc. 2006. "The Struggle for Indigenous Rights in Latin America." *Journal of Latin American Anthropology* 11 (1): 208–10.

Postero, Nancy, and Leon Zamosc. 2004. "Indigenous Movements and the Indian Question in Latin America." In *The Struggle for Indigenous Rights in Latin America*, edited by Nancy Postero and Leon Zamosc, 1–31. London: Sussex Academic Press.

Prentice, Ross L., Benjamin J. Williams, and Arthur V. Peterson. 1981. "On the Regression Analysis of Multivariate Failure Time Data." *Biometrika* 68 (2): 373–79.

Prevost, Gary, Carlos Oliva Campos, and Harry E. Vanden. 2012. *Social Movements and Leftist Governments in Latin America: Confrontation or Co-optation?* London: Zed Books.

Pringle, Rosemary, and Sophie Watson. 1992. "Women's Interests and the Poststructuralist State." In *Destabilizing Theory: Contemporary Feminist Debates*, edited by M. Barrett and A. Phillips, 53–73. Stanford, CA: Stanford University Press.

Programa Orígenes. 2008. "Re-Conocer. Pacto Social por la Multiculturalidad." Programa Orígenes, Santiago.

Quilaqueo, Daniel, and Segundo Quintriqueo. 2010. "Saberes educativos mapuches: un análisis desde la perspectiva de los kimches." *Polis. Revista Latinoamericana* 9 (26): 337–60.

Ray, Leslie. 2007. *Language of the Land: The Mapuche in Argentina and Chile*. Copenhagen: International Work Group for Indigenous Affairs (IWGIA).

Read, Jason. 2009. "A Genealogy of Homo-Economicus: Neoliberalism and the Production of Subjectivity." *Foucault Studies* 6:25–36.

Rehren, Alfredo. 1991. "El impacto de las políticas autoritarias a nivel local: Implicancias para la consolidación democrática en Chile." *Estudios Públicos* 44:207–46.

Rehren, Alfredo. 1996. "Corruption and Local Politics in Chile." *Crime, Law and Social Change* 25 (4): 323–34.

Rehren, Alfredo. 2008. "La evolución de la agenda de transparencia en los gobiernos de la concertación." *Temas de la Agenda Pública* 3 (18).

Reyes, R., and H. Nelson. 2014. "A Tale of Two Forests: Why Forests and Forest Conflicts are Both Growing in Chile." *International Forestry Review* 16 (4): 379–88.

Rice, Roberta. 2012. *The New Politics of Protest: Indigenous Mobilization in Latin America's Neoliberal Era*. Tucson: University of Arizona Press.

Richards, Patricia. 2010. "Of Indians and Terrorists: How the State and Local Elites Construct the Mapuche in Neoliberal Multicultural Chile." *Journal of Latin American Studies* 42 (1): 59–90.

Richards, Patricia. 2013. *Race and the Chilean Miracle: Neoliberalism, Democracy, and Indigenous Rights*. Pittsburgh: University of Pittsburgh Press.

Richards, Patricia, and Jeffrey A. Gardner. 2013. "Still Seeking Recognition: Mapuche Demands, State Violence, and Discrimination in Democratic Chile." *Latin American and Caribbean Ethnic Studies* 8 (3): 255–79.

Roberts, Kenneth M. 2002. "Social Inequalities without Class Cleavages in Latin America's Neoliberal Era." *Studies in Comparative International Development* 36 (4): 3–33.

Rodríguez, Jorge Pinto. 2015. *Conflictos étnicos, sociales y económicos: Araucanía 1900–2014*. Santiago: Pehuén Editores.

Rodriguez, Patricia, and David Carruthers. 2008. "Testing Democracy's Promise: Indigenous Mobilization and the Chilean State." *Revista Europea de Estudios Latinoamericanos y del Caribe/European Review of Latin American and Caribbean Studies* 85:3–21.

Rose, Nikolas. 1999. *Powers of Freedom: Reframing Political Thought*. Cambridge: Cambridge University Press.

Rose, Nikolas, and Peter Miller. 1992. "Political Power beyond the State: Problematics of Government." *British Journal of Sociology* 43 (2): 173–205.

Ross-Schneider, Ben, and Blanca Heredia. 2003. *Reinventing Leviathan: the Politics of Administrative Reform in Developing Countries*. Miami, FL: North-South Center Press.

Rucht, Dieter, and Friedhelm Neidhardt. 1999. "Methodological Issues in Collecting Protest Event Data: Units of Analysis, Sources and Sampling, Coding Problems." In *Acts of Dissent: New Developments in the Study of Protest*, edited by Dieter Rucht, Ruud Koopmans, and Friedhelm Neidhardt, 65–89. Lanham, MD: Rowman & Littlefield.

Sanhueza, Cristián, Daniel Saber, James Cavallaro, Jorge Contesse, and César Rodríguez. 2013. *No nos toman en cuenta: pueblos indígenas y consulta previa en las pisciculturas de la Araucanía*. Santiago: Universidad Diego Portales.

Santos, Boaventura de Sousa. 2010. *Refundación del estado en América Latina: perspectivas desde una epistemología del Sur*. Lima: Instituto Internacional de Derecho y Sociedad.

Santos, Boaventura de Sousa, and César A. Rodríguez-Garavito. 2005. "Law, Politics and the Subaltern in Counter-Hegemonic Globalization." In *Law and Globalization from Below: Towards a Cosmopolitan Legality*, edited by Boaventura de Sousa Santos and César A. Rodríguez-Garavito, 1–26. Cambridge: Cambridge University Press.

Sassen, Saskia. 2013. "When Territory Deborders Territoriality." *Territory, Politics, Governance* 1 (1): 21–45.

Seguel, Alfredo. 2007. "Crónicas de desencuentros: el gobierno de Ricardo Lagos versus el movimiento social mapuche." In *El gobierno de Lagos, los pueblos indígenas y el "nuevo trato*," edited by Nancy Yañez y José Aylwin, 59–80. Santiago: LOM Ediciones, 2007.

Selee, Andrew D., and Enrique Peruzzotti. 2009. *Participatory Innovation and Representative Democracy in Latin America*. Baltimore: Johns Hopkins University Press.

Selligson, Mitchell, Nathalie Jaramillo, Juan Pablo Luna, Valentina Salas and Sergio Toro. 2012. "Cultura política de la democracia en Chile y en las Américas, 2012: Hacia la igualdad de oportunidades." Santiago: UC-UCT-U Vanderbilt.

Siavelis, Peter. 2009. "Elite-Mass Congruence, Partidocracia and the Quality of Chilean Democracy." *Journal of Politics in Latin America* 1 (3): 3–31.

Sieder, Rachel. 2002. *Multiculturalism in Latin America*. New York: Palgrave Macmillan.

Sil, Rudra, and Peter J. Katzenstein. 2010. "Analytic Eclecticism in the Study of World Politics: Reconfiguring Problems and Mechanisms across Research Traditions." *Perspectives on Politics* 8 (2): 411–31.

Silva, Eduardo. 2009. *Challenging Neoliberalism in Latin America*. New York: Cambridge University Press.

Silva, Eduardo, and Patricio Rodrigo. 2010. "Contesting Private Property Rights: The Environment and Indigenous Peoples." In *The Bachelet Government: Conflict and Consensus in Post-Pinochet Chile*, edited by Silvia Borzutzky and Gregory B. Weeks, 181–214.

Silva, Patricio. 1991. "Technocrats and Politics in Chile: from the Chicago Boys to the CIEPLAN Monks." *Journal of Latin American Studies* 23 (2): 385–410.

Silva, Patricio. 2004. "Doing Politics in a Depoliticised Society: Social Change and Political Deactivation in Chile." *Bulletin of Latin American Research* 23 (1): 63–78.

Silva, Patricio. 2008. *In the Name of Reason: Technocrats and Politics in Chile.* University Park: Pennsylvania State University Press.

Simpson, Audra. 2014. *Mohawk Interruptus: Political Life across the Borders of Settler States.* Durham, NC: Duke University Press.

Springer, Simon. 2011. "Articulated Neoliberalism: the Specificity of Patronage, Kleptocracy, and Violence in Cambodia's Neoliberalization." *Environment and Planning* 43 (11): 2554–70.

Svampa, Maristella. 2013. "Resource Extractivism and Alternatives: Latin American Perspectives on Development." In *Beyond Development: Alternative Visions from Latin America*, edited by M. Lang and D. Mokrani, 43–73. Amsterdam and Quito: Transnational Institute and Rosa Luxemburg Foundation.

Sylvander, Nora. 2018. "Saneamiento Territorial in Nicaragua, and the Prospects for Resolving Indigenous-Mestizo Land Conflicts." *Journal of Latin American Geography* 17 (1): 166–94.

Thiesenhusen, William C. 1995. *Broken Promises: Agrarian Reform and the Latin American Campesino.* Boulder, CO: Westview Press.

Tilly, Charles. 1978. *From Mobilization to Revolution.* New York: McGraw-Hill.

Tinsman, Heidi. 2002. *Partners in Conflict: The Politics of Gender, Sexuality, and Labor in the Chilean Agrarian Reform, 1950–1973.* Durham, NC: Duke University Press.

Tockman, Jason, and John Cameron. 2014. "Indigenous Autonomy and the Contradictions of Plurinationalism in Bolivia." *Latin American Politics and Society* 56 (3): 46–69.

Toro Maureira, Sergio, and Nathalie Jaramillo-Brun. 2014. "Despejando mitos sobre el voto indígena en Chile: Preferencias ideológicas y adhesión étnica en el electorado Mapuche." *Revista de ciencia política* 34 (3): 583–604.

Torres, Robinson, Gerardo Azócar, Jorge Rojas, Aldo Montecinos, and Patricio Paredes. 2015. "Vulnerability and Resistance to Neoliberal Environmental Changes: An Assessment of Agriculture and Forestry in the Biobio Region of Chile (1974–2014)." *Geoforum* 60:107–22.

Tricot, Tito. 2013. *Autonomía: el movimiento Mapuche de resistencia.* Santiago: CEIBO Ediciones.

Tricot, Tito. 2014. *Palabras de tierra: cronicas de la resistencia mapuche*. Santiago: CEIBO Ediciones.

Tricot, Tito. 2017. "Violencia histórica chilena y contra-violencia política mapuche." *Persona y Sociedad* 31 (2): 35–71.

United Nations Commission on Human Rights. 2006. "Indigenous Issues: Human Rights and Indigenous Issues, Report of the Special Rapporteur on the Situation of Human Rights and Fundamental Freedoms of Indigenous People." Rodolfo Stavenhagan, Addendum, January 17, 2006, E/CN.4/2006/78, https://undocs.org/E/CN.4/2006/78.

Valdivia, Verónica, Rolando Álvarez, and Karen Donoso. 2012. *La alcaldización de la política. Los municipios en la dictadura pinochetista*. Santiago: LOM Ediciones.

Valenzuela, Arturo. 1977. *Political Brokers in Chile: Local Government in a Centralized Polity*. Durham, NC: Duke University Press.

Van Cott, Donna Lee. 2000. *The Friendly Liquidation of the Past: the Politics of Diversity in Latin America*. Pittsburgh, PA: University of Pittsburgh Press.

Van Cott, Donna Lee. 2002. "Constitutional Reform in the Andes: Redefining Indigenous-State Relations." In *Multiculturalism in Latin America: Indigenous Rights, Diversity and Democracy*, edited by Rachel Sieder, 45–73. New York: Palgrave Macmillan.

Van Cott, Donna Lee. 2007. *From Movements to Parties in Latin America: The Evolution of Ethnic Politics*. New York: Cambridge University Press.

Van Cott, Donna Lee. 2008. *Radical Democracy in the Andes*. New York: Cambridge University Press.

van der Haar, Gemma. 2000. "The Contested Nature of Land Tenure Regulation." In *Current Land Policy in Latin America: Regulating Land Tenure under Neo-Liberalism*, edited by Annelies Zoomers and Gemma van der Haar, 271–87. Amsterdam: Royal Tropical Institute, KIT Publishers.

Veltmeyer, Henry. 2005. "The Dynamics of Land Occupations in Latin America." In *Reclaiming the Land: The Resurgence of Rural Movements in Africa, Asia, and Latin America*, edited by Sam Moyo and Paris Yeros, 285–316. London: Zed Books.

Veltmeyer, Henry. 2016. "Investment, Governance and Resistance in the New Extractive Economies of Latin America." In *Mining in Latin America: Critical Approaches to the New Extraction*, edited by Kalowatie Deonandan and Michael L. Dougherty, 27–44. New York: Routledge.

Veltmeyer, Henry, and James Petras. 2014. *The New Extractivism in Latin America*. London: Zed Books.

Vergara, Jorge Iván, Rolf Foerster, and Hans Gundermann. 2004. "Más acá de la legalidad. La CONADI, la Ley Indígena y el pueblo mapuche (1989–2004)." *Polis: Revista Latinoamericana* 8:381–405.

Wainwright, Joel, and Joe Bryan. 2009. "Cartography, Territory, Property: Postcolonial Reflections on Indigenous Counter-Mapping in Nicaragua and Belize." *Cultural Geographies* 16 (2): 153–78.

Wallmapuwen, Partido Mapuche. 2009. "La violencia colonial en Wallmapu." https://www.mapuche-nation.org/espanol/html/documentos/doc-90.htm.

Webb, Andrew. 2014. "Articulating the Mapu: Land as a Form of Everyday Ethnicity among Mapuche Youth of Chile." *Latin American and Caribbean Ethnic Studies* 9 (3): 222–46.

Weyland, Kurt. 1999. "Economic Policy in Chile's New Democracy." *Journal of Interamerican Studies and World Affairs* 41 (3): v–96.

Weyland, Kurt. 2004. "Neoliberalism and Democracy in Latin America: A Mixed Record." *Latin American Politics and Society* 46 (1): 135–57.

Yashar, Deborah J. 1999. "Democracy, Indigenous Movements, and Postliberal Challenge in Latin America." *World Politics* 52 (1): 76–104.

Yashar, Deborah J. 2005. *Contesting Citizenship in Latin America: the Rise of Indigenous Movements and the Postliberal Challenge.* New York: Cambridge University Press.

Yates, Julian S., and Karen Bakker. 2013. "Debating the 'Post-Neoliberal Turn' in Latin America." *Progress in Human Geography* 38 (1): 62–90.

Yrigoyen Fajardo, Raquel. 2010. *Pueblos indígenas. Constituciones y reformas políticas en América Latina.* Lima: Editorial Gráfica Kuatro.

Zoomers, Annelies, and Gemma van der Haar. 2000a. "Introduction: Regulating Land Tenure under Neo-Liberalism." In *Current Land Policy in Latin America: Regulating Land Tenure under Neo-Liberalism*, edited by Gemma van der Haar and Annelies E. B. Zoomers. Amsterdam: Royal Tropical Institute, KIT Publishers.

Zoomers, Annelies, and Gemma van der Haar. 2000b. *Land in Latin America: New Context, New Claims, New Concepts.* Amsterdam: Royal Tropical Institute, KIT Publishers.

Zuñiga Navarro, Gerardo. 1998. "Los procesos de constitución de territorios indígenas en América Latina." *Nueva Sociedad* 153:141–55.

INDEX